AWS Scripted 2

AWS Scripted 2

Essential Security, SSH and MFA

A QuickStepApps Guide

By Christian Cerri

(First Edition 2015)

Table of Contents

Introduction

Welcome to the second book from QuickStepApps on Amazon Web Services. In the first of the series, "AWS Scripted: How to Automate the Deployment of Secure and Resilient Websites with Amazon Web Services VPC, ELB, EC2, RDS, IAM, SES and SNS", I examined advanced AWS CLI scripting for Web and Database services. I have been busy expanding on what is certainly the most important aspect of Cloud Computing: Security. The book starts with basic security concepts and securing your tools. I then move on to the most important security technique of all: Multi-Factor Authentication, or MFA. I show you how to apply MFA to the AWS Console, the AWS CLI and SSH. Finally, I examine Bastion Hosts and Secure Internal Servers.

This book represents the sum total of my knowledge as regards implementing real world security for AWS Servers. These techniques work, I've used most of them in real-world production environments. At every stage I have done my best to provide working scripts to automate security techniques as much as possible. All the code in this book is available for free for download at **http://www.quickstepapps.com**. It's been tested on OSX and AWS Linux. Windows users can knock up an AWS instance and run it from there, which is a lot easier than trying this sort of stuff with PuTTY or the Windows shell. An excellent AWS document for using PuTTY for this purpose is available at **http://docs.aws.amazon.com/AWSEC2/latest/UserGuide/putty.html** .

In **Chapter 1 - Know Your Enemy**, a general approach to security is discussed. I look at the sorts of Attackers you are likely to meet out there on the Internet and the Vulnerabilities they will try to exploit. MFA is discussed and finally the art of Writing Down Passwords.

In **Chapter 2 - Securing Basic AWS Access**, I discuss how to set up your AWS Account and your AWS CLI (Command Line Interface) securely. Also of vital importance is the Secure Laptop strategy (readers of my first book will be familiar with this already).

In **Chapter 3 - AWS Security Groups**, the main implementer of AWS security is discussed - the Security Group. I discuss how they work and how to manage them, from the Console and with CLI commands. Then I provide some useful scripts for managing Security Groups which also showcase how to use the aforementioned CLI commands. I also take a look at Network Access Control Lists, a second layer of network security.

In **Chapter 4 - MFA for AWS CLI**, I show you how to implement MFA for AWS CLI. This means that whenever you want to use CLI commands, you'll need to enter an MFA code (which lasts up to one hour). It is essential security and, in my opinion, the most important chapter of the book. First are the scripts to set it all up. Then scripts to Sign In and Sign Out. Last, I show you how to include AWS CLI MFA in your other scripts.

In **Chapter 5 - SSH**, that most fundamental and important service, SSH - the Secure Shell, is discussed. I look at general security considerations. Then how to ssh into a new instance. Next, I show you how to automate the SSH sign in process. The default SSH configuration isn't secure enough, so you'll see how to change the user who can ssh in, 'harden' SSH and how to set up a daily email which contains the SSH logs (because we all know vigilance is key to security). Scripts to build this hardened box are provided.

In **Chapter 6 - SSH with Password**, I show you how to reconfigure SSH to require a password, rather than an SSH Key. Scripts to build and configure such a server are provided. Then, there are scripts to automate the SSH sign in process.

In **Chapter 7 - SSH with Password/MFA**, I get to the really cool stuff and see how to implement SSH with MFA - for free and with no external service providers! Scripts are provided to build and configure this type of server and also to automate SSH access.

In **Chapter 8 - SSH with Password/MFA/Sudo-Password**, I build on the last chapter to build the mother of all secure servers, the "SSH with Password/MFA and Sudo-Password Server". I discuss 'sudo' and how to change it to make it more secure. Then there are the usual scripts to build and access this new type of server.

In **Chapter 9 - Using a Bastion Host**, I discuss Bastion Hosts, which are ultra-secure gateways to the rest of your network. I look at the technique of using servers that are not directly connected to the Internet (but still accessible via things like Elastic Load Balancers) and how to allow Outbound Internet Access to these sorts of very secure servers. Then I provide scripts to build a Bastion Host and configure it. In a demo network, I build a couple of 'Internal Servers' which are only accessible via the Bastion. Then, I provide scripts to configure internal servers and update them. A Master Script is provided for a breathtaking experience. Finally, I conclude with the connect scripts to get a shell on all the created servers.

In **Appendix A - VPC**, the script for creating the VPC used throughout the book is provided.

In **Appendix B - Fun with Expect**, I explore 'expect', a terribly useful utility which lets you automate commands and keyboard entry.

In **Appendix C - OTP Manager for OSX**, there are details on a very useful App for generating MFA codes on your computer (rather than your unwieldy smartphone).

In **Appendix D - Automating MFA**, I show you how to generate codes with PHP and on the command line - strictly for development only!

In **Appendix E - UnBrick a Brick**, you will find a script for fixing a server you can't ssh to because you screwed the sshd config file (commonly known as 'bricking').

In **Appendix F - Bash Script Essentials**, I run you through the basics of bash scripting with all sorts of invaluable techniques.

Apologies, this is an edited reprint from my first book, however, many people have commented that they found it extremely useful. If you don't have that book, you'll find this Appendix very handy.

Note that all the MFA implementations I use are FREE and work with the Google Authenticator App available on iOS and Android, as well as most other MFA OTP generators. There is no requirement to use external MFA Service Providers.

And remember, this book is fully supported at **http://www.quickstepapps.com**. You can download all the code examples in this book, read extra articles, ask questions and participate in the forums.

AWS CLI Version

My version of AWS CLI is 1.7.26. Here is my '--version' output:

```
$ aws --version
aws-cli/1.7.26 Python/2.7.6 Darwin/14.3.0
```


How to use the code provided

Download the zip available at **http://www.quickstepapps.com**. The direct link is **http://www.quickstepapps.com/wp-content/uploads/2015/06/awsscripted2.zip**.

From a Linux instance, you can use:

```
wget http://www.quickstepapps.com/wp-
content/uploads/2015/06/awsscripted2.zip
  unzip awsscripted2.zip
```

Once unzipped, you need to edit the top level globals.sh file.

The default file looks like this:

```
[globals.sh]

#!/bin/bash
```

```
# shared variables for ALL scripts in ALL chapters

# this may change so find the latest from the aws console
# 'EC2' > 'Launch Instance' and copy the AMI ID
# must match the region used in 'aws configure'
# as of publishing, the following were valid:
# us-east-1 ami-1ecae776
# us-west-1 ami-d114f295
# us-west-2 ami-e7527ed7
# eu-west-1 ami-a10897d6
# eu-central-1 ami-a8221fb5
# ap-southeast-1 ami-68d8e93a
# ap-southeast-2 ami-fd9cecc7
# ap-northeast-1 ami-cbf90ecb
# sa-east-1 ami-b52890a8
# Amazon Linux AMI, HVM (ap-southeast-1)
baseami=ami-68d8e93a

# the name of the VPC to launch into
# see Appendix A
vpcname=MYVPC

# zones are sub regions
# must match the region used in 'aws configure'
# normally, zones are the same with a, b, c appended
# as of publishing, the following were valid:
# us-east-1 a b c e (ie us-east-1a us-east-1b us-east-1c us-east-
1e)
# us-west-1 a c
# us-west-2 a b c
# eu-west-1 a b c
# eu-central-1 a b
# ap-southeast-1 a b
# ap-southeast-2 a b
# ap-northeast-1 a c
# sa-east-1 a b c
deployzone=ap-southeast-1a
deployzone2=ap-southeast-1c

# SSH defaults to port 22
# this is changed to a new port as defined below
sshport=38142

# the email address to send sshd logs to
emailaddress=user@youremail.com

# the new ssh username
sshuser=ssher
```

Change the definitions to suit your needs.

'baseami' is the AMI ID of the latest Amazon Linux HVM AMI. This changes every few months and region by region, so find the latest one on the first page when you launch a new instance in the AWS Console. Make sure the value matches whatever you use as your 'aws configure' region. It may work with the value provided, but you should check and update this as soon as you start.

When configuring SSH, the SSH port is changed from the default of 22. The new port is configurable in 'sshport'. Just make sure you don't pick a conflicting value or anything below 1024. The SSH user (that is the user who can ssh in) is also changed: I use 'ssher' but you can and should choose what you like.

Finally, most servers are configured with email logging for SSH. To define the email address these logs are sent to, edit the 'emailaddress' variable. The default won't crash but the emails won't get received by anyone.

I've done it like this so you don't have to change multiple variable definition files. The 'globals.sh' is used by almost all of the scripts that follow. Most chapters have an additional file, 'vars.sh' which defines variables specific to that chapter. When you create your scripts, feel free to copy and paste definitions as required. My advice is to try to keep each variable definition in as few places as possible, ideally only once, so you don't accidentally forget to change one.

All code examples in this book use a created VPC, not the default one. I do it like this because code changes if you are using the default VPC, and some readers may have multiple VPCs. VPCs are also free, so making a new one is hip. The VPC is identified and tagged by a VPC Name which you can set with the 'vpcname' variable in globals.sh. You also need to choose 2 deployment zones which match your 'aws configure' region and put them in the 'deployregion' and 'deployregion2' variables. The script to create the VPC used and more information can be found in **Appendix A - VPC**.

The code examples in the zip use 'expect'. On OSX, this works out of the box. If you are running from an AWS instance, install it with:

```
yum -y install expect
```

Last of all let me discuss some of the scripting conventions I use. The first is the use of *template* scripts. These always have filenames X_template.Y or X_template (for instance install_template.sh or sshd_config_template). What I do is use 'sed' to search and replace strings in a template file to create a finalised file. So, the files X_template.Y or X_template would be 'sed'ed to create the files X.Y or X respectively (for instance install_template.sh becomes install.sh, sshd_config_template becomes sshd_config). Replaced strings are always of the form 'SED***SED', such as 'SEDsshuserSED'. Here's an example template file:

```
# this is a demo template file, demo_template.txt
echo SEDstring1SED
echo SEDstring2SED
```

If you ran the following 'sed' command:

```
sed -e "s/SEDstring1SED/hello/g" -e "s/SEDstring2SED/world/g"
demo_template.txt > demo.txt
```

you'd create the following file 'demo.txt':

```
# this is a demo template file, demo_template.txt
echo hello
echo world
```

The reason I do it like this is that it works for all types of files (scripts, configuration files, text files). You could theoretically call scripts with arguments, but this won't work for non-executable configuration files, for instance.

The next thing to mention is the heavy use of 'expect' to automate commands *as though you were typing them on the keyboard*. This means you can automate all sorts of useful commands which require keyboard entry, like ssh with password or changing a user password.

There's a lot more on 'expect' in **Appendix B - Fun with Expect**, but just to get a taste, this is an example script:

```
#!/usr/bin/expect -f
set timeout -1
spawn ssh ec2-user@100.100.100.100
expect "Password:"
send "1234\n"
interact
```

The above script runs the command 'ssh ec2-user@100.100.100.100', waits for 'Password:' and types in '1234' then return (the '\n'). 'interact' tells the script to start running. You would run it in a similar way to a bash script:

```
chmod +x expect.sh
./expect.sh
```

I also like to build my expect scripts dynamically from within other scripts, because this keeps the command flow sequence in the original script, rather than having to look at another external file. The other advantage is that you can dynamically include bash variables, rather than using sed to finalise a template expect script. If you squint a bit you can get round the excessive escaping:

```
#!/bin/bash
# make and run expect script
# use timeout -1 for no timeout
echo "#!/usr/bin/expect -f" > expect.sh
echo "set timeout -1" >> expect.sh
echo "spawn ssh -p $sshport $sshuser@$ip_address" >> expect.sh
echo "expect \"Password:\"" >> expect.sh
echo "send \"$ssherpassword\n\"" >> expect.sh
echo "expect \"Verification code:\"" >> expect.sh
echo "send \"$mfacode\n\"" >> expect.sh
echo "interact" >> expect.sh
chmod +x expect.sh
./expect.sh
rm -f expect.sh
```

There's more about essential bash techniques in **Appendix F - Bash Script Essentials**. And if you get stuck, can't get a script to work or need to do something not in this book, feel free to drop a post at **http://www.quickstepapps.com** - I won't ignore you!

Code Listings

All code in this book can be found in the downloadable zip. Code from the zip is normal and unindented. However, for readability, when code is listed in this book, beginnings of lines are indented with 2 spaces. Lines that wrap are not indented. Multiple wrapped lines will also not indent. The reason is that given the vast number of platforms on which you can read this document, it's impossible to specify the exact width of listings. Here's an example:

```
#!/bin/bash

# this is a new line (indented by 2 spaces)

# this is a new line, but at some point I will wrap and the
wrapped part will not be indented, to repeat, at some point I will
wrap and the wrapped part will not be indented, to repeat, at some
point I will wrap and the wrapped part will not be indented, to
repeat, ...
```

Hopefully, this helps with reading code listings in this book. Obviously, for development purposes, you should always work from downloaded code which is not indented. I also recommend setting your e-reader to as wide a format as possible, so use 'one page landscape' rather than a double page view.

Note that many scripts are similar to each other, however, I realise that many readers are just looking for a quick script which will 'fix the problem'. So, I have tried to provide ready-to-use scripts in as many cases as possible so you can just download or copy and paste them and get going with the minimum of fuss.

Chapter 1 - Know Your Enemy

Key Security Concepts

In order to defend successfully against attack, you need to understand your opponents. Sounds like something out of Art of War... Well, 'war' is a good way to think about it, because there are people and programs out there who want to steal, take over or break your stuff. And they will, if you let them.

So, the first thing to emphasise is that the security of any system is only as good as its Weakest Link. It's no good having massive security on one entry to a server (like SSH) but then running a poorly written website on the same server which is vulnerable to SQL Injection attacks. Any hacker could ignore your SSH security (because it's too hard to circumvent) but still download your database. You need to protect each and every way into your servers to a level which prevents malicious activity. SSH is one service which is relatively easy to secure properly, compared, for instance, to securing a complex PHP website. However, if SSH is compromised on any of your servers, the results can be catastrophic, so securing this service is essential.

Next, I need to differentiate between 'security layer' and 'security bloat'. Good security has several layers. Bad security has one bloated layer. A layer is different from another layer if and only if it is qualitatively different and by that I mean that it can't be hacked in the same way.

To see these layers in action, let's start with an example of bad security and progressively move to better security setups. I'll use SSH as the example:

1. (BAD) SSH is open on port 22; the AWS Security Group is permanently open to the world (CIDR 0.0.0.0/0); you use the default username (ec2-user) and a simple password to sign in; the ability to 'sudo su' without password is left on. Well, you'll be

what's known as 'rooted' in no time, that is, a brute force attack will get into your server via SSH, root permissions will be obtained, and then you'll find your server is serving porn quicker than you can say WTF! I know, it happened to me a long, long time ago in a data centre far, far away...

2 (PRETTY BAD) SSH is open on port 22; the AWS Security Group is permanently open to a fixed IP, say your company's leased line; you use the default username (ec2-user) and a simple password to sign in; the ability to 'sudo su' without password is left on. The reason this is 'pretty bad' is anyone using your leased line would be able to get access to your SSH daemon. So, if you had lax WiFi security, or if another employee ran one of those funny little exes 'a friend sent them' and installed a virus, your server would be vulnerable to a brute force attack.

3 (STILL PRETTY BAD) SSH is open on port 22; the AWS Security Group is permanently open to a fixed IP, say your company's leased line; you use a non default username and an SSH Key to sign in; the ability to 'sudo su' without password is left on. The problem here is that you have a single line of defence: the laptop or desktop you connect with which has the SSH Key as a file. If that computer is compromised, like losing it or getting a virus, you have a potential breach.

4 (GETTING BETTER) SSH is open on a new port (say 38142); the AWS Security Group is normally closed and only opened to your IP when you need SSH access; you use a non default username and an SSH Key to sign in; 'sudo su' requires a reasonable password which is not stored on the same laptop as the SSH Key. You might get away with this setup. By changing the SSH port, you would avoid a lot of the automated attacks that are out there on the Internet. Not that it matters, since by keeping the AWS Security Group closed until you need it, you're only vulnerable when connected. And by editing /etc/security/limits.conf, you can limit the number of SSH sessions to yours alone. But what really differentiates this setup from the previous ones is that the 'sudo su' password is NOT on the same computer as the SSH Key, or perhaps not on a computer at all. You

now have 2 security layers. You might still get hacked, but it just got an order of magnitude harder.

5 (GOOD) SSH is open on a new port (say 38142); the AWS Security Group is normally closed and only opened to your IP when you need SSH access; AWS CLI is protected with MFA; you use a non default username and an SSH Key to sign in; 'sudo su' requires a reasonable password which is not stored on the same laptop as the SSH Key. This setup has 3 layers. A hacker would need 1) your SSH Key 2) your AWS CLI MFA device and 3) your 'sudo su' password. You are still slightly vulnerable because you might forget to close the AWS Security Group and a hacker with your SSH Key brutes your 'sudo su' password or uses another privilege escalation technique.

6 (BEST) SSH is open on a new port (say 38142); the AWS Security Group is normally closed and only opened to your IP when you need SSH access; AWS CLI is protected with MFA; SSH is protected with a non default username and MFA; 'sudo su' requires a reasonable password which is not stored on the same laptop as the SSH Password. This setup would have 3 and a half or 4 layers depending on whether you have one or two MFA devices. Two MFA devices would be best, but may be slightly overkill. The point is, even if something goes wrong and a hacker with an SSH Password gets access to the SSH port, they still need the second MFA code. However, unless you really need it, this setup is slightly impractical because it needs 3 separate credential tokens, and you start to get to a stage when the likelihood of losing a password or an MFA device outweighs the security benefit.

7 (GOOD AND PRACTICAL) SSH is open on a new port (say 38142); the AWS Security Group is normally closed and only opened to your IP when you need SSH access; AWS CLI is protected with MFA; SSH is protected with a non default username and MFA; the ability to 'sudo su' without password is disabled BUT the password is automated. This is the setup I normally use. I would rate it 3 layers. When I need to connect, I enable AWS CLI with MFA. Then I run a connect script (which has my SSH password). But I also need to MFA the SSH login. Practically

speaking, I have the laptop and the MFA device, my smartphone, which is passcode locked. The password for SSH is ultra-tough, because it's stored on my laptop and automated. Now, if I lost my laptop, which is encrypted, normally locked and always used securely, hackers might somehow manage to get into it, but without the MFA device they can't crack SSH - especially because MFA SSH sign in is rate limited to 1 per minute. If I forget to close as AWS Security Group port, it still doesn't matter - brute force is out because of my heinous SSH user password and SSH MFA sign in. I drop the requirement to store the 'sudo su' password on a different medium because of all the features, it is the least effective - any decent hacker might be able to escalate privileges anyway. And I can do away with one set of credentials (the 'sudo su' password), which I could potentially lose and thus lock myself out of my server. It's pretty quick to sign in, just run a script and enter 2 MFA codes (they're on different accounts so you can get away with entering 2 at the same time). I'm unlikely to lose my laptop or my smartphone and in any case, all the important codes are stored cryptically on paper in the company safe I have access to only via someone else. So I could recreate SSH passwords or MFA devices if needed.

So, let's return to what 'qualitatively different' means with reference to security layers and having seen several example setups. It means that there is a separate mechanism which needs to be compromised. Just adding another password to a setup is not adding a new layer if that password is stored in the same place as the first one. It's just bloat. Yes, it would slow down brute force attacks, but most likely any hacker would get into your laptop, at which point having one or two passwords is moot. And your biggest friend in this respect is MFA - bang! instant new and free security layer. It's also pretty simple to setup for protecting SSH, the AWS CLI or PHP websites, as will be explained in subsequent chapters.

Sometimes, people refer to this as the Security Onion. Onions have layers, and the more the better. If the layers are a little thick, that's good too. But too thick is bad - you get big chunks when you chop it up and we all like our onion diced up nice and fine, now don't we? Examples of layers that are too thick: having to input ridiculously long passwords by hand; or having to cart around 17 different MFA devices.

The last important point is that your own colleagues (bless them) are your biggest threat. You need to be fighting a war of attrition against people in your own organisation, funny as that may sound. People always want quick and easy access to everything. You enforce a strong password policy, and the next day it's post-it noted to their monitor. You give them an MFA device and they lose or break it accidentally-on-purpose and then it's YOUR fault they can't do their work! Yes, people will need access to data, but at all times you need to follow the principle of Least Privileges. That is, if someone only needs to read how much AWS cost last month, then give them an IAM account which can do that and ONLY that. Don't just hand over an account with Admin privileges. Even better, if your organisation is big enough, have very few people able to access the AWS infrastructure and route requests via those people. It's not a bad idea to have one person whose only job it is is to access and manage AWS, especially in a development environment. What, you allow your developers to access your Production AWS resources? Madness, madness I tell you! Here you really need that go-to guy.

However, in the most likely event that people will need more access, always try to do it via a secure website. Direct database access is completely out. I may sound belligerent when discussing my fellow employees, but really I always do my best to give them tailored PHP websites which actually do what they want. It's a lot cheaper than giving them SQL training, if that is even on the cards. With some scripts from later in the book, PHP MFA and good database security you can get excellent results. And, of course, it's vital to do the basic security training: what not to install on company computers; no-one will ever ask you for passwords over the phone and so on.

Before I end this discussion, I should address one common criticism of Cloud Computing. Shared Hardware is the issue, especially in business areas with strong Compliance requirements, such as Finance. Your Compliance Officer might specifically rule out shared Cloud resources.

Practically speaking, I haven't heard of vulnerabilities in something like VMWare, which does the actual virtualisation of servers and spreads them across hardware, but that doesn't mean they aren't there. So, a cpu might be crunching your sensitive data one minute and someone else's the next. And theoretically, you could get hacked at the source. It's also highly likely that various Organisations we all know and love have back door access. I suppose if you're not doing something bad you shouldn't be worried, right?

To alleviate these concerns, AWS has introduced a new class of instance, the Dedicated Instance, which 'guarantees' you your own hardware. This is a possible option. But if this is relevant to your business, you should of course speak to Amazon. They want your cash and will no doubt have answers for even the toughest of Compliance Officers. There is also the option of encrypted volumes.

Attacker Types

Who are these people that are messing with my servers? Here are 5 Attacker Types, rated 1 to 5 from least to most dangerous:

Level 1

Fully Automated Scripts

The Internet is rife with hosts infected with worms, malware, port scanners, bot-net recruiters and the like. Generally, these are self-propagating viruses used to infect new hosts for various nefarious purposes, like bot-nets or hacker data collection. They are unintelligent, but run a standard array of attacks ranging from brute force to SQL Injection to bug exploits. Your servers MUST absolutely be able to withstand such attacks on any ports open to the world, because AWS IP ranges are well known and are being constantly scanned. Last time I launched an AWS website, I was seeing funny requests in the logs within seconds! Yes, seconds, not hours or days. It's no good saying, "Oh, no one knows about my website yet, I haven't linked up the DNS..." Luckily, protection for this lowest level of threat is available from packages such as ModSecurity for Apache. Other open services need to be protected from brute force attacks, so implement MFA. And keep packages up to date for any security updates - a daily 'yum update' can't be bad.

Level 2

Script Kiddies

This rather derogatory appellation refers to entry level hackers, who hate it. Google it and you'll find dozens of example scripts and programs you can point at your website for a little out-of-the-box hacking. A famous example is Havij - give it a go! Just be careful what you install it on though, I bet it's heavily infected... The threat level is not much greater than Level 1, but it is a different type. Similar measures need to be taken to counter.

Level 3

Competent, but not Malicious

There are quite a few people out there with a decent knowledge of security. They know what a SQL attack is, they can paste a bit of Javascript into one of your forms and so on. Mainly they are just playing, seeing if what they read about works or not. There's no plan to hack you. Still, you need to disappoint them - they might unwittingly do some damage.

Level 4

The Insider

This is the most likely attack you will get which might actually work. Candidates include a disgruntled employee, a corporate spy, a traitor. Remember that surly IT hire you fired a few months ago? They can steal data, hand over credentials or reveal security infrastructure. This might also include disgruntled customers - they already have credentials to get into your system, which is why when designing websites, security after authentication needs to be even tighter! Don't just assume that because someone is signed in they aren't going to mess with your stuff. The best approach to countering these sorts of attacks is Least Privileges and proactive logging, so at least you limit the damage and also you can work out who it was that did the deed.

Level 5

Intelligent, Competent and Determined Hacker

If you ever become the target of this kind of attacker, watch out! Unless your security is 100%, they will get in. They include Industrial Espionage, Government Agencies and High Level Hacker Groups. They will use a mixture of computer, human and physical based hacking, such as viruses, worms, physical key-loggers and calls to employees or service providers impersonating IT support. If you're a small to mid-sized organisation, you're unlikely to run into this opponent. But you hear of large corporations getting hacked all the time - shame on them!

Threats and Vulnerabilities

Given the types of attacker you will encounter on the Internet, here is a list of attack vectors, listed from most likely to least likely. Included are the likely types of attackers who could perpetrate the attack (in the 'level' section).

Forgetfulness

enabled by: human imperfection, laziness
succeeds because: security measures do not automatically expire or reset
countered by: MFA, auto expiring security measures (like assuming a role for AWS CLI)
level: 12345

Brute Force

enabled by: open ports/services
succeeds because: weak passwords; no password rotation policy; lack of log monitoring
countered by: MFA, strong passwords, password rotation and log monitoring
level: 1245

Vulnerable Software

enabled by: periodic flaws in trusted software (like Apache) or protocols (like SSL)
succeeds because: updates are not implemented; reliance on a single layer of security
countered by: staying informed on security news; applying updates; assuming vulnerabilities exist and adding more security
level: 1245

Network Sniffer

enabled by: shared network connections (even encrypted wifi, from a different infected client)
succeeds because: plain-text passwords/cookies are used (no encryption or SSL)
countered by: encryption, SSL and MFA
level: 2345

AWS Scripted 2

No Encryption

enabled by: lack of SSL on websites
succeeds because: web sessions can be hijacked by reading cookies
countered by: using SSL
level: 2345

Poor Database Security

enabled by: storing un-hashed passwords; not using parameterised queries; not using database users or stored procedures to control access; having a database accessible from the internet
succeeds because: SQL Injection Attack is common
countered by: proper database security
level: 12345

Overconfidence and Complacency

enabled by: human nature
succeeds because: lack of logging and automation; excessive trust in security systems
countered by: proper logging and constant effort
level: 12345

Employees

enabled by: granting access to people who do not understand security implications
succeeds because: humans are easier to hack than computers
countered by: least privileges; training; threat of dismissal
level: 45

Key Logger

enabled by: using an insecure platform to access private services
succeeds because: all authentication tokens are static and entered via keyboard
countered by: OSX Terminal 'Secure Keyboard Entry'; MFA (with no code reuse)
level: 45

Infected Client

enabled by: using an insecure platform to access private services
succeeds because: all authentication tokens are static and on the client
countered by: MFA, Secure Laptop
level: 45

Infected Software

enabled by: installing server software from untrusted repositories
succeeds because: outbound security on server is lax
countered by: use yum with trusted (AWS) repositories; download RPMs from trusted source; limit outbound destinations; use internal servers with no Public Internet IP address
level: 45

Development Back-Door

enabled by: shortcuts to develop faster (like disabling MFA for development)
succeeds because: shortcuts are not tracked or documented; large software projects become unwieldy
countered by: strict tracking of development back-doors; multiple eyes; final project inspection (peer review)
level: 45

Weak Services Security

enabled by: lax security for adjunct services such as DNS provider, SSL Certificate provider
succeeds because: services accessed from insecure client; weak passwords; no MFA
countered by: Secure Laptop; service providers with MFA; locking services
level: 45

Electronic Storage

enabled by: all computer based storage is theoretically vulnerable
succeeds because: security credentials are stored electronically all in one place
countered by: splitting up credentials storage; pen and paper and the company safe
level: 45

Writing Down Passwords

enabled by: doing it
succeed because: everyone can read
countered by: using a cypher; securing the password sheet
level: 45

Development and Production

enabled by: sharing accounts between development and production
succeeds because: security during development tends to be lax
countered by: developing with one account and shifting to a new one for production
level: 45

Excessive Access

enabled by: not using Least Privileges principle
succeed because: employees often don't understand security
countered by: Least Privileges
level: 45

Account Hijacking

enabled by: incorrect setup of an AWS account
succeed because: all humans can be hacked
countered by: proper setup of AWS Security Questions; not using root credentials
level: 45

It is very useful when evaluating your security to use a list such as this. Just consider each vector in turn and ponder how your security stacks up. You can even document the process - if the 'proverbial' hits the fan later on, at least you can show 'reasonable care'! Just remember to secure this document if you create it as it will reveal key points of your security infrastructure.

Multi-Factor Authentication

MFA is the single greatest addition to your security arsenal. It's pretty simple to implement... with the scripts from this book! It's secure. With the Google Authenticator App it's basically free to implement. And most people actually prefer typing in an MFA code to remembering a password. You probably already use MFA for Gmail and if you don't you should!

You can apply MFA technology to: your AWS account; the AWS CLI; SSH connections; and PHP websites. You should use it whenever possible.

How does MFA work? Well, MFA with Google Authenticator is a time-based code generator. Basically, when MFA is set up for a particular service and user, a random string is generated. The server has a copy of this string and the user does too (typed or scanned into the MFA app). Both parties use the string and the current time to generate a 6 digit number. The number changes every 30 seconds. If they match, access is granted.

How secure is MFA? First of all it's not reversible. That means that you can't generate the original key from a number of codes. And knowing some codes won't help in predicting future codes. However, because it's a time-based algorithm, MFA normally includes what's called a 'window of error'. So, the current code will work, and the previous one and the next one. This is because the time on the server and the time on the App might not be exactly the same. You can also extend the window further, so 2 or even 3 codes either side are acceptable. The larger the 'window', the larger the time discrepancy can be. In general, try to keep the window at 3, so that only 3 codes will work. I haven't had any problems with a window of 3.

The problem is, then, that 6 digits is not really a lot of security. It's only a million possibilities. And with the error window set at 3, this falls to 333,333! Normally with cryptography you are talking billions, trillions or even "it won't happen in the lifetime of the Universe!" This makes MFA amenable to brute-force attacks. The main counter measure to this is called 'rate-limiting', that is limiting the number of attempts to 1 per minute or similar. This option is automatic with AWS Account MFA and AWS CLI MFA. You can also enable it for SSH MFA. For PHP MFA, you need to implement it, so only allow one logon attempt per minute. A hacker might get lucky and get a working code within a few minutes, but it's still hundreds of thousands to one. And that is only if MFA is the only credential being forced - if it's combined with a password and rate-limiting is enabled, it becomes very, very unlikely. But you should still check logs - they will tell you if someone is brute forcing you and you can take action (like ban their IP).

Another issue is MFA code reuse. Imagine someone is intercepting your network packets and can decrypt them or is listening in on your keyboard with a key-logger. They might get your password and MFA code and use them while the MFA code is still active. The counter for this is to disable code reuse, so a code used once won't work again, even if it's valid. This is the case with AWS Account MFA and AWS CLI MFA. It can be enabled for SSH MFA. For PHP MFA, you need to implement it. Be aware that restrictions on code reuse only apply to the last code used, so if you open up the MFA time 'window' too much and use several MFA codes, a used code might become valid.

The SSH MFA setup scripts later in this book enable both rate-limiting and no-code-reuse.

Always enable both rate-limiting and no-code-reuse and your MFA will be highly secure. And combine MFA with a password, which will thwart brute force attacks. Talk about a force multiplier!

Writing Down Passwords

Some people may disagree with me, but I like writing down passwords. Done correctly, it prevents the possibility of losing access to your servers and data. I don't write down passwords for everyday use - that is bad. But as a backup for a lost laptop or MFA device, it's a must.

You don't need to write down passwords which can be recreated or reset. For instance, if an IAM user loses his password, you can just sign in to the AWS Console as an Admin to reset it. Same goes for your AWS CLI credentials. You also don't need to write down passwords which are stored electronically AND backed up. For instance, if you set up SSH to require username and password and automate in a seriously hard password, you should have a Time Machine backup of your machine (encrypted, of course) and this will back up the password in question. Just make sure the backup media is kept separate from the original, otherwise you cold lose both at the same time. But, consider an MFA password you have typed into your smartphone. If you lose your phone, there is no backup of that MFA code and bang! you lost access to your server.

So that's something you would write down.

I do 2 things to ensure security. First, I store the piece of paper somewhere secure. If you have a company safe, use it. Otherwise, fold it up and hide it in a book in your library. Under your mattress? Perhaps.

Second, I use a trick my father taught me. He was always forgetting his ATM card PIN codes. So he used a simple cypher: pick a word with 10 letters and all letters different (you can search the internet, there are many lists). I'll tell you his word (because he's not using it any more): RESPUBLICA. Then convert your numeric code to letters by substituting R for 0, E for 1, S for 2, etc. So, 3852 becomes PCBS. He used to write the code on the back of the card. Without the cypher word, you can't break it (but only because ATMs aren't good candidates for brute force attacks).

With a slight improvement to the cypher, you can encode any alphanumeric string. First, choose a suitable cypher word (10 letters all different), I'll use HYPODERMIC. Write the word out and the numbers underneath:

```
H Y P O D E R M I C
0 1 2 3 4 5 6 7 8 9
```

Next write out the alphabet and then the numbers in a column. Then next to each letter, write an ascending number, starting from 10. Next to the number use the cypher above to write 2 letters (for instance 10 = YH). So you get:

```
A 10 YH
B 11 YY
C 12 YP
D 13 YO
E 14 YD
F 15 YE
G 16 YR
H 17 YM
I 18 YI
J 19 YC
K 20 PH
L 21 PY
M 22 PP
N 23 PO
O 24 PD
P 25 PE
Q 26 PR
```

```
R  27  PM
S  28  PI
T  29  PC
U  30  OH
V  31  OY
W  32  OP
X  33  OO
Y  34  OD
Z  35  OE
0  36  OR
1  37  OM
2  38  OI
3  39  OC
4  40  DH
5  41  DY
6  42  DP
7  43  DO
8  44  DD
9  45  DE
```

Now, here's an MFA code I received a few months back and is no longer in use: ELP5TREKK84JXN1Q. Conversion using the table above results in:

```
E   L   P   5   T   R   E   K   K   8   4   J   X   N   1   Q
YD  PY  PE  DY  PC  PM  YD  PH  PH  DD  DH  YC  OO  PO  OM  PR
```

or: YDPYPEDYPCPMYDPHPHDDDHYCOOPOOMPR

Now write this code down rather than the original password. Remember your cypher word. Reverse the process to decode. Destroy the paper you used to work the codes out on - and by 'destroy' I mean burn or shred it, preferably burn. Don't write a script to automate this process. It needs to be non-electronic for maximum effectiveness. Sometimes, pencil and paper are best.

It's not unbreakable. If Alan Turing got hold of it, it would probably only take him half an hour to decipher it. But it will stop most hackers or anyone who casually happens to see your paper. And it would certainly give you the few hours you need to change all your passwords in the event of a breach. Also, you don't need a computer to encode or decode, so nothing is in electronic format.

Note that MFA codes are case-insensitive, which is handy when you're typing them into your smartphone. If you use this method to encode other passwords, either use case-insensitive passwords, or modify the cypher method above to list lowercase letters and then uppercase ones.

The only problem with this is that if you get run over by a bus, and then your company needs to access these codes, they won't be able to. You'll have to work out who to trust with your cypher word and your method! Or institute a policy that in the event of your demise, such and such an envelope should be opened and all passwords should be changed. It's worth it just to send your boss an email starting with "In the event of my death..." What dedication!

Chapter 2 - Securing Basic AWS Access

Secure Laptop

The importance of a secure environment when running AWS CLI scripts cannot be over-emphasised. When you sign in to the AWS Console on the Internet, you have good protection with MFA (Multi-Factor Authentication). With AWS CLI all your credentials are on the client and if a hacker compromised you they would have full control over your servers. Even if you use the MFA scripts later in this book, you are temporarily vulnerable. Hence a Secure Laptop is vital and also a must for accessing services outside of AWS, like your DNS and SSL providers.

Because we are using AWS Linux, a Mac laptop is highly recommended. The Mac bash shell is the same as the Linux one (for our purposes), so you can test commands from your Mac. Things like file permissions can be carried over for transferred files, for instance the fact that scripts are executable. In addition, Macs are much more secure than most other platforms and also rather pleasant on the eyes. A Linux environment would also work. And if you feel confident you can secure a Windows installation - go for it! I say Laptop because laptops feel inherently more secure than desktops. You can put a laptop in a safe. It's quite hard to take them apart. And so on.

Here are some steps you should take to secure a Mac Laptop for this purpose:

Administrator Account

Use a very long and difficult password for the Administrator Account, something like a phrase with numbers interspersed, at least 30 or 40 characters. From this account you need to create your day to day account with heavy restrictions.

Users and Groups

From your Administrator Account, go to Users and Groups in Settings. Turn off the Guest Account. Add a new account with a long password, at least 20 characters. For this new user uncheck 'Allow user to administer this computer' and turn on Parental Controls.

Parental Controls

For your new user, on the Apps Tab, check Limit Applications. Don't allow App Store Apps. From the list of available apps, select the absolute minimum you will need: Calculator, ksadmin (otherwise it prompts you every few minutes), Mission Control, Safari and TextEdit; from the Utilities, select only Terminal.

On the Web Tab, select 'Allow access to only these websites', and add in any websites you will need. The first will be AWS at aws.amazon.com, and then any others such as your Domain Name Provider, Gmail and any other services which need to be secure.

What I mean by secure is this: there is no point having hyper-security on your AWS and servers if your DNS account can be hacked, as this could compromise your Application in a major way. Similarly, if you use a provider such as Digicert for you SSL keys, this account also needs to be secure. All these peripheral service accounts should be created from your Secure Laptop and should never be used from any other computer.

Do not add in things like Google (for searching) or your personal email account or similar. This laptop is not for development, not for reading emails, not for updating your FB page! Only access things that need to be secured, only access those secure services from the laptop and don't ever be tempted to open up access to potential threats for the sake of convenience. Then it will be impossible for you to download a key-logger or other malware, which would be a disaster for your organisation.

Secure Settings

Always 'Click the lock to prevent further changes'. Also, in Terminal, turn on 'Secure Keyboard Entry' under the Terminal menu option.

Security and Privacy

From the Security and Privacy Settings panel, select 'Require password IMMEDIATELY after sleep or screensaver begins'. Turn on FileVault to encrypt your drive and set a recovery key. Only the Administrator Account should be able to to unlock the disk.

On the Firewall Tab, enable the firewall and in Firewall Options enable 'Block All Incoming Connections' and 'Enable Stealth Mode'.

Other Services

Don't set up anything else, such as iCloud, your Apple ID, or Sharing. You should set up Time Machine (a good way to do this is to an SD Card) and Encrypt Backups. To copy files to the Secure Laptop, you should use a USB stick, not file sharing. And preferably a new USB stick at that.

General Use

Now sign out of the Administrator Account and sign back in as your new user. Day to day, you will use this account. Minimise signing in as the Administrator. On the rare occasions that you need to add a new website (because it is a secure service) or make a new App available you can do this from the new account by typing the Administrator Password.

Storing Passwords

Because you are using long and complex passwords, you should write them down. You are using FileVault and other measures which mean that if you do lose access you really won't be able to fix it. And if you lose access to your Secure Laptop, you could lose access to all your servers, which could be a disaster. So, contrary to popular opinion, write your passwords down on one sheet of paper with a cypher and then secure that sheet, in a safe, under a floorboard or with your organisation's secure storage facility. See **Chapter 1 - Writing Down Passwords** for some useful tips

Once your Secure Laptop is ready, you can proceed to the next section to create your AWS Account. Do it from the Secure Laptop, especially for an AWS Account which will host Production Servers.

AWS Console

You are doing this from your Secure Laptop, yes?

Go to **https://aws.amazon.com** and do the steps to create a new account. It's a little involved - Amazon rings you back to confirm your telephone number, but all in all it's not rocket science. Just be careful with creating too many accounts. I have been blocked on my third account linked to the same credit card and no amount of pleading with support changed that.

In terms of security, you MUST ABSOLUTELY WITHOUT FAIL set up MFA AND your Security Questions.

You can set up MFA for your AWS Account by clicking your Account Name top right and selecting Security Credentials. On the first page that appears, click the plus next to Multi-Factor Authentication (MFA) and proceed with the setup. Then, when you need to sign in to the AWS Console you will need to enter an MFA code.

To set up your Security Questions, from the Console, click your Account Name top right and select My Account. On the first page which appears, scroll down to Configure Security Challenge Questions, select three questions and type responses which are 6 digit random numbers. DO NOT use real world answers, because this sort of data is probably readily available on the Internet for you - from your Blog, your Facebook or LinkedIn profile etc. Stick to numbers as these are easy to read out to support if you should ever need to. Write the questions down then encode the answers with the cypher shown in **Chapter 1 - Writing Down Passwords** and write those down as well. Then secure the sheet of paper.

The Security Questions are vital because there are stories going round of hackers calling AWS and gaining access to someone's account by 'human hacking' AWS Support. Amazon have probably tightened this up, but using random digit Security Question answers will prevent this.

Next create an IAM User with Admin privileges. Do not create root account keys. To create the IAM user, click Services top left, select IAM, click Users on the left menu and select Create New Users. Type an appropriate name, like 'admin', and then Create bottom right. On the resulting page, click Show User Security Credentials and copy and paste the Access Key ID and Secret Access Key to your Secure Laptop. Then click Close twice (you don't need to download the credentials because you copied and pasted them). From the Users list page, click the user you just created, then click the Attach Policy button. From the Attach Policy page, select AdministratorAccess and then the Attach Policy button bottom right. Now you can use the copied credentials for setting up the AWS CLI in the next section.

AWS CLI

OSX

On Mac OSX, you can install the AWS CLI (Command Line

Interface) with a few commands in Terminal:

```
sudo easy_install pip
sudo pip install awscli
```

Next, open your .profile file with:

```
sudo vi ~/.profile
```

Paste in the following 2 lines at the bottom:

```
export LC_ALL=en_US.UTF-8
export LANG=en_US.UTF-8
```

(press 'i' to insert, paste with command-V, press Escape, save and quit with :wq)

Next (in Terminal):

```
aws configure
```

and paste in your Access Key ID and Secret Access Key you just copied from your newly created admin user. You should set your default region here too, such as us-west-1 or eu-west-1, and set the Default output format to json. At this point, it's probably worth deleting wherever you copied and pasted your admin credentials to.

Restart your Terminal Window. That's it. The 'aws' command will now work from any Terminal Window, normally I have at least 6 open.

AWS Linux

On the latest Amazon Linux AMIs, the 'aws' command works out of the box. You just need to do 'aws configure' as per the last section.

If you don't have a Mac or don't want to use it because it's not secure enough, using an AWS instance to create and manage your

Cloud Application is very possible and very easy. Just launch an instance from the AWS Console and get a shell on it with whichever SSH client you use. You can send files to it with 'scp'. You can download the code for this book direct to the box with 'wget', see the **Introduction**. It all works.

Chapter 3 - AWS Security Groups

How Security Groups Work

AWS Security Groups are pretty cool and simple. They specify a set of Inbound rules and a set of Outbound rules which permit network traffic to pass or not. Rules are specified with three parameters: Protocol, Port Range and Source (for Inbound rules) or Destination (for Outbound rules). There's no order to the rules and they are all ALLOW rules.

When a Security Group is created, all Outbound traffic is permitted. You need to specify Inbound Rules. To allow all traffic in to a website from the whole Internet, select Protocol: TCP, Port Range: 80 and Source: Anywhere. To allow traffic in to SSH from only your IP, select Protocol: TCP, Port Range:22 and Source: My IP. IP addresses and ranges are specified in CIDR notation: 0.0.0.0/0 means Anywhere, w.x.y.z/32 means only from w.x.y.z and x.y.z.0/24 means x.y.z.*, that is a 255.255.255.0 subnet (24 bits) or IP addresses x.y.z.1 to x.y.z.255.

Security Groups can also refer to other Security Groups. This is how you open up connectivity between your instances. You could use internal or Private IP addresses, but in certain situations these can change, so it's best to link to other Security Groups, which don't change. A good example is connecting to a database: if your web server has Security Group A and your RDS instance has Security Group B, you allow the web server to talk to your RDS instance by adding an Inbound rule to Security Group B with Protocol: TCP, Port Range: 3306 (the MySQL port), Source: Security Group A. It's similar for an ELB: for an ELB distributing web traffic, the ELB Security Group would have an Inbound rule allowing traffic into it from the Internet, and each instance receiving traffic from the ELB would have an Inbound rule allowing traffic from the ELB Security Group.

Once a Security Group is created, it can be attached to a resource, which can be an EC2 instance, an ELB (Elastic Load Balancer) or an RDS database, amongst other things. Basically, anything which can send or receive traffic can have a Security Group attached. You can attach more than one Security Group to a resource, and you can attach a Security Group to multiple resources.

Personally, I like one Security Group per resource, and a unique Security Group per resource, then you don't inadvertently open up ports on a server you don't want to. I like to use a standard naming convention, whereby the Security Group name is the resource name with 'sg' appended. When I create an instance, I give it a unique key name, like 'webphp1', I tag it with the same name [instancename=webphp1]. Then I attach a Security Group I have created with the name webphp1sg and tagged with [sgname=webphp1sg]. I always append the 'sg' to the key or tag name of the server so I can always work out the Security Group name in question and retrieve its ID by tag.

In general, you will have 2 kinds of Security Group, temporary and permanent. For instance, for a web server, you would have permanent rules allowing Inbound ports 80 (HTTP) and 443 (HTTPS). When you need to do some work on the server, you would open up port 22 (SSH) temporarily, do what needs to be done, and then close it. Connect scripts provided later in this chapter automate this process: they open the SSH port before connecting and when SSH is done, they close the port in the Security Group.

Security Groups are 'stateful', which means any traffic leaving your server as a result of an Inbound network connection (like a reply to a web request) is allowed. So, you don't need to specify rules for replies to Inbound requests, as you do with NACLs (see later in this Chapter) or 'iptables'. If your server never uses outgoing connections, you could remove the default Outbound rule which is Protocol: All, Port Range 0-65535, Destination: Anywhere (0.0.0.0/0). This does however mean you won't be able to install or update software with yum or connect out. A possibility after you have set up your server.

Managing Security Groups

AWS Console

You create a Security Group from the Security Groups section in the EC2 or VPC Console section. After pressing Create Security Group, enter a Security group name and a Description; select a VPC the Security Group will be in; then add some Inbound rules below and click Create. The Console interface is very helpful when referring to other Security Groups. Just select 'Custom IP' and type 's' and a tagged list will pop up for you to select from.

AWS CLI

Here are some example AWS CLI commands which show you how to do what you generally need to do to manage Security Groups.

Make a Security Group called 'mysg', described as 'my security group' (description is required) in the VPC $vpc_id:

```
aws ec2 create-security-group --group-name mysg --description "my
security group" --vpc-id $vpc_id
```

You don't need to define a Security Group inside a VPC (Virtual Private Cloud), but in practice you always need to because your resources are in a VPC. To get a VPC ID to use in the 'aws ec2 create-security-group' you can use:

```
vpc_id=$(aws ec2 describe-vpcs --filters Name=tag-
key,Values=vpcname Name=tag-value,Values=MYVPC --output text
--query 'Vpcs[*].VpcId')
echo $vpc_id
```

(assuming you tagged your VPC with [vpcname=MYVPC] - see **Appendix A - VPC** for a script to set up the VPC used throughout this book).

In practice, when you create a Security Group, you actually want to get back its ID so you can then tag and configure it:

```
sgid=$(aws ec2 create-security-group --group-name mysg
--description "my security group" --vpc-id $vpc_id --output text
--query 'GroupId')
echo sgid=$sgid
```

Getting a Security Group ID after you have created it is best done by filtering for a tag. You attach a tag with:

```
aws ec2 create-tags --resources $sgid --tags
Key=sgname,Value=mysg
```

Use a standard naming convention for Security Group name and tag values, I always just append 'sg' to the instance name it will be attached to. Or 'elbsg' if it's attached to an ELB. Or 'dbsg' if it's attached to an RDS Database.

You retrieve the ID from the tag with:

```
sgid=$(aws ec2 describe-security-groups --filters Name=tag-
key,Values=sgname Name=tag-value,Values=mysg --output text --query
'SecurityGroups[*].GroupId')
echo sgid=$sgid
```

The reason that in many of my scripts you will see me make a Security Group, tag it and then re-retrieve the ID by tag is that I like to make make my scripts re-runnable, that is they will work even if it's not the first time they have been called without having to undo everything from the previous call. So by 'making, tagging, retrieving by tag' it will work a second time around: the make fails (already exists), the add tag fails ($sgid is empty), but retrieve by tag works (and you get a working $sgid to use) because the Security Group already exists and was tagged when created.

Now that you have a working Security Group ID (in $sgid), you can use AWS CLI to add or revoke Inbound rules. Here's how to add a rule to allow everyone to access a website on port 80:

```
aws ec2 authorize-security-group-ingress --group-id $sgid
--protocol tcp --port 80 --cidr 0.0.0.0/0
```

It's more common to limit access to a specific IP, but to do this you need to get your IP into a bash variable:

```
myip=$(curl http://checkip.amazonaws.com/)
echo myip=$myip
```

Now, open up SSH to your IP only:

```
aws ec2 authorize-security-group-ingress --group-id $sgid
--protocol tcp --port 22 --cidr $myip/32
```

And close it when you're done:

```
aws ec2 revoke-security-group-ingress --group-id $sgid --protocol
tcp --port 22 --cidr $myip/32
```

To allow traffic between instances, use the '--source-group' parameter:

```
aws ec2 authorize-security-group-ingress --group-id $sgid
--source-group $sg2id --protocol tcp --port 22
```

which would allow TCP traffic from any instance with Security Group $sg2id attached to port 22 on the instance tagged with Security Group $sgid.

A shorthand for specifying ALL ports and protocols is ' --protocol -1', for example:

```
aws ec2 authorize-security-group-ingress --group-id $sgid
--source-group $sg2id --protocol -1
```

which would allow ALL traffic from $sg2id to $sgid.

Deleting Security Groups is a little more complex because a Security Group can't be deleted if it is referred to by any other Security Group. So, before deleting, you need to remove any references to it from other Security Groups. In practice, I don't often delete Security Groups, so it's not a big issue. But I normally have a 'master delete' script which removes all the resources I have created. In that I just remove all rules from all Security Groups, and then actually delete the Security Groups with:

```
aws ec2 delete-security-group --group-id $sgid
```

Useful Scripts

Here are 2 useful scripts which demonstrate some techniques for handling Security Groups. They help with the security sensitive task of closing temporary ports used to administer servers.

The first script closes any CIDR rules for the specified port in the specified Security Group.

[chapter3/closeports.sh]

```bash
#!/bin/bash

# this script closes any cidr rules for the specified port for
the specified security group
# call it with 2 arguments
# ./closeports <sg_tag_value> <port>
# eg ./closeports xxxsg 22 would close port 22 rules in xxx
security group (tagged xxxsg)

# when we create a security group, we always tag it
[sgname=xxxsg] with:
# aws ec2 create-tags --resources <security group id> --tags
Key=sgname,Value=xxxsg

# read arguments
sgtag=$1
port=$2

# get the group id of the sg from the tag
sgid=$(aws ec2 describe-security-groups --filters Name=tag-
key,Values=sgname Name=tag-value,Values=$sgtag --output text
--query 'SecurityGroups[*].GroupId')
echo sgid=$sgid

echo closing any port $port inbound rules in sg $sgid tagged
$sgtag

# get the cidrs for the ingress rule
rules=$(aws ec2 describe-security-groups --group-ids $sgid
--output text --query 'SecurityGroups[*].IpPermissions')

# if no rules, quit
if test "$rules" = ""; then
        echo "no rules found, exiting"
        exit
fi

# rules will contain something like:
# 22 tcp 22
# IPRANGES 108.42.177.53/32
# IPRANGES 10.0.0.0/16
# 80 tcp 80
# IPRANGES 0.0.0.0/0

# luckily, aws returns all ipranges per port grouped together

# flag for if we are reading ipranges
reading=0
# loop returned lines
```

```
while read -r line; do
        # split the line up
        rulebits=($line)
        # check if if we are reading ssh port ipranges
        if [ $reading -eq 0 ] ; then
                # we are not reading ipranges
                # assuming port==22, check if '22 tcp 22'
                if [ ${rulebits[0]} == "$port" ] && [ $
{rulebits[1]} == "tcp" ] && [ ${rulebits[2]} == "$port" ] ; then
                        # found it
                        reading=1
                fi
        else
                # we are reading ipranges
                # check if first word is 'IPRANGES'
                if [ ${rulebits[0]} == "IPRANGES" ] ; then
                        # found a cidr for open ssh port
                        cidr=${rulebits[1]}
                        echo found port $port open cidr $cidr
closing...
                        # close it
                        aws ec2 revoke-security-group-ingress
--group-id $sgid --protocol tcp --port $port --cidr $cidr
                else
                        # new port
                        reading=0
                fi
        fi
    done <<< "$rules"
```

You should call it with:

```
./closeports.sh <sg tag name> <port>
```

The second script uses the first script to loop across all Security
Groups to close any CIDR rules for the specified port in all
Security Groups.

[chapter3/closeportsallsgs.sh]

```
#!/bin/bash

# this script closes any cidr rules for the specified port for
all security group
# call it with 1 argument
# ./closeportsallsgs <port>
# eg ./closeportsallsgs 22 would close port 22 cidr rules in all
security groups

# this script calls the closeports.sh script

# read arguments
port=$1

# get all security groups with specified port open with cidr rule
sgs=$(aws ec2 describe-security-groups --output text --query
'SecurityGroups[*].Tags[*].Value')

# loop through found security groups
for sg in $sgs
do
```

```
          # call sub script
          echo $'\n' calling    . ./closeports.sh $sg $port
          . ./closeports.sh $sg $port

done
```

You should call it with:

```
./closeportsallsgs.sh <port>
```

Here is a test script which makes some Security Groups, adds some rules, calls the above scripts, then deletes the new Security Groups:

[Chapter3/testclose.sh]

```
#!/bin/bash

# this script tests out security group port closing scripts
# it makes 2 security groups, adds some rules, then tests the
close scripts
# finally, it deletes the security groups
# for this test, for simplicity, we are not using a vpc

echo $'\n' making new sgs and rules $'\n'

# make my1 sg
my1sgid=$(aws ec2 create-security-group --group-name my1sg
--description "my1 security group" --output text --query 'GroupId')
# tag it
aws ec2 create-tags --resources $my1sgid --tags
Key=sgname,Value=my1sg
# get the sg id by tag
my1sgid=$(aws ec2 describe-security-groups --filters Name=tag-
key,Values=sgname Name=tag-value,Values=my1sg --output text --query
'SecurityGroups[*].GroupId')
echo my1sgid=$my1sgid

# make my2 sg
my2sgid=$(aws ec2 create-security-group --group-name my2sg
--description "my2 security group" --output text --query 'GroupId')
# tag it
aws ec2 create-tags --resources $my2sgid --tags
Key=sgname,Value=my2sg
# get the sg id by tag
my2sgid=$(aws ec2 describe-security-groups --filters Name=tag-
key,Values=sgname Name=tag-value,Values=my2sg --output text --query
'SecurityGroups[*].GroupId')
echo my2sgid=$my2sgid

# create some inbound rules on tcp port 22 (they are unattached
sgs so no security issues...)
# my1: from 0.0.0.0/0; from 10.0.10.0/24; from 192.168.1.1/32
# my2: from 10.0.10.0/24; from my1
# also create some tcp port 80 rules, to check they are
unaffected
# my1: from 0.0.0.0/0
# my2: from 0.0.0.0/0

aws ec2 authorize-security-group-ingress --group-id $my1sgid
--protocol tcp --port 22 --cidr 0.0.0.0/0
aws ec2 authorize-security-group-ingress --group-id $my1sgid
```

```
--protocol tcp --port 22 --cidr 10.0.10.0/24
  aws ec2 authorize-security-group-ingress --group-id $my1sgid
--protocol tcp --port 22 --cidr 192.168.1.1/32

  aws ec2 authorize-security-group-ingress --group-id $my2sgid
--protocol tcp --port 22 --cidr 10.0.10.0/24
  aws ec2 authorize-security-group-ingress --group-id $my2sgid
--protocol tcp --port 22 --source-group $my1sgid

  aws ec2 authorize-security-group-ingress --group-id $my1sgid
--protocol tcp --port 80 --cidr 0.0.0.0/0
  aws ec2 authorize-security-group-ingress --group-id $my2sgid
--protocol tcp --port 80 --cidr 0.0.0.0/0

  # describe the groups
  echo $'\n' describing new sgs $'\n'
  aws ec2 describe-security-groups --group-id $my1sgid --output
text
  aws ec2 describe-security-groups --group-id $my2sgid --output
text

  # lets close cidr 22s in my2sg
  echo $'\n' closing 22 cidrs in my2sg$ with . ./closeports.sh
my2sg 22 $'\n'
  . ./closeports.sh my2sg 22

  # then describe my2sg
  echo $'\n' describing my2sg $'\n'
  aws ec2 describe-security-groups --group-id $my2sgid --output
text
  echo $'\n' note 'IPRANGES     10.0.10.0/24' is no longer listed

  # make my2sg rules again
  echo $'\n' remaking my2sg 10.0.10.0/24:22 rule
  aws ec2 authorize-security-group-ingress --group-id $my2sgid
--protocol tcp --port 22 --cidr 10.0.10.0/24

  # describe my2sg again
  echo $'\n' describing my2sg $'\n'
  aws ec2 describe-security-groups --group-id $my2sgid --output
text

  # close all cidr 22s in all sgs
  echo $'\n' closing 22 cidrs in all sgs with .
./closeportsallsgs.sh 22
  . ./closeportsallsgs.sh 22
  echo $'\n' finished . ./closeportsallsgs.sh 22

  # describe the groups
  echo $'\n' describing after all closed $'\n'
  aws ec2 describe-security-groups --group-id $my1sgid --output
text
  aws ec2 describe-security-groups --group-id $my2sgid --output
text
  echo $'\n' note there are no port 22 cidr rules

  # delete the sgs
  # first revoke the link between sgs (or they can't be deleted)
  aws ec2 revoke-security-group-ingress --group-id $my2sgid
--protocol tcp --port 22 --source-group $my1sgid
  # now delete
  aws ec2 delete-security-group  --group-id $my1sgid
  aws ec2 delete-security-group  --group-id $my2sgid
  echo $'\n' deleted groups
```

Run it with:

```
./testclose.sh
```

and the resulting output is:

[chapter3/testclose_results.txt]

```
$ ./testclose.sh

  making new sgs and rules

  my1sgid=sg-7f0d552a
  my2sgid=sg-790d552c

  describing new sgs

  SECURITYGROUPS          my1 security group      sg-7f0d552a
my1sg   xxxxxxxxxxxxx
   IPPERMISSIONS 22        tcp     22
   IPRANGES       0.0.0.0/0
   IPRANGES       10.0.10.0/24
   IPRANGES       192.168.1.1/32
   IPPERMISSIONS 80        tcp     80
   IPRANGES       0.0.0.0/0
   TAGS   sgname  my1sg
   SECURITYGROUPS          my2 security group      sg-790d552c
my2sg   xxxxxxxxxxxxx
   IPPERMISSIONS 22        tcp     22
   IPRANGES       10.0.10.0/24
   USERIDGROUPPAIRS        sg-7f0d552a     my1sg   xxxxxxxxxxxxx
   IPPERMISSIONS 80        tcp     80
   IPRANGES       0.0.0.0/0
   TAGS   sgname  my2sg

  closing 22 cidrs in my2sg$ with . ./closeports.sh my2sg 22

  sgid=sg-790d552c
  closing any port 22 inbound rules in sg sg-790d552c tagged my2sg
  found port 22 open cidr 10.0.10.0/24 closing...

  describing my2sg

  SECURITYGROUPS          my2 security group      sg-790d552c
my2sg   xxxxxxxxxxxxx
   IPPERMISSIONS 22        tcp     22
   USERIDGROUPPAIRS        sg-7f0d552a     my1sg   xxxxxxxxxxxxx
   IPPERMISSIONS 80        tcp     80
   IPRANGES       0.0.0.0/0
   TAGS   sgname  my2sg

  note IPRANGES           10.0.10.0/24 is no longer listed

  remaking my2sg 10.0.10.0/24:22 rule

  describing my2sg

  SECURITYGROUPS          my2 security group      sg-790d552c
my2sg   xxxxxxxxxxxxx
   IPPERMISSIONS 22        tcp     22
   IPRANGES       10.0.10.0/24
   USERIDGROUPPAIRS        sg-7f0d552a     my1sg   xxxxxxxxxxxxx
   IPPERMISSIONS 80        tcp     80
   IPRANGES       0.0.0.0/0
   TAGS   sgname  my2sg

  closing 22 cidrs in all sgs with . ./closeportsallsgs.sh 22
```

```
 calling . ./closeports.sh my2sg 22
sgid=sg-790d552c
closing any port 22 inbound rules in sg sg-790d552c tagged my2sg
found port 22 open cidr 10.0.10.0/24 closing...

 calling . ./closeports.sh my1sg 22
sgid=sg-7f0d552a
closing any port 22 inbound rules in sg sg-7f0d552a tagged my1sg
found port 22 open cidr 0.0.0.0/0 closing...
found port 22 open cidr 10.0.10.0/24 closing...
found port 22 open cidr 192.168.1.1/32 closing...

 finished . ./closeportsallsgs.sh 22

 describing after all closed

 SECURITYGROUPS          my1 security group       sg-7f0d552a
my1sg   xxxxxxxxxxxx
 IPPERMISSIONS 80        tcp      80
 IPRANGES        0.0.0.0/0
 TAGS  sgname  my1sg
 SECURITYGROUPS          my2 security group       sg-790d552c
my2sg   xxxxxxxxxxxx
 IPPERMISSIONS 22        tcp      22
 USERIDGROUPPAIRS        sg-7f0d552a    my1sg    xxxxxxxxxxxx
 IPPERMISSIONS 80        tcp      80
 IPRANGES        0.0.0.0/0
 TAGS  sgname  my2sg

 note there are no port 22 cidr rules

 deleted groups
```

Network ACLs

Network ACLs are a second layer of port control. Whereas Security Groups are attached to resources, NACLs are attached to subnets and are applied to all resources in that subnet. They are almost exactly the same as iptables, but applied to a whole network.

AWS provides a good comparison of Security Groups vs NACLs at **http://docs.aws.amazon.com/AmazonVPC/latest/UserGuide/VPC_Security.html#VPC_Security_Comparison**.

In general, I stick to Security Groups because I like to have fine grain control. However, if you are doing VPC or Subnet wide things, like limiting Inbound/Outbound traffic to your Corporate Headquarters, NACLs are very useful. Just remember that they operate differently from Security Groups and much more like 'iptables'. They are still a *second* layer of security - so I would also keep any rules in the corresponding Security Group.

In terms of providing extra security, this is a case of 'security bloat'. The point is, if a hacker can mess with your Security Groups, they can also mess with your NACLs, for instance, if they have stolen your AWS Credentials or hacked into your AWS Console. So adding NACLs which restate rules already in Security Groups doesn't really do much. It's not as though Security Groups are going to stop working for a bit, so it's lucky I had those NACLs! On the other hand, you could grant permissions to edit Security Groups and NACLs to different IAM Users, so if one set of credentials is compromised, your network security would still be intact.

Chapter 4 - MFA for AWS CLI

It took me a long time to get this to work. I had to get my head around some pretty heavy documentation and, as usual, the main problem was the documentation itself! It's fragmented and nowhere does it say here's a list of commands to 'do it'. Even the AWS blogs were pretty cryptic. But, in my opinion, this is the most important chapter of the book, so it has been worth it. If the only thing you implement from this book is AWS CLI MFA, you will have added a strong defence against malicious activity, because CLI credentials are inherently insecure. They're just 2 strings stored unencrypted in a file on your laptop. It's the same as putting your AWS Console username and password in a text file on your Desktop and not turning on Console MFA. Anyone with access to your computer (like when you go to get that coffee) can just read the file.

Basically, what you can do is have an AWS CLI setup which permits you to do nothing other than request more privileges. To do this you need to enter an MFA code. Once the privileges are requested and obtained, you can do what you want. The privileges assigned automatically expire after a certain time (max 1 hour). So you are protecting your AWS CLI access with MFA.

Some basic concepts you need to understand:

An 'IAM User' is an entity which can act in your AWS Account with specific privileges. IAM Users have a 'Policy' attached to them which grants privileges. They can also have an MFA Device assigned to them. When you set up AWS CLI in **Chapter 2 - AWS CLI**, you made an IAM User called 'admin' with full permissions.

An 'IAM Role' defines a set of permissions which can be attached to a resource, such as an EC2 Instance or IAM User. Roles have an 'Assume Policy', which specifies who or what can 'assume' them, and a 'Policy', which defines privileges available once assumed.

An IAM User is entitled to assume a Role if they are listed in the

Role's Assume Policy. When they assume the Role, they receive privileges as defined by the Role's Policy.

MFA is linked into the whole process in the Role's Assume Policy: you can specify that a Role can only be assumed by such and such a User if and only if they have authenticated with MFA.

The next section describes the setup process and provides the scripts to do it. I don't recommend setting this up in the AWS Console for three reasons. First, it's very complex - for example, policies need to refer to each other and so things need to be done in the right order. Second, The AWS Console interface for creating Users and Roles is a bit 'wizardy', so you can't just make a role with such and such a policy, you need to make one, remove the policy then add another one. Last, the setup script actually makes the Sign In and Sign Out scripts that you will need for day to day use. If you do it from AWS Console you will have to manually build these scripts.

Setup MFA for AWS CLI

Setting up MFA for AWS CLI can be done in the AWS Console but it is a complete nightmare, so do it with the scripts provided. The general process is as follows:

- create an IAM User 'assumer'
- create an IAM Role 'adminrole'
- attach an 'assume-policy' to adminrole which lets assumer assume it if MFA is active
- attach a 'role-policy' to adminrole with admin privileges
- create an IAM Role 'connectrole'
- attach an 'assume-policy' to connectrole which lets assumer assume it if MFA is active
- attach a 'role-policy' to connectrole with connect privileges
- attach a 'policy' to assumer which allows commands to assume the adminrole or the connectrole, and permits nothing else

- make an access key for assumer and download credentials
- make a new virtual MFA device
- enable the MFA device and attach it to assumer

Now, you have lots of choices as regards how to implement this. You can have multiple IAM Users, each of whom can assume one or more IAM Roles. Each IAM User has their own MFA device. Each IAM Role has its own set of privileges, which is useful as you can separate permission sets into, for example, one for day to day connecting to instances and one for full admin access. You need to decide how to play it. For instance, if you are the only person to access AWS via the CLI, you would probably go for 1 User (assumer) and 2 Roles (connectrole and adminrole), which means you would use the same MFA generator for assuming both roles. If you want to be more secure and have separate MFA devices for each role, you would use 2 Users and 2 Roles: adminuser who can assume adminrole and connectuser who can assume connectrole. And if you have many people connecting, you can have multiple users, multiple MFA devices and multiple roles.

In my own CLI setup, I use 1 IAM User, 'assumer' and 2 roles which can be assumed: 'adminrole' and 'connectrole'. I use the same MFA device for assuming both roles. It's still very secure and when I only need connect privileges, I obey Least Privileges and don't assume admin status. When I need to build resources, I assume the admin role and I can do anything. This is how the scripts are configured in this chapter. If you want something different, you'll need to edit them to suit your needs.

Before I get into the heavy scripting, here are the various policies which you can copy and paste into AWS Console, if that's how you choose to do it. There are 3 types of policy: the user policy attached to a user (which only allows 'aws sts assume-role ...'); the role assume policy attached to a role (which specifies who can assume the policy and with what conditions); and the role policy attached to a role (which specifies the privileges obtained when the role is successfully assumed). The first two (user policy and role assume policy) are standard and for our purposes their structure doesn't change. These two policies are slightly complicated by the fact that they need to refer to each other. For the third type (the role policy), you can use a standard policy structure - I provide 2, full admin and connect only.

So let's start with the assumer user policy, which when attached to a user allows only the assumption of a specific role:

[chapter4/assumeruserpolicy.txt]

```
# assumer user policy
# can only run 'aws sts assume-role --role-arn ***ROLEARN*** ...'
{
        "Version": "2012-10-17",
        "Statement":
        [
                {
                        "Effect": "Allow",
                        "Action": "sts:AssumeRole",
                        "Resource": "***ROLEARN***"
                }
        ]
}

# to put this policy into a bash variable, use:
userpolicy="{\"Version\": \"2012-10-17\",\"Statement\":
[{\"Effect\": \"Allow\",\"Action\": \"sts:AssumeRole\",\"Resource\"
: \""
userpolicy+=$rolearn
userpolicy+="\"}]}"
echo userpolicy=$userpoli
```

You'll notice the string '***ROLEARN***' - this is the ARN of the role that can be assumed. Role ARNs have a standard format: 'arn:aws:iam::[AWS Account Number]:role/[rolename]' (you need to update [AWS Account number] with your 12 digit account number, available in My Account, and [rolename] with the name of the role). In my scripts, I don't build the ARN, I retrieve it when I create the role.

Next there is the assume-role policy, which needs to be attached to a role and specifies who can assume the role:

[chapter4/assumerolepolicy.txt]

```
# assume-role policy
{
        "Version": "2012-10-17",
        "Statement": [
                {
```

```
                    "Sid": "",
                    "Effect": "Allow",
                    "Principal": { "AWS": "***USERARN***" },
                    "Action": "sts:AssumeRole",
                    "Condition": { "Bool":
{ "aws:MultiFactorAuthPresent": true } }
                }
            ]
    }

    # to put this policy into a bash variable, use:

    assumerolepolicy="{\"Version\": \"2012-10-17\",\"Statement\":
[{\"Sid\": \"\",\"Effect\": \"Allow\",\"Principal\": {\"AWS\": \""
    assumerolepolicy+=$userarn

assumerolepolicy+="\"},\"Action\": \"sts:AssumeRole\",\"Condition\"
: { \"Bool\": { \"aws:MultiFactorAuthPresent\": true } }}]}"
    echo assumerolepolicy=$assumerolepoli
```

You'll notice the string '***USERARN***' - this is the ARN of the user that can assume the role. User ARNs have a standard format: 'arn:aws:iam::[AWS Account Number]:user/[username]' (you need to update [AWS Account number] with your 12 digit account number, available in My Account, and [username] with the name of the user). In my scripts, I don't build the ARN, I retrieve it when I create the user.

This is a policy which allows full admin access, which can be attached to a user or a role, however, I will attach it to a role:

[chapter4/adminrolepolicy.txt]

```
    # user or role policy for admin privileges

    {
            "Version": "2012-10-17",
            "Statement": [
                    {
                            "Effect": "Allow",
                            "Action": "*",
                            "Resource": "*"
                    }
            ]
    }
    # to put this policy into a bash variable, use:

    rolepolicy="{\"Version\": \"2012-10-17\",\"Statement\":
[{\"Effect\": \"Allow\",\"Action\": \"*\",\"Resource\": \"*\"}]}"
```

This is a policy which allows connect access, which can be attached to a user or a role, however, I will attach it to a role. The connect role allows only 4 'aws ec2' commands: describe-instances, describe-security-groups, authorize-security-group-ingress and revoke-security-group-ingress. These are the only commands you need to connect to instances with ssh. Basically, you can query information (like getting Security Group IDs or instance Public IP Addresses) and open and close ports. Why assume Admin privileges when you don't need them? By separating admin and connect, you are more secure. The connect policy looks like this:

```
[chapter4/connectrolepolicy.txt]

# user or role policy for connect privileges

{
        "Version": "2012-10-17",
        "Statement": [
                {
                        "Effect": "Allow",
                        "Action": [
                                "ec2:DescribeInstances",
                                "ec2:DescribeSecurityGroups",
"ec2:AuthorizeSecurityGroupIngress",
                                "ec2:RevokeSecurityGroupIngress"
                        ],
                        "Resource": "*"
                }
        ]
}

# to put this policy into a bash variable, use:

rolepolicy="{\"Version\": \"2012-10-17\",\"Statement\":
[{\"Effect\": \"Allow\",\"Action\":
[\"ec2:DescribeInstances\", \"ec2:DescribeSecurityGroups\", \"ec2:A
uthorizeSecurityGroupIngress\", \"ec2:RevokeSecurityGroupIngress\"]
,\"Resource\": \"*\"}]}"
```

OK, so by now you're probably thoroughly confused, I know I am... Keep calm, the scripts that follow don't require a Degree in IAM.

This setup script creates one IAM User 'assumer' with one MFA Device. 'assumer' can do nothing other than assume one of 2 roles, 'adminrole' or 'connectrole' and will need to enter an MFA code to do so. The script also creates two more scripts, signin.sh and signout.sh, both in the chapter4/output folder. These two scripts are what you use day to day to sign in and out of AWS CLI. They are completely relocatable and rely on no other files, so you can copy them where you want and use them easily in other scripts. They also pose no security threat because an MFA code is required to assume higher privileges. All the scripts in Chapter 4 expect to be run from the 'chapter4' folder, so 'cd' there before starting. The main setup script is as follows:

[chapter4/mfa_setup.sh]

```
#!/bin/bash

# interactive script to set up a secure user with mfa
# make a new user 'assumer' who can only execute 'aws sts assume-role'
# make 2 new roles which can only be assumed by this user
# the new adminrole has full admin privileges
# the new connectrole has connect privileges
# also make a virtual mfa device, configure it
# and attach it to the user assumer

# make new user
# we need the user arn for the role policy used in 'aws iam create-role'
echo creating iam user assumer
userarn=$(aws iam create-user --user-name assumer --output text --query 'User.Arn')
echo userarn=$userarn

# let the user cook
# else upcoming 'aws iam create-role' fails
sleep 5

# create a role policy that allows assumption by the user
echo creating assume role policy that can be assumed by $username only
assumerolepolicy="{\"Version\": \"2012-10-17\",\"Statement\": [{\"Sid\": \"\",\"Effect\": \"Allow\",\"Principal\": {\"AWS\": \""
assumerolepolicy+=$userarn

assumerolepolicy+="\"},\"Action\": \"sts:AssumeRole\",\"Condition\" : { \"Bool\": { \"aws:MultiFactorAuthPresent\": true } }}]}"
echo assumerolepolicy=$assumerolepolicy

# create the admin role
echo creating admin role with this assume role policy
adminrolearn=$(aws iam create-role --role-name assumer_adminrole --assume-role-policy-document "$assumerolepolicy" --output text --query 'Role.Arn')
echo adminrolearn=$adminrolearn

# create the connect role
echo creating connect role with this assume role policy
connectrolearn=$(aws iam create-role --role-name assumer_connectrole --assume-role-policy-document "$assumerolepolicy" --output text --query 'Role.Arn')
echo connectrolearn=$connectrolearn

# attach an admin role policy to the admin role with admin privileges
rolepolicy="{\"Version\": \"2012-10-17\",\"Statement\": [{\"Effect\": \"Allow\",\"Action\": \"*\",\"Resource\": \"*\"}]}"
echo rolepolicy=$rolepolicy
aws iam put-role-policy --role-name assumer_adminrole --policy-name assumer_adminrole_policy --policy-document "$rolepolicy"
```

```
# attach a connect role policy to the connect role with connect
privileges
   rolepolicy="{\"Version\": \"2012-10-17\",\"Statement\":
[{\"Effect\": \"Allow\",\"Action\":
[\"ec2:DescribeInstances\", \"ec2:DescribeSecurityGroups\", \"ec2:A
uthorizeSecurityGroupIngress\", \"ec2:RevokeSecurityGroupIngress\"]
,\"Resource\": \"*\"}]}"
   echo rolepolicy=$rolepolicy
   aws iam put-role-policy --role-name assumer_connectrole --policy-
name assumer_connectrole_policy --policy-document "$rolepolicy"

   # create the policy for the user
   # can only run 'aws sts assume-role ...' for the two roles
   userpolicy="{\"Version\": \"2012-10-17\",\"Statement\": ["

userpolicy+="{\"Effect\": \"Allow\",\"Action\": \"sts:AssumeRole\",
\"Resource\": \""
   userpolicy+=$adminrolearn
   userpolicy+="\"},"

userpolicy+="{\"Effect\": \"Allow\",\"Action\": \"sts:AssumeRole\",
\"Resource\": \""
   userpolicy+=$connectrolearn
   userpolicy+="\"}"
   userpolicy+="]}"
   echo userpolicy=$userpolicy

   # attach the policy to the user
   echo attaching this policy to assumer
   aws iam put-user-policy --user-name assumer --policy-name
assumer_policy --policy-document "$userpolicy"

   # make an access key for the user
   # we need to get 2 values from this returned data but can only
call the function once
   # so we can't use '--query'
   cred=$(aws iam create-access-key --user-name assumer --output
text)
   bits=($cred)
   AccessKeyId=${bits[1]}
   SecretAccessKey=${bits[3]}

   # request user installs mfa app
   echo Install the Google Authenticator App on your mobile device
   echo THEN press a key
   read -n 1 -s

   # make a new mfa device
   echo making a new virtual mfa device
   mfaserial=$(aws iam create-virtual-mfa-device --virtual-mfa-
device-name assumer_mfa_device --outfile mfa.png --bootstrap-method
QRCodePNG --output text --query 'VirtualMFADevice.SerialNumber')
   echo mfaserial=$mfaserial

   # request user scans QR code
   # QR code here is a must because AWS uses very long MFA keys
   # you will make a mistake if you try to type it by hand...
   echo open mfa.png in a image viewing app and scan it
   echo THEN press a key
   read -n 1 -s

   # alternatively, if you are using something like OTP Manager
   # which allows copy and paste of the mfa seed
   # you could use:
   #mfaserial=$(aws iam create-virtual-mfa-device --virtual-mfa-
device-name assumer_mfa_device --outfile mfa.txt --bootstrap-method
Base32StringSeed --output text --query
'VirtualMFADevice.SerialNumber')
```

AWS Scripted 2   64

```
#echo copy and paste the following seed into OTP Manager:
#cat mfa.txt

# get 2 mfa codes
read -p "Enter an MFA code (6 numbers): " mfacode1
read -p "Enter the next MFA code (6 numbers): " mfacode2

# enable the mfa device
aws iam enable-mfa-device --user-name assumer --serial-number
$mfaserial --authentication-code-1 $mfacode1 --authentication-code-
2 $mfacode2
echo mfa device enabled

# delete the QR code
rm -f mfa.png
# or the txt file
#rm -f mfa.txt
echo MFA Key deleted

echo finished mfa setup

echo now building sign in and sign out scripts

# sign in script
# create safe versions of the strings to be inserted
# ie escape / \ and &
adminrolearnsafe=$(echo $adminrolearn | sed -e 's/\\/\\\\/g' -e
's/\//\\\//g' -e 's/&/\\\&/g')
echo adminrolearnsafe=$adminrolearnsafe
connectrolearnsafe=$(echo $connectrolearn | sed -e 's/\\/\\\\/g'
-e 's/\//\\\//g' -e 's/&/\\\&/g')
echo connectrolearnsafe=$connectrolearnsafe
mfaserialsafe=$(echo $mfaserial | sed -e 's/\\/\\\\/g' -e
's/\//\\\//g' -e 's/&/\\\&/g')
echo mfaserialsafe=$mfaserialsafe
sed -e "s/SEDadminrolearnSED/$adminrolearnsafe/g" -e
"s/SEDconnectrolearnSED/$connectrolearnsafe/g" -e
"s/SEDmfaserialSED/$mfaserialsafe/g" -e
"s/SEDusernameSED/assumer/g" mfa_signin_template.sh >
output/signin.sh
chmod +x output/signin.sh
echo new signin.sh saved to output/signin.sh

# sign out script
# create safe versions of the strings to be inserted
# ie escape / \ and &
AccessKeyIdsafe=$(echo $AccessKeyId | sed -e 's/\\/\\\\/g' -e
's/\//\\\//g' -e 's/&/\\\&/g')
echo AccessKeyIdsafe=$AccessKeyIdsafe
SecretAccessKeysafe=$(echo $SecretAccessKey | sed -e
's/\\/\\\\/g' -e 's/\//\\\//g' -e 's/&/\\\&/g')
echo SecretAccessKeysafe=$SecretAccessKeysafe
sed -e "s/SEDAccessKeyIdSED/$AccessKeyIdsafe/g" -e
"s/SEDSecretAccessKeySED/$SecretAccessKeysafe/g" -e
"s/SEDusernameSED/assumer/g" mfa_signout_template.sh >
output/signout.sh
chmod +x output/signout.sh
echo new signout.sh saved to output/signout.sh

echo finished mfa setup
echo use \'signout.sh\' to sign out of your current AWS CLI
account and enable the assumer user
echo use \'signin.sh admin\' or \'signin.sh connect\' to assume
privileges for 1 hour
```

Call this script with:

```
./mfa_setup.sh
```

This script doesn't like being called if there are already resources defined, like an IAM User 'assumer' or either of the two roles. To delete everything, it's a lot easier to do it in AWS Console - just delete assumer from Users and adminrole and connectrole from Roles.

After running mfa_setup.sh with the above arguments, you can see what has been created in the AWS Console in the IAM section - check out 'assumer' in Users and 'adminrole' and 'connectrole' in Roles. Note that there's no need to save MFA seeds in case you lose the MFA device (for instance your smartphone). You can just use the AWS Console to delete everything (IAM User and IAM Roles) and then rerun the setup script with a new phone. Note also that the setup script mfa_setup.sh does not change your actual AWS CLI credentials - for that you need to use the generated files signout.sh and signin.sh in the next section.

If you are running the code on an AWS instance, you won't be able to view the mfa.png file with the QR Code to set up your MFA device. You can download from your instance with:

```
 scp -i [keyname] ec2-user@[PublicIP]:code/chapter4/mfa.png
mfa.png
```

assuming that you unzipped the code zip in /home/ec2-user.

Now everything is in place to secure the AWS CLI with MFA. Daily use involves Signing In and Signing Out.

Signing In and Signing Out

2 scripts control the AWS CLI MFA process. They are generated by 'mfa_setup.sh' from the last section. They are signin.sh and signout.sh. These scripts are completely self-contained and contain all the data required to do their business. This is because when you are signed in as 'assumer' and have no privileges, you can't actually run commands like 'get me the ARN of this role' or 'get me the

serial of this MFA device'.

The first script is the Sign Out Script. It overwrites the current AWS CLI credentials with the credentials of the 'assumer user' - remember this user has no AWS privileges except the ability to assume the 'adminrole' Role or the 'connectrole' Role (if they have authenticated with MFA) with the 'aws sts assume-role ...' command. This is the template script, which is used by mfa_setup.sh:

```
[chapter4/mfa_signout_template.sh]

#!/bin/bash

# script to change security credentials to the 'assumer user'
# that is, a user with no privileges except for 'aws sts assume-role'

# this script is a template to be searched and replaced by
mfa_setup.sh
# replaced strings:
# SEDAccessKeyIdSED
# SEDSecretAccessKeySED
# SEDusernameSED

# the output from 'sed' can be found in
chapter4/output/signout.sh
# signout.sh relies on nothing and can be moved anywhere

# the assumer user's credentials
AccessKeyId=SEDAccessKeyIdSED
SecretAccessKey=SEDSecretAccessKeySED

# clear aws cli auth
export AWS_SECRET_KEY=
export AWS_ACCESS_KEY=
export AWS_DELEGATION_TOKEN=
rm ~/.aws/credentials

# now set assumer user to be the default user
echo [default] > ~/.aws/credentials
echo aws_access_key_id=$AccessKeyId >> ~/.aws/credentials
echo aws_secret_access_key=$SecretAccessKey >> ~/.aws/credentials
chmod 600 ~/.aws/credentials
# other options are in ~/.aws/config
# like region and output format
# but we don't need to touch this file

# now any aws commands will be run as the assumer user
# everything will fail except 'aws sts assume-role'
echo aws credentials reset to assumer user \'SEDusernameSED\'
echo access to everything but \'aws sts assume-role\' is disabled
```

Here is the script produced by mfa_setup.sh using mfa_signout_template.sh (the actual credentials have been starred out):

[chapter4/signout_example.sh]

```bash
#!/bin/bash

# script to change security credentials to the 'assumer user'
# that is, a user with no privileges except for 'aws sts assume-
role'

# this script is a template to be searched and replaced by
mfa_setup.sh
# replaced strings:
# AKIA***********N3PA
# hD2L*******************************mRbx
# assumer

# the output from 'sed' can be found in
chapter4/output/signout.sh
# signout.sh relies on nothing and can be moved anywhere

# the assumer user's credentials
AccessKeyId=AKIA***********N3PA
SecretAccessKey=hD2L********************************mRbx

# clear aws cli auth
export AWS_SECRET_KEY=
export AWS_ACCESS_KEY=
export AWS_DELEGATION_TOKEN=
rm ~/.aws/credentials

# now set assumer user to be the default user
echo [default] > ~/.aws/credentials
echo aws_access_key_id=$AccessKeyId >> ~/.aws/credentials
echo aws_secret_access_key=$SecretAccessKey >> ~/.aws/credentials
chmod 600 ~/.aws/credentials
# other options are in ~/.aws/config
# like region and output format
# but we don't need to touch this file

# now any aws commands will be run as the assumer user
# everything will fail except 'aws sts assume-role'
echo aws credentials reset to assumer user \'assumer\'
echo access to everything but \'aws sts assume-role\' is disabled
```

When you ran the MFA Setup Script 'mfa_setup.sh' from the last section, you would have had AWS privileges to do so (for example Admin privileges). By running the generated script './signout.sh' from the output folder, you will wipe those credentials (which can be recreated from the AWS Console, if necessary) and replace them with the user 'assumer' credentials. You can restore default Admin privileges by following the instructions in **Chapter 2 - Securing Basic AWS Access**.

After running signout.sh, all 'aws' commands except 'aws sts assume-role' will fail. You can test this with an example:

```
aws ec2 describe-key-pairs
```

AWS Scripted 2

which will return:

```
A client error (UnauthorizedOperation) occurred when calling the
DescribeKeyPairs operation: You are not authorized to perform this
operation.
```

The second script is the Sign In Script. It uses an MFA code to
assume a role and overwrites the current AWS CLI credentials
with the temporary credentials returned. This is the template script,
which is used by mfa_setup.sh:

[chapter4/mfa_signin_template.sh]

```
#!/bin/bash

# interactive script to change security credentials
# to the admin or connect role

# call with 1 argument: admin or connect, ie
# ./signin.sh admin
# ./signin.sh connect

# this script is a template to be searched and replaced by
mfa_setup.sh
# replaced strings:
# SEDadminrolearnSED
# SEDconnectrolearnSED
# SEDmfaserialSED
# SEDusernameSED

# the output from 'sed' can be found in chapter4/output/signin.sh
# signin.sh relies on nothing and can be moved anywhere

# this script only works if the current user is 'assumer'
# ie, signout.sh needs to have been called first

# the role arns we will be assuming
adminrolearn=SEDadminrolearnSED
connectrolearn=SEDconnectrolearnSED

rolearn=none
if test "$1" = "admin"; then
        rolearn=$adminrolearn
elif test "$1" = "connect"; then
        rolearn=$connectrolearn
else
        echo 'usage: ./signin.sh <admin or connect>'
        exit
fi

# username and virtual mfa device serial
username=SEDusernameSED
mfaserial=SEDmfaserialSED

# prompt the user for an mfa code
read -p "Enter an MFA code for $username: " mfacode

# assume the role
# we need to get 3 values from this returned data but can only
call the function once
# so we can't use '--query'
```

```
cred=$(aws sts assume-role --role-arn $rolearn --role-session-
name rolesession --serial-number $mfaserial --token-code $mfacode
--duration-seconds 3600 --output text)

    # let's check we assumed the role ok
    # perhaps we made a mistake with the mfa code
    if test "$cred" = ""; then
            # it didn't work
            echo ensure you are signed in as the assumer user
            echo by running signout.sh
            echo or please retry with new mfa code
            echo assume role $1 FAILED
            exit
    fi

    # ok it worked, get the credentials
    bits=($cred)
    AccessKeyId=${bits[4]}
    SecretAccessKey=${bits[6]}
    SessionToken=${bits[7]}

    # clear aws cli auth
    export AWS_SECRET_KEY=
    export AWS_ACCESS_KEY=
    export AWS_DELEGATION_TOKEN=
    rm ~/.aws/credentials

    # now set aws credentials with the temporary ones received
    echo [default] > ~/.aws/credentials
    echo aws_access_key_id=$AccessKeyId >> ~/.aws/credentials
    echo aws_secret_access_key=$SecretAccessKey >> ~/.aws/credentials
    echo aws_session_token=$SessionToken >> ~/.aws/credentials
    chmod 600 ~/.aws/credentials
    # other options are in ~/.aws/config
    # like region and output format
    # but we don't need to touch this file

    # now all aws commands will work for 1 hour
    # after expiry, call signout.sh to reinstate the 'assumer user'
    # and then run this script again if you need credentials again
    echo $1 assumed SUCCESS
```

Here is the script produced by mfa_setup.sh using
mfa_signin_template.sh (the AWS Account numbers have been
zeroed):

[chapter4/signin_example.sh]

```
#!/bin/bash

# interactive script to change security credentials
# to the admin or connect role

# call with 1 argument: admin or connect, ie
# ./signin.sh admin
# ./signin.sh connect

# this script is a template to be searched and replaced by
mfa_setup.sh
# replaced strings:
# arn:aws:iam::000000000000:role/assumer_adminrole
# arn:aws:iam::000000000000:role/assumer_connectrole
# arn:aws:iam::000000000000:mfa/assumer_mfa_device
```

```
# assumer

# the output from 'sed' can be found in chapter4/output/signin.sh
# signin.sh relies on nothing and can be moved anywhere

# this script only works if the current user is 'assumer'
# ie, signout.sh needs to have been called first

# the role arns we will be assuming
adminrolearn=arn:aws:iam::000000000000:role/assumer_adminrole
connectrolearn=arn:aws:iam::000000000000:role/assumer_connectrole

rolearn=none
if test "$1" = "admin"; then
      rolearn=$adminrolearn
elif test "$1" = "connect"; then
      rolearn=$connectrolearn
else
      echo 'usage: ./signin.sh <admin or connect>'
      exit
fi
# get the virtual mfa device serial
username=assumer
mfaserial=arn:aws:iam::000000000000:mfa/assumer_mfa_device

# prompt the user for an mfa code
read -p "Enter an MFA code for $username: " mfacode

# assume the role
# we need to get 3 values from this returned data but can only
call the function once
# so we can't use '--query'
cred=$(aws sts assume-role --role-arn $rolearn --role-session-
name rolesession --serial-number $mfaserial --token-code $mfacode
--duration-seconds 3600 --output text)
echo $cred

# let's check we assumed the role ok
# perhaps we made a mistake with the mfa code
if test "$cred" = ""; then
      # it didn't work
      echo ensue you are signed in as the assumer user
      echo by running signout.sh
      echo or please retry with new mfa code
      echo assume role $1 FAILED
      exit
fi

# ok it worked, get the credentials
bits=($cred)
AccessKeyId=${bits[4]}
SecretAccessKey=${bits[6]}
SessionToken=${bits[7]}

# clear aws cli auth
export AWS_SECRET_KEY=
export AWS_ACCESS_KEY=
export AWS_DELEGATION_TOKEN=
rm ~/.aws/credentials

# now set aws credentials with the temporary ones received
echo [default] > ~/.aws/credentials
echo aws_access_key_id=$AccessKeyId >> ~/.aws/credentials
echo aws_secret_access_key=$SecretAccessKey >> ~/.aws/credentials
echo aws_session_token=$SessionToken >> ~/.aws/credentials
chmod 600 ~/.aws/credentials
# other options are in ~/.aws/config
# like region and output format
```

```
# but we don't need to touch this file

# now all aws commands will work for 1 hour
# after expiry, call signout.sh to reinstate the 'assumer user'
# and then run this script again if you need credentials again
echo $1 assumed SUCCESS
```

signin.sh takes one argument: admin or connect, depending on which privileges you want to assume. Before running the Sign In Script, make sure you have set up the user 'assumer' by running the Sign Out Script above. Test it out by issuing any 'aws' command. It will work. If the 1 hour runs out, calls with the 'aws' command will fail. Run the Sign In Script again to get new credentials.

Example Script Use

One of the really handy things about the Sign In and Sign Out scripts in the last section is that you can use them in scripts... They are self-contained and can be copied anywhere and will work. Here's an example:

[chapter4/mfa_examplescriptuse.sh]

```
#!/bin/bash

# interactive script to show how mfa sign in and sign out can be
used in a script

# sign out
./output/signout.sh

# try a command (it won't work)
aws ec2 describe-instances

# sign in (you'll need to enter an mfa code)
./output/signin.sh admin

# now you can do whatever - run a script or some commands
# we'll use a test command
echo RUNNING PRIVILEGED COMMANDS
aws ec2 describe-instances
echo FINISHED PRIVILEGED COMMANDS

# when you're finished, sign out again
./output/signout.sh

# try a command (it won't work)
aws ec2 describe-key-pairs

# now sign in as connect (you'll need to enter an mfa code)
./output/signin.sh connect

# now you can run:
# describe-instances
```

```
# describe-security-groups
# authorize-security-group-ingress
# revoke-security-group-ingress

# we'll use a test command
echo RUNNING PRIVILEGED COMMANDS
# this will work
aws ec2 describe-instances
# this won't
aws ec2 describe-key-pairs
echo FINISHED PRIVILEGED COMMANDS

# when you're finished, sign out again
./output/signout.sh

# try a command (it won't work)
aws ec2 describe-instances
```

The output from the above script is:

[chapter4/mfa_examplescriptuse_results.txt]

```
$ ./mfa_examplescriptuse.sh
aws credentials reset to assumer user 'assumer'
access to everything but 'aws sts assume-role' is disabled

A client error (UnauthorizedOperation) occurred when calling the
DescribeInstances operation: You are not authorized to perform this
operation.
  Enter an MFA code for assumer: 817829
  admin assumed SUCCESS
  RUNNING PRIVILEGED COMMANDS
  {
      "Reservations": []
  }
FINISHED PRIVILEGED COMMANDS
aws credentials reset to assumer user 'assumer'
access to everything but 'aws sts assume-role' is disabled

A client error (UnauthorizedOperation) occurred when calling the
DescribeKeyPairs operation: You are not authorized to perform this
operation.
  Enter an MFA code for assumer: 685434
  connect assumed SUCCESS
  RUNNING PRIVILEGED COMMANDS
  {
      "Reservations": []
  }

A client error (UnauthorizedOperation) occurred when calling the
DescribeKeyPairs operation: You are not authorized to perform this
operation.
  FINISHED PRIVILEGED COMMANDS
  aws credentials reset to assumer user 'assumer'
  access to everything but 'aws sts assume-role' is disabled

A client error (UnauthorizedOperation) occurred when calling the
DescribeInstances operation: You are not authorized to perform this
operation.
```

Chapter 5 - SSH

SSH Security Considerations

The default EC2 SSH installation for an Amazon Linux AMI is relatively secure in that it is impossible that it will be hacked via a brute force attack. They SSH Key system which is used is akin to SSH with a very long and nasty password. However, if someone got hold of your Key, and they have access to the SSH port, they can get in easily. Given a simple setup where you have a computer with AWS CLI installed and the SSH Key on it, the risk of a breach is quite high because if your computer is compromised, it's pretty simple to steal SSH Keys and AWS CLI credentials.

Accessing SSH is a two stage process: Stage 1 is to gain network access; Stage 2 is to sign in with ssh. Both stages can be protected.

As regards Stage 1, gaining network access, let's assume that in a normal situation, your SSH port is closed to everyone, and that means anyone on the Internet and also anything from within your VPC. An SSH breach is impossible because there is no network access. What would a hacker have to do to gain network access and which security measures would be the most effective defence?

Well, the first thing that would need to be done is to open a route to the SSH port to allow access. This requires a breach of your AWS Account. I am going to assume that your AWS Console access is secured with MFA and a good password. That means they cannot get in there - and if they could, all bets are off because they can destroy your infrastructure, make and download snapshots of your drives, even change your credentials to lock you out! So the only way to breach your AWS Account is via your AWS CLI credentials, and any hacker who infects your computer and gets privileges to run code can do so by looking at your ~/.aws/credentials file, which contains unencrypted credentials. By plugging these credentials into another AWS CLI, they can do everything you can do. Or they could just execute 'aws' commands from your computer. So an important security measure is using a Secure Laptop. A Secure Laptop *can* be breached, but you need to be a target, that is someone needs explicitly to try to get in. A Secure Laptop strategy will almost certainly prevent accidental infection and will also make targeted attacks much harder.

As well as the Secure Laptop, the most important defence is securing your AWS CLI with MFA, as explained in **Chapter 4 - MFA for AWS CLI**. If you want good security, do it. It means if your computer is infected and an attacker can run code on it, they still can't assume your Admin credentials because they need an MFA code. Does this protect you 100%? Unfortunately not. Imagine you are infected. You sit down at your computer, activate AWS CLI by running the Sign In script and entering an MFA code. Your new credentials are downloaded and installed. Now, your credentials can still be stolen and used for 1 hour. So you are vulnerable. OK, it's still a big improvement - you need a really dedicated and smart hacker to be able to listen in to what you are doing on your computer and real-time hack you. But you can do better and thwart even this attack by securing Stage 2, the process of signing in to SSH.

By installing MFA for SSH, you will need to enter another MFA code during ssh sign in. This means that a hacker, *even with* AWS CLI credentials that allow them to open up network access to SSH, *even with* SSH passwords downloaded from your computer, cannot get in. They could try a brute force attack with a 1 in 333,333 chance per attempt. But because you enabled rate limiting on your SSH MFA sign in, they are limited to a very small number of attempts. They can't reuse the code you entered, even though it is valid for a minute more, because you enabled 'no MFA code reuse'. And by editing /etc/security/limits.conf, there can be only one active SSH Session, and you've got it. Now you are very secure.

But, let's assume this ultra-hacker is key logging you or using a man-in-the-middle attack and has everything set up to do a hyper-speed hack. They've looked at your scripts and know what's going to happen. You sign in to AWS CLI and they steal your temporary credentials as well as your SSH sign in password, which is on disk.

They open a port to your SSH. As you type the MFA password for SSH, they scan it and use it before you do. Bang, they're in. Your ssh fails. And now you can't get in because SSH sessions are limited to 1. Time to panic! Or sit back and admire a very skilful hacker... Could you protect against this?

Your last line of defence is securing the ability to do 'sudo su', that is requiring a password to do it. It's not a great defence though for several reasons. First, you *can* get root privileges on a system by privilege escalation, no need for 'sudo su', although this is very hard and normally requires bad file permissions (like world writable and executable files) or system reboots. However, it's not impossible. Second, where is the password for 'sudo su' stored? If it's on the infected computer, it's useless, bearing in mind that the hacker has already raped several other credentials from you. It might be in your head or on a piece of paper. That's better, but you still needed to type it in in the first place (so it was in electronic format at some point) AND you'll need to type it to do the 'sudo su' at which point the hacker has it. Even if you change your 'sudo su' password every time you use it, you still typed it in, so it's compromised.

What about Secure Keyboard Entry in OSX Terminal, I hear you ask? It's a good layer of protection, for sure, but not against an attacker with root privileges. Root can see everything, do everything... But, of course, you should still turn it on.

So, I conclude that the 'sudo su' password option is not useless but also not perfect as the third line of defence in an attack scenario as outlined above. However, it is useful for a different situation. Let's imagine that your laptop is secure, you aren't infected, no hacker is looking over your shoulder. But one night, very late, something goes wrong with your port closing script, and you leave blurry-eyed for the long weekend with the SSH port open to your Corporate Intranet. Some malicious programs are sniffing packets and start to brute force your SSH. They might get in, even with MFA. A good 'sudo su' password would help enormously in this situation, because on a properly secured system, privilege escalation is almost impossible and the hackers could do little *even though* they cracked your SSH. And in this situation, it doesn't really matter if your 'sudo su' password is stored electronically with your other credentials. You are protecting against a port accidentally left open, not a hacker who has infected you. If we assume the open SSH port is discovered by scanning or the like, that attacker will not know where the 'sudo su' password is stored, will not have hacked your computer and so on. So, an electronically stored 'sudo su' password is useful against some attacks.

In conclusion, then, if you want a properly secure way to access SSH you need to do the following:

On the client:

- use a Secure Laptop
- secure AWS Console with MFA and strong password
- secure AWS CLI with MFA
- open SSH ports only when needed and always close them
- open SSH ports from your IP, not the world

On the server:

- harden the SSH config file
- change the default ssh user from ec2-user to something else (ssher)
- enable MFA for SSH with rate-limiting and no-code-reuse
- require a password for 'sudo su' (and storing this password electronically is acceptable)
- use nasty passwords when they are automated

Passwords

In all the scripts that follow, I have set passwords to be simple, like '1234' or '222222', so it's easy to test things like signing in to ssh. Obviously, you should change these to suit your needs. Here is a good way to generate hard passwords:

```
openssl rand -hex 8
```

This will return a an 8 byte random password in hex, that is 16 characters 0-9 and a-f. Change the 8 to more or less as required. A value of 16 produces a 32 character password which is utterly impossible to break. It's quite useful to use the hex notation as there are no special characters (like '/') which don't work without escaping for commands like 'sed'.

Normally I automate the password generation by running a script which looks something like this before any builds:

[chapter5/makepasswords.sh]

```
#!/bin/bash

# generates a file passwords.sh with all passwords

# password for ssher
ssherpassword=$(openssl rand -hex 8)

# password for root
rootpassword=$(openssl rand -hex 8)

# mysql root password
mysql_rootpassword=$(openssl rand -hex 8)

# db
db_webpass=$(openssl rand -hex 8)

# make the AES key (64 characters) for PHP sessions
aes=$(openssl rand -hex 32)

# write file
echo "#!/bin/bash" > passwords.sh
echo "ssherpassword=$ssherpassword" >> passwords.sh
echo "rootpassword=$rootpassword" >> passwords.sh
echo "mysql_rootpassword=$mysql_rootpassword" >> passwords.sh
echo "db_webpass=$db_webpass" >> passwords.sh
echo "aes=$aes" >> passwords.sh
chmod +x passwords.sh
```

The generated file is as follows (passwords will change for every execution):

[chapter5/passwords.sh]

```
#!/bin/bash
ssherpassword=dfd3b1f3511d7bdb
rootpassword=83d3a4a6b62b58f4
mysql_rootpassword=b7cbe02bc9eb2384
db_webpass=b2fc0d3da82bfdad

aes=a8026b1366ae4938fc811cb8a89cbb97dc78f3363f3b57ddfe63d0ac653247d
6
```

Then, in any script which needs passwords, which is most of them, I include the passwords with:

```
. ./passwords.sh
```

Host Key Checking

Please note the following about Strict Host Key checking with the ssh command. When ssh connects using an SSH Key, it verifies the key against a copy stored in ~/.ssh/known_hosts, that is the ssh/known_hosts file in the current user's home directory. The first time you connect, if the key is not in this file, ssh will prompt for if you want to add it. This also applies if you change the SSH port, so a reconnect to the same instance with a new port will force a prompt. For scripting purposes, this is annoying as you have to type 'yes', and within the authentication time limit. So for the first ssh connection (or scp command) to any instance and port, use the StrictHostKeyChecking option as follows:

```
ssh -i [keyfile] -o StrictHostKeyChecking=no ec2-
user@[instance_public_ipaddress]
```

By adding '-o StrictHostKeyChecking=no', ssh will not prompt for if you want to add the key, it will just do it. For subsequent calls to ssh, you don't need to use the option, as the key is already stored. However, if you have done something like terminate a server, or changed keys or changed port, some scripts won't work because the new key and the stored key don't match. In a Production Environment, this should not be a problem, as you're unlikely to be building and terminating servers. But when developing, this might happen. Note that by setting StrictHostKeyChecking to no, it doesn't mean the keys aren't checked - they are always checked whatever this setting, but you are not prompted to add or override a key.

It can be useful to delete the known_hosts file if you've just replaced servers with:

```
rm -f ~/.ssh/known_hosts
```

You should generally keep StrictHostKeyChecking to the default value of 'ask'. This means if keys are different, you will be prompted to continue and will therefore be warned of a man-in-the-middle or trojan attack. If you set it to 'no', you will still get a message, but it will continue automatically. For Bastion Hosts (see **Chapter 9 - Using a Bastion Host**), or other servers with Public IP addresses, it's important to check you are connecting to the right instance, because you are connecting over the Internet and so could be the target of a man-in-the-middle attack. But when you connect from a Bastion to an internal server, it's less important - if a hacker can launch a MITM attack on your internal AWS network, they have already breached your security.

Basic SSH to an AWS EC2 Instance

The first thing you will almost always have to do after creating an Amazon Linux AMI is ssh to it. It's pretty simple, but there are some prerequisites. The command you will issue to ssh in is:

```
ssh -i [keyfile] ec2-user@[instance_public_ipaddress]
```

Replace [keyfile] with the name or path of the file you downloaded when you created your instance and [instance_public_ipaddress] with the Public IP Address of the new instance. The prerequisites you will need to confirm are:

- your VPC needs to be set up correctly, so that Internet traffic actually reaches you instance - see **Appendix A - VPC** for a guide
- your SSH key must not be publicly readable (or 'ssh' will reject it) - use the following to fix it:

```
chmod 600 <keyfile>
```

- there needs to be an Inbound Rule in the Security Group attached to the instance with Protocol: TCP, Port Range: 22, Source: MyIP
- the SSH daemon needs to be running on the instance (it

may take a couple of minutes to start even if the instance state is 'running')

In practice, once you have done it once, it becomes second nature. If you find you really can't connect, check the Security Group rule in case your IP has changed. And if you've been playing with the SSH config on the server, you may have bricked it, see **Appendix E - UnBrick a Brick**.

Automating Basic SSH Access

The normal procedure for connecting to your AWS box with SSH is as follows:

- open AWS Console - EC2
- in Security Groups, add an Inbound rule for port 22 from MyIP to the server in question
- cd to the directory containing the .pem file for the server
- execute an ssh command, for instance:

```
ssh -i server.pem ec2-user@100.100.100.100
```

- when finished, close the SSH session
- in Security Groups, remove the Inbound rule for port 22 from MyIP to the server in question

It's not a very complex procedure, but it is pleasant to automate it. Well, you save a sign in to AWS Console. Here is a bash script which does it:

[chapter5/connectssh.sh]

```
#!/bin/bash

# open an ssh session to a server
# opens the associated Security Group port
# exit from ssh to remove the Security Group ingress rule

# call with one parameter, the key name for the server
# eg if you connect with server.pem use:
# ./connectssh.sh server

# assumes each key is only used for one server
```

```
# assumes server has only one security group

# ssh port on server
sshport=22
# ssh user to connect with
sshuser=ec2-user

echo connecting ssh to $1 on $sshport with user $sshuser

# get my IP
myip=$(curl -s http://checkip.amazonaws.com/)
echo my IP is $myip

# get ip of server
ip_address=$(aws ec2 describe-instances --filters Name=key-
name,Values=$1 --output text --query
'Reservations[*].Instances[*].PublicIpAddress')
echo connecting to $ip_address

# get security group id of server
sgid=$(aws ec2 describe-instances --filters Name=key-
name,Values=$1 --output text --query
'Reservations[*].Instances[*].SecurityGroups[*].GroupId')
echo security group id is $sgid

# allow ssh in sg
echo authorising ingress
aws ec2 authorize-security-group-ingress --group-id $sgid
--protocol tcp --port $sshport --cidr $myip/32 --output text

echo ssh command:
echo ssh -i $1.pem -p $sshport $sshuser@$ip_address

# wait for ssh
echo -n "waiting for ssh"
while ! ssh -i $1.pem -p $sshport -o ConnectTimeout=5 -o
BatchMode=yes $sshuser@$ip_address > /dev/null 2>&1 true; do
  echo -n . ; sleep 5;
done; echo " ok"

# now connect
ssh -i $1.pem -p $sshport $sshuser@$ip_address

# exit ssh to close the security group port

# remove ssh in sg
echo revoking ingress
aws ec2 revoke-security-group-ingress --group-id $sgid --protocol
tcp --port $sshport --cidr $myip/32 --output text
```

Put the script in the same folder as your key. To make the script executable use:

```
# you only need to do this once
chmod +x connectssh.sh
```

If your key is called server.pem, call with:

```
./connectssh.sh server
```

There are some assumptions made by the script:

- you have AWS CLI installed and working
- the .pem key is attached only to one server
- the server has only one security group
- SSH is on port 22 (discouraged)

The assumptions are normal for most situations, but if not you may need the script below.

If you are using one key for multiple servers, first ask yourself why, as it is a bad idea. Nonetheless, you could get the server IP address and server Security Group by filtering for tag name. Say your server was tagged with [instancename=server1], use the argument "server1" instead of key name and use the script below. If your server has more than one Security Group, you only need to authorise it one group. The 'get security group id of server' command will return a list and the following script reduces that list to just the first Security Group ID:

[chapter5/connectsshbytag.sh]

```
#!/bin/bash

# open an ssh session to a server
# opens the associated Security Group port
# exit from ssh to remove the Security Group ingress rule

# call with one parameter, the tag name for the server
# eg if the server is tagged as [Name=server1]:
# ./connectsshbytag.sh server1

# does not assume each key is only used for one server
# does not assume server has only one security group

# assumes that if the key name for the server is eg serverkey,
the file serverkey.pem is in the same directory as the script

# ssh port on server
sshport=22
# ssh user to connect with
sshuser=ec2-user

echo connecting ssh to $1 on $sshport with user $sshuser

# get my IP
myip=$(curl -s http://checkip.amazonaws.com/)
echo my IP is $myip

# get ip of server
# use 'Name=instance-state-name,Values=running'
# in case you just deleted an instance with the same key...
ip_address=$(aws ec2 describe-instances --filters Name=tag-
key,Values=instancename Name=tag-value,Values=$1 Name=instance-
state-name,Values=running --output text --query
```

```
'Reservations[*].Instances[*].PublicIpAddress')
  echo connecting to $ip_address

  # get security group id of server
  sgid=$(aws ec2 describe-instances --filters Name=tag-
key,Values=instancename Name=tag-value,Values=$1 Name=instance-
state-name,Values=running --output text --query
'Reservations[*].Instances[*].SecurityGroups[*].GroupId')
  echo security group id is $sgid

  # if multiple ids, only use the first with
  sgids=($sgid)
  sgid=${sgids[0]}
  echo security group id is $sgid

  # get key name for server
  keyname=$(aws ec2 describe-instances --filters Name=tag-
key,Values=instancename Name=tag-value,Values=$1 Name=instance-
state-name,Values=running --output text --query
'Reservations[*].Instances[*].KeyName')
  echo connecting with key $keyname

  # allow ssh in sg
  echo authorising ingress
  aws ec2 authorize-security-group-ingress --group-id $sgid
--protocol tcp --port $sshport --cidr $myip/32 --output text

  echo ssh command:
  echo ssh -i $keyname.pem -p $sshport $sshuser@$ip_address

  # wait for ssh
  echo -n "waiting for ssh"
  while ! ssh -i $keyname.pem -p $sshport -o ConnectTimeout=5 -o
BatchMode=yes $sshuser@$ip_address > /dev/null 2>&1 true; do
    echo -n . ; sleep 5;
  done; echo " ok"

  # connect
  ssh -i $keyname.pem -p $sshport $sshuser@$ip_address

  # exit ssh to close the security group port

  # remove ssh in sg
  echo revoking ingress
  aws ec2 revoke-security-group-ingress --group-id $sgid --protocol
tcp --port $sshport --cidr $myip/32 --output text
```

In both the above scripts, change the 'sshport' and 'sshuser' variables to match your situation. The shown values are the default ones. Finally note that if you 'sudo su' on the box, you need to do a double 'exit' - one for the sudo and one for the ssh.

Changing the SSH User

Changing the user who can sign in with ssh is not a huge security upgrade. After all, anyone who can steal you SSH Keys form your client computer can read your scripts and see what this username is. However, it does provide extra security against brute force attacks, and it's likely that implementing this feature will stop all automated attacks on SSH. It's also not so complicated to do and gives you a good understanding of how SSH and users interact.

The steps to changing the SSH user are as follows:

- ssh to your instance
- 'sudo su' as you'll need root permissions
- create a new group, I'll use 'ssher' but you should pick something different
- create a new user, I'll use 'ssher' but you should pick something different
- set ssher's password
- update the sshd config to allow ssher only to ssh in
- update the sudoers config to allow ssher to do 'sudo su'
- move the SSH Key from ec2-user to ssher
- restart sshd
- exit and ssh back in as ssher
- optionally delete the ec2-user account

OK, so launch an instance and ssh in with your key:

```
ssh -i <key> ec2-user@<PublicIP>
```

Become root with:

```
sudo su
```

Now let's make ssher:

```
groupadd ssher
useradd -g ssher ssher
```

You can verify ssher has a home directory with:

```
ls -al /home
```

which outputs:

```
drwx------ 3 ec2-user ec2-user 4096 Jun  3 03:17 ec2-user
```

```
drwx------ 2 ssher     ssher     4096 Jun  3 03:18 ssher
```

Change ssher's password (although if you stick with SSH Keys you won't need this):

```
passwd ssher
[then type password twice]
```

Update the sshd_config:

```
vi /etc/ssh/sshd_config
```

Paste in at the bottom (type i to insert):

```
AllowUsers ssher
```

Then save by pressing Escape and typing :wq!

Allow ssher to do 'sudo su':

```
vi /etc/sudoers.d/cloud-init
```

Then change the 3 occurrences of ec2-user to ssher: type i to insert, make the changes, press Escape and save with :wq!.

The file /etc/sudoers.d/cloud-init should look like this:

```
ssher ALL = NOPASSWD: ALL

# User rules for ssher
ssher ALL=(ALL) NOPASSWD:ALL
```

Next, move the SSH Key:

```
cd /home/ssher
mkdir .ssh
chown ssher:ssher .ssh
chmod 700 .ssh
mv /home/ec2-user/.ssh/authorized_keys .ssh
chown ssher:ssher .ssh/authorized_keys
chmod 600 .ssh/authorized_keys
```

And restart the SSH daemon:

```
/etc/init.d/sshd restart
```

Quit ssh and 'sudo su' with:

```
exit
exit
```

And ssh in again with:

```
ssh -i [key] ssher@[PublicIP]
```

All done! You can verify 'sudo su' works, and clean up by deleting ec2-user with:

```
sudo su
userdel -r ec2-user
```

From here on, all the scripts in this book will implement this procedure and will use the new ssh username as defined in the top level file 'globals.sh' which by default is 'ssher'.

So who can sign in?

It can be a little confusing working out who exactly can or cannot sign in on your instance.

The first place which defines who can sign in with ssh is /etc/ssh/sshd_config, specifically the lines:

```
PermitRootLogin no
AllowUsers ssher
```

which allows only ssher to connect and denies the root user.

Another important file is /etc/passwd, which doesn't actually store passwords, but defines the shell when running as a user. This is the file on an EC2 instance (with the ssher user added):

[chapter5/cat_etc_passwd.txt]

```
# cat /etc/passwd
root:x:0:0:root:/root:/bin/bash
bin:x:1:1:bin:/bin:/sbin/nologin
daemon:x:2:2:daemon:/sbin:/sbin/nologin
adm:x:3:4:adm:/var/adm:/sbin/nologin
lp:x:4:7:lp:/var/spool/lpd:/sbin/nologin
```

```
sync:x:5:0:sync:/sbin:/bin/sync
shutdown:x:6:0:shutdown:/sbin:/sbin/shutdown
halt:x:7:0:halt:/sbin:/sbin/halt
mail:x:8:12:mail:/var/spool/mail:/sbin/nologin
uucp:x:10:14:uucp:/var/spool/uucp:/sbin/nologin
operator:x:11:0:operator:/root:/sbin/nologin
games:x:12:100:games:/usr/games:/sbin/nologin
gopher:x:13:30:gopher:/var/gopher:/sbin/nologin
ftp:x:14:50:FTP User:/var/ftp:/sbin/nologin
nobody:x:99:99:Nobody:/:/sbin/nologin
ntp:x:38:38::/etc/ntp:/sbin/nologin
saslauth:x:499:76:"Saslauthd
user":/var/empty/saslauth:/sbin/nologin
mailnull:x:47:47::/var/spool/mqueue:/sbin/nologin
smmsp:x:51:51::/var/spool/mqueue:/sbin/nologin
sshd:x:74:74:Privilege-separated
SSH:/var/empty/sshd:/sbin/nologin
dbus:x:81:81:System message bus:/:/sbin/nologin
ec2-user:x:500:500:EC2 Default User:/home/ec2-user:/bin/bash
ssher:x:501:501::/home/ssher:/bin/bash
```

Any user whose line ends with '/sbin/nologin' can't have a session
running (so you can't su to them). You can filter the above list
with:

```
cat /etc/passwd | grep -v nologin
```

which outputs:

```
# cat /etc/passwd | grep -v nologin
root:x:0:0:root:/root:/bin/bash
sync:x:5:0:sync:/sbin:/bin/sync
shutdown:x:6:0:shutdown:/sbin:/sbin/shutdown
halt:x:7:0:halt:/sbin:/sbin/halt
ec2-user:x:500:500:EC2 Default User:/home/ec2-user:/bin/bash
ssher:x:501:501::/home/ssher:/bin/bash
```

As you can see, only root, ec2-user and ssher can get a bash shell.

The other important file to have a look at is /etc/shadow. It lists the
hashed passwords for users.

```
[chapter5/cat_etc_shadow.txt]
```

```
# cat /etc/shadow
root:
$6$7YhGRUW0$Fa6Jxn3iwGTOKcu8lu9OyfR9E6TgwbCwcKeuR3bShc3G.RdalxHtRPh
4U.wRewJwW2UTZRM.NXeP7BiPFGDuQ0:16590:::::::
bin:*:16323:0:99999:7:::
daemon:*:16323:0:99999:7:::
adm:*:16323:0:99999:7:::
lp:*:16323:0:99999:7:::
sync:*:16323:0:99999:7:::
shutdown:*:16323:0:99999:7:::
halt:*:16323:0:99999:7:::
mail:*:16323:0:99999:7:::
```

```
uucp:*:16323:0:99999:7:::
operator:*:16323:0:99999:7:::
games:*:16323:0:99999:7:::
gopher:*:16323:0:99999:7:::
ftp:*:16323:0:99999:7:::
nobody:*:16323:0:99999:7:::
ntp:!!:16512:::::
saslauth:!!:16512:::::::
mailnull:!!:16512:::::::
smmsp:!!:16512:::::::
sshd:!!:16512:::::::
dbus:!!:16512:::::::
ec2-user:!!:16590:0:99999:7:::
ssher:
$6$p0veThQg$BmqIrGowmauNkZU6lFLXTZjGp5M/T3UKJqv9yfREQgl0Goetak23iB0
fTT2ZOLNe0SNP0E9Ls1XEemUd.2wW10:16590:0:99999:7:::
```

Each line denotes a user and the password is after the first colon. There are 3 options: a valid password hash (which looks like a long string of mumbo jumbo); '*' for disabled and '!!' for unset. You can verify this because with the above file you can 'su ec2-user' (password in /etc/shadow is '!!' and shell in /etc/passwd is '/bin/bash').

So by looking at a combination of /etc/passwd and /etc/shadow you can see potential users that can be 'su'ed to. For an EC2 instance, the default is root and ec2-user, so you don't have to worry about anyone getting a shell as some other weird user (like saslauth).

Hardening SSH

SSH on an Amazon Linux AMI is configured in the file /etc/ssh/sshd_config. In it's original form it looks like this:

[chapter5/sshd_config_original.txt]

```
#       $OpenBSD: sshd_config,v 1.89 2013/02/06 00:20:42 dtucker
Exp $

# This is the sshd server system-wide configuration file.  See
# sshd_config(5) for more information.

# This sshd was compiled with PATH=/usr/local/bin:/bin:/usr/bin

# The strategy used for options in the default sshd_config
shipped with
# OpenSSH is to specify options with their default value where
# possible, but leave them commented.  Uncommented options
override the
# default value.

# If you want to change the port on a SELinux system, you have to
```

```
tell
  # SELinux about this change.
  # semanage port -a -t ssh_port_t -p tcp #PORTNUMBER
  #
  #Port 22
  #AddressFamily any
  #ListenAddress 0.0.0.0
  #ListenAddress ::

  # The default requires explicit activation of protocol 1
  #Protocol 2

  # HostKey for protocol version 1
  #HostKey /etc/ssh/ssh_host_key
  # HostKeys for protocol version 2
  #HostKey /etc/ssh/ssh_host_rsa_key
  #HostKey /etc/ssh/ssh_host_dsa_key
  #HostKey /etc/ssh/ssh_host_ecdsa_key

  # Lifetime and size of ephemeral version 1 server key
  #KeyRegenerationInterval 1h
  #ServerKeyBits 1024

  # Logging
  # obsoletes QuietMode and FascistLogging
  #SyslogFacility AUTH
  SyslogFacility AUTHPRIV
  #LogLevel INFO

  # Authentication:

  #LoginGraceTime 2m
  #PermitRootLogin yes
  # Only allow root to run commands over ssh, no shell
  PermitRootLogin forced-commands-only
  #StrictModes yes
  #MaxAuthTries 6
  #MaxSessions 10

  #RSAAuthentication yes
  #PubkeyAuthentication yes

  # The default is to check both .ssh/authorized_keys and
.ssh/authorized_keys2
  # but this is overridden so installations will only check
.ssh/authorized_keys
  AuthorizedKeysFile .ssh/authorized_keys

  #AuthorizedPrincipalsFile none

  #AuthorizedKeysCommand none
  #AuthorizedKeysCommandUser nobody

  # For this to work you will also need host keys in
/etc/ssh/ssh_known_hosts
  #RhostsRSAAuthentication no
  # similar for protocol version 2
  #HostbasedAuthentication no
  # Change to yes if you don't trust ~/.ssh/known_hosts for
  # RhostsRSAAuthentication and HostbasedAuthentication
  #IgnoreUserKnownHosts no
  # Don't read the user's ~/.rhosts and ~/.shosts files
  #IgnoreRhosts yes

  # To disable tunneled clear text passwords, change to no here!
  #PasswordAuthentication yes
  #PermitEmptyPasswords no
  # EC2 uses keys for remote access
```

```
PasswordAuthentication no

# Change to no to disable s/key passwords
#ChallengeResponseAuthentication yes
ChallengeResponseAuthentication no

# Kerberos options
#KerberosAuthentication no
#KerberosOrLocalPasswd yes
#KerberosTicketCleanup yes
#KerberosGetAFSToken no
#KerberosUseKuserok yes

# GSSAPI options
#GSSAPIAuthentication no
#GSSAPICleanupCredentials yes
#GSSAPIStrictAcceptorCheck yes
#GSSAPIKeyExchange no

# Set this to yes to enable PAM authentication, account
processing,
# and session processing. If this is enabled, PAM authentication
will
# be allowed through the ChallengeResponseAuthentication and
# PasswordAuthentication.  Depending on your PAM configuration,
# PAM authentication via ChallengeResponseAuthentication may
bypass
# the setting of "PermitRootLogin without-password".
# If you just want the PAM account and session checks to run
without
# PAM authentication, then enable this but set
PasswordAuthentication
# and ChallengeResponseAuthentication to 'no'.
# WARNING: 'UsePAM no' is not supported in Fedora and may cause
several
# problems.
#UsePAM no
# Leaving enabled as described so that account and session checks
are run
UsePAM yes

#AllowAgentForwarding yes
#AllowTcpForwarding yes
#GatewayPorts no
#X11Forwarding no
X11Forwarding yes
#X11DisplayOffset 10
#X11UseLocalhost yes
#PrintMotd yes
# Explicitly enable
PrintLastLog yes
#TCPKeepAlive yes
#UseLogin no
UsePrivilegeSeparation sandbox          # Default for new
installations.
#PermitUserEnvironment no
#Compression delayed
#ClientAliveInterval 0
#ClientAliveCountMax 3
#ShowPatchLevel no
#UseDNS yes
#PidFile /var/run/sshd.pid
#MaxStartups 10:30:100
#PermitTunnel no
#ChrootDirectory none
#VersionAddendum none

# no default banner path
```

```
#Banner none

# Accept locale-related environment variables
AcceptEnv LANG LC_CTYPE LC_NUMERIC LC_TIME LC_COLLATE LC_MONETARY
LC_MESSAGES
AcceptEnv LC_PAPER LC_NAME LC_ADDRESS LC_TELEPHONE LC_MEASUREMENT
AcceptEnv LC_IDENTIFICATION LC_ALL LANGUAGE
AcceptEnv XMODIFIERS

# override default of no subsystems
Subsystem sftp          /usr/libexec/openssh/sftp-server

# Uncomment this if you want to use .local domain
#Host *.local
#       CheckHostIP no

# Example of overriding settings on a per-user basis
#Match User anoncvs
#       X11Forwarding no
#       AllowTcpForwarding no
#       ForceCommand cvs server
```

This is a hardened form of the file, set up for Key-based SSH:

[chapter5/sshd_config_hardened.txt]

```
# hardened sshd config file
# uses Key-based authentication

# change the default ssh port
Port 38142

# use better security protocols
Protocol 2

# log to authriv
SyslogFacility AUTHPRIV
# log info messages
LogLevel INFO

# don't permit root login, or root forced commands
PermitRootLogin no

# where the access keys can be found
AuthorizedKeysFile    .ssh/authorized_keys

# turn off various things
HostbasedAuthentication no
IgnoreRhosts yes
X11Forwarding no

# password authentication off
PasswordAuthentication no
ChallengeResponseAuthentication no

# only ssher can sign in
AllowUsers ssher
# run user and session checks
UsePAM yes

# when last signed in
PrintLastLog yes

# more secure way to run the sshd
UsePrivilegeSeparation sandbox
```

```
# max seconds to sign in after connecting
LoginGraceTime 60

# max authentication attempts per connect
# setting this any lower can cause problems
MaxAuthTries 3

# max multiplexed ssh sessions
# to limit sesions add to /etc/security/limits.conf
#ec2-user - maxlogins 1
MaxSessions 1

# max concurrent unauthenticated sessions
MaxStartups 1

# check no world writeable files left in user home directory
StrictModes yes

# no empty passwords
PermitEmptyPasswords no

# allows scp
Subsystem       sftp       /usr/libexec/openssh/sftp-server
```

Note that in what follows I assume you've changed the ssh user from ec2-user to ssher. If you haven't it will still work, but replace ssher with ec2-user. Also, in the sshd_config file above you'll need to change 'AllowUsers ssher' to 'AllowUsers ec2-user'.

To install the hardened config, copy the file to the instance, move it to /etc/ssh/sshd_config, set ownership root:root, set permissions to 400 (root can only read) and restart the sshd daemon. This procedure is used throughout the book for all scripts which follow where I build and automate successively more secure SSH installations.

You can upload the file by using scp from your client computer:

```
scp -i [key] sshd_config_hardened.txt ssher@[PublicIP]:
```

The commands to do it if the new sshd_config is in /home/ssher:

```
sudo su
cd /home/ssher
mv sshd_config_hardened.txt /etc/ssh/sshd_config
chown root:root /etc/ssh/sshd_config
chmod 400 /etc/ssh/sshd_config
/etc/init.d/sshd restart
exit
exit
```

The commands to do it with copy and paste are:

```
sudo su
# wipe the old file (but keep it and its permissions)
echo "" > /etc/ssh/sshd_config
# paste in with vi
# copy the sshd_config_hardened.txt listing above
vi /etc/ssh/sshd_config
# in vi, press i, press command-V (paste), press Escape, then
type ":wq!"
/etc/init.d/sshd restart
exit
exit
```

If you do install this config file, you'll need to update the port in your ssh command:

```
ssh -i server.pem -p 38142 ssher@100.100.100.100
```

And you'll need to change the Security Group port from 22 to 38142.

If you want to limit concurrent SSH sessions, you need to edit /etc/security/limits.conf and paste in at the bottom:

```
ssher - maxlogins 1
```

This is good security practice because you can be sure that, while your port is open and you are 'ssh'ed in, no-else can be connected. Obviously, if you're a multi-window fiend, set it to 2, 3 or 4! Just make sure when you open up the port that you've got all the available sessions.

SSH Logging

The following lines in the sshd_config file enable logging:

```
SyslogFacility AUTHPRIV
LogLevel INFO
```

You'll find the sshd log in /var/log/secure. It lists sshd daemon starts and stops, ssh sign ins and uses of 'sudo'. Now, you don't really want to have to sign in every day to check this log, do you? It would be much more useful if you received a daily email with the last day's log.

Sendmail is installed by default and running on the Amazon Linux AMIs. Okay, we all know the problems with SPAM sent from AWS Instances... Just remember to 'unspam' the first few emails you get and Gmail will get the idea. Also, don't abuse sendmail - Amazon are very touchy about spammers and will not tolerate excessive emails. One or two a day per instance is fine, though.

So here's a script you can cron as root which emails the current sshd log file, then appends it to an old version of the log and clears the current log file. You'll need to change 'youremail@address.com' to your email address.

[chapter5/emailsshlog.sh]

```
#!/bin/bash

# a script to send an email with the last days sshd log
# old log entries are moved to secureold

echo "." >> /var/log/secure
/usr/sbin/sendmail youremail@address.com < /var/log/secure
cat /var/log/secure >> /var/log/secureold
echo "" > /var/log/secure
chown root:root /var/log/secureold
chmod 600 /var/log/secureold
```

Upload or paste this script to /home/root, set the file owner to be root:root and file permissions to be 500 (Read and Execute). To cron the job every day at 5 minutes past midnight, use:

```
line="5 0 * * * /root/emailsshlog.sh"
(crontab -u root -l; echo "$line" ) | crontab -u root -
```

In addition, it would be useful to receive an immediate email in the event of a possible breach attempt. Now, there are several ways to get root permissions on an instance, the main two being:

```
sudo su
# or
su root
```

The difference between the two is whether a password is requested: 'sudo su' can be used password-less because this is allowed in /etc/sudoers (or more precisely /etc/sudoers.d/cloud-init); 'su root' requires the root password (which is initially set but unknown for new AWS instances). In later chapters, I reconfigure 'sudo' to require a root password, so it behaves much as 'su root'. However, logging for the two is different.

For 'sudo su', we can have an email sent immediately whenever this command is used (or any 'sudo). To do this, edit '/etc/sudoers.d/cloud-init' and add in the following line at the end:

```
Defaults mailto="youremail@address.com",mail_always
```

For 'su root', we can configure the root login script for root (/root/.bashrc) to send an email when run. Add the following line to '/root/.bashrc':

```
echo Subject: Root Access$'\n'$(who) | sendmail
youremail@address.com
```

This means when you do a 'sudo su' you'll actually get two emails (one from each method), but this is worth it to ensure 'su root' is also checked. Note that if you set a proper root password (like a 32 character random hexadecimal value), they're never going to crack it, but it is important to know if anyone is trying to assume privileges on your servers when they shouldn't be, and for that notification to be immediate. Obviously, it's a trifle annoying to get 50 emails when you are updating your servers or the like, so you might wish to disable these modifications during development or configuration. However, for stable production servers which you rarely ssh into, these notifications are vital.

These logging configurations are used and installed in the next 3 Chapters where I build and automate successively more secure SSH installations.

Building a Server

Scripts which build a server to show the above techniques can be found in chapter5/build. cd to 'chapter5/build' and run with:

```
./make.sh
```

This will build a server which retains SSH Keys but hardens SSH, changes the ssh user to 'sshuser' and sets up SSH email logging. Frankly, if you're running a low security server and employ good Secure Laptop habits, this server will probably be secure enough and involves a minimum of hassle.

You can change settings for the server in vars.sh:

[chapter5/build/vars.sh]

```
#!/bin/bash

# include globals
. ./../../globals.sh

# shared variables for scripts in chapter5//build

# the base name for the instance
# this string is used for key name, instance and sg names and
tags
ibn=sshhard
```

The script make.sh, which launches the instance, transfers files and runs them is as follows:

[chapter5/build/make.sh]

```
#!/bin/bash

# makes an ec2 instance
# the ssh user is changed and ssh is hardened
# SSH Keys are retained

# include chapter6 variables
. ./vars.sh

# show variables
echo AMI: $baseami
echo instance base name: $ibn
echo VPC name: $vpcname
echo new SSHD port: $sshport
echo logging to email address: $emailaddress
echo sshuser: $sshuser

# get our ip from amazon
myip=$(curl http://checkip.amazonaws.com/)
echo myip=$myip

# make a new keypair
echo "making keypair"
rm "$ibn".pem
aws ec2 delete-key-pair --key-name "$ibn"
aws ec2 create-key-pair --key-name "$ibn" --query 'KeyMaterial'
--output text > "$ibn".pem
chmod 600 "$ibn".pem
echo "$ibn" keypair made
```

```
# get the vpc id
vpc_id=$(aws ec2 describe-vpcs --filters Name=tag-
key,Values=vpcname Name=tag-value,Values=$vpcname --output text
--query 'Vpcs[*].VpcId')
echo vpc_id=$vpc_id

# make a security group
sgid=$(aws ec2 create-security-group --group-name "$ibn"sg
--description "$ibn security group" --vpc-id $vpc_id --output text
--query 'GroupId')
# tag it
aws ec2 create-tags --resources $sgid --tags
Key=sgname,Value="$ibn"sg
# now get the security group id again by using the tag
sgid=$(aws ec2 describe-security-groups --filters Name=tag-
key,Values=sgname Name=tag-value,Values="$ibn"sg --output text
--query 'SecurityGroups[*].GroupId')
echo sgid=$sgid

# allow ssh in on port 22 from our ip only
aws ec2 authorize-security-group-ingress --group-id $sgid
--protocol tcp --port 22 --cidr $myip/32

# get a vpc subnet
subnet_id=$(aws ec2 describe-subnets --filters Name=vpc-
id,Values=$vpc_id Name=tag-key,Values=subnet Name=tag-
value,Values=1 --output text --query 'Subnets[*].SubnetId')
echo subnet_id=$subnet_id

# make the instance
instance_id=$(aws ec2 run-instances --image $baseami --key "$ibn"
--security-group-ids $sgid --instance-type t2.micro --subnet-id
$subnet_id --associate-public-ip-address --output text --query
'Instances[*].InstanceId')
echo instance_id=$instance_id

# tag the instance (so we can get it later)
aws ec2 create-tags --resources $instance_id --tags
Key=instancename,Value="$ibn"

# wait for it
echo -n "waiting for instance"
while state=$(aws ec2 describe-instances --instance-ids
$instance_id --output text --query
'Reservations[*].Instances[*].State.Name'); test "$state" =
"pending"; do
  echo -n . ; sleep 3;
done; echo " $state"

# get the new instance's public ip address
ip_address=$(aws ec2 describe-instances --instance-ids
$instance_id --output text --query
'Reservations[*].Instances[*].PublicIpAddress')
echo ip_address=$ip_address

# wait for ssh to work
echo -n "waiting for ssh"
while ! ssh -i "$ibn".pem -o ConnectTimeout=5 -o BatchMode=yes -o
StrictHostKeyChecking=no ec2-user@$ip_address > /dev/null 2>&1
true; do
  echo -n . ; sleep 5;
done; echo " ssh ok"

# remove old files
rm -f install.sh
rm -f emailsshlog.sh
rm -f sshd_config
```

AWS Scripted 2

```
# sed the install script
sed -e "s/SEDsshuserSED/$sshuser/g" -e "s/SEDemailaddressSED/
$emailaddress/g" install_template.sh > install.sh

# sed the email logging script
sed -e "s/SEDemailaddressSED/$emailaddress/g"
emailsshlog_template.sh > emailsshlog.sh

# sed the sshd_config file
sed -e "s/SEDsshportSED/$sshport/g" -e "s/SEDsshuserSED/
$sshuser/g" sshd_config_template > sshd_config

# make the scripts executable
chmod +x install.sh
chmod +x emailsshlog.sh

# send required files
echo "transferring files"
scp -i "$ibn".pem install.sh ec2-user@$ip_address:
scp -i "$ibn".pem sshd_config ec2-user@$ip_address:
scp -i "$ibn".pem emailsshlog.sh ec2-user@$ip_address:
echo "transferred files"

# remove sent files
rm -f install.sh
rm -f emailsshlog.sh
rm -f sshd_config

# run the install script
ssh -i "$ibn".pem -t -o ConnectTimeout=60 -o BatchMode=yes ec2-
user@$ip_address sudo ./install.sh

# drop the port 22 rule
aws ec2 revoke-security-group-ingress --group-id $sgid --protocol
tcp --port 22 --cidr $myip/32

# open up the new ssh port
aws ec2 authorize-security-group-ingress --group-id $sgid
--protocol tcp --port $sshport --cidr $myip/32

echo
echo now ssh to the box with:
echo ssh -i "$ibn".pem -p $sshport "$sshuser"@"$ip_address"
echo 'sudo su' still works
echo remove ec2-user with: userdel -r ec2-user

echo
echo while sshed in from one terminal, try again from another
echo you will get: Too many logins for 'ssher'.

echo
echo when finished, terminate the server or close the 22 inbound
port
echo "eg aws ec2 revoke-security-group-ingress --group-id $sgid
--protocol tcp --port $sshport --cidr $myip/32"
```

The install.sh script which is run on the instance is generated from the following file:

[chapter5/build/install_template.sh]

```
#!/bin/bash

# this script needs to be run on the instance as root
```

```
# it changes the ssh user to ssher
# it hardens sshd
# it sets up a daily email of the sshd log file

# the following strings are replaced:
# SEDsshuserSED
# SEDemailaddressSED

# update yum
yum -y update

# add ssher user
groupadd SEDsshuserSED
useradd -g SEDsshuserSED SEDsshuserSED

# actually, as we are still using ssh keys,
# we don't need to change ssher's password

# allow ssher to 'sudo su'
sed -e "s/ec2-user/SEDsshuserSED/g" /etc/sudoers.d/cloud-init
> /etc/sudoers.d/cloud-init2
cat /etc/sudoers.d/cloud-init2 > /etc/sudoers.d/cloud-init
rm /etc/sudoers.d/cloud-init2
cat /etc/sudoers.d/cloud-init

# move the ssh key
cd /home/SEDsshuserSED
mkdir .ssh
chown SEDsshuserSED:SEDsshuserSED .ssh
chmod 700 .ssh
ls -al
mv /home/ec2-user/.ssh/authorized_keys .ssh
chown SEDsshuserSED:SEDsshuserSED .ssh/authorized_keys
chmod 600 .ssh/authorized_keys
ls -al .ssh

# update sshd config
cd /home/ec2-user
mv sshd_config /etc/ssh/sshd_config
chown root:root /etc/ssh/sshd_config
chmod 600 /etc/ssh/sshd_config

# set the max concurrent ssh sessions
echo "SEDsshuserSED - maxlogins 1" >> /etc/security/limits.conf

# restart sshd
# careful, sshd doesn't seem to like
# being restarted just as you end an ssh session
/etc/init.d/sshd restart
sleep 5

# set up email logging
mv emailsshlog.sh /root/emailsshlog.sh
chown root:root /root/emailsshlog.sh
chmod 500 /root/emailsshlog.sh

# run daily at 12:05am
line="5 0 * * * /root/emailsshlog.sh"
(crontab -u root -l; echo "$line" ) | crontab -u root -

# send immediate email for sudo use
 echo 'Defaults mailto="SEDemailaddressSED",mail_always' >>
/etc/sudoers.d/cloud-init

 # send immediate email for root signin
 echo "echo Subject: Root Access\$'\n'\$(who) | sendmail
SEDemailaddressSED" >> /root/.bashrc
```

```
# delete this script
rm -f install.sh
```

install.sh uses two files to complete the configuration of the instance. The new sshd_config is generated from this file:

`[chapter5/build/sshd_config_template]`

```
# hardened sshd config file
# turns off Key access
# turns on Password access

# the following strings are replaced:
# SEDsshportSED
# SEDsshuserSED

# change the default ssh port
Port SEDsshportSED

# use better security protocols
Protocol 2

# log to authriv
SyslogFacility AUTHPRIV
# log info messages
LogLevel INFO

# don't permit root login, or root forced commands
PermitRootLogin no

# TURNED OFF
# where the access keys can be found
#AuthorizedKeysFile    .ssh/authorized_keys

# turn off various things
HostbasedAuthentication no
IgnoreRhosts yes
X11Forwarding no

# TURNED ON
# password authentication
PasswordAuthentication yes
ChallengeResponseAuthentication yes

# only SEDsshuserSED can sign in
AllowUsers SEDsshuserSED
# run user and session checks
UsePAM yes

# when last signed in
PrintLastLog yes

# more secure way to run the sshd
UsePrivilegeSeparation sandbox

# max seconds to sign in after connecting
LoginGraceTime 60

# max authentication attempts per connect
# setting this any lower can cause problems
MaxAuthTries 3

# max multiplexed ssh sessions
# to limit sessions add the following to
```

```
/etc/security/limits.conf:
  #ssher - maxlogins 1
  MaxSessions 1

  # max concurrent unauthenticated sessions
  MaxStartups 1

  # check no world writeable files left in user home directory
  StrictModes yes

  # no empty passwords
  PermitEmptyPasswords no

  # allows scp
  Subsystem      sftp      /usr/libexec/openssh/sftp-server
```

And email logging of SSH logs is accomplished from this script:

[chapter5/build/emailsshlog_template.sh]

```
#!/bin/bash

# a script to send an email with the last days sshd log
# old log entries are moved to secureold

# the following strings are replaced:
# SEDemailaddressSED

echo "." >> /var/log/secure
/usr/sbin/sendmail SEDemailaddressSED < /var/log/secure
cat /var/log/secure >> /var/log/secureold
echo "" > /var/log/secure
chown root:root /var/log/secureold
chmod 600 /var/log/secureold
```

You can also use the two connect scripts shown earlier in this chapter, connectssh.sh and connectsshbytag.sh to connect to your new server. In each file, change the sshuser and sshport definitions to:

```
sshport=38142
sshuser=ssher
```

Or whatever you changed them to in globals.sh. Then copy the key, sshhard.pem, to the chapter5 directory. From the chapter5 directory, you can run:

```
./connectssh.sh sshhard
```

Or:

```
./connectsshbytag.sh sshhard
```

Chapter 6 - SSH with Password

Requiring an SSH Password

Instead of using the default SSH system of Keys, you can turn off Keys and require a normal Password sign in. Actually, this is less secure than using Keys, so I don't recommend using this method. However, for the sake of completeness, I am, in Chapters 6, 7 and 8, building progressively more secure SSH systems. So I have included this as the first step.

The steps involved to switch to an SSH password are as follows:

- ssh to the instance with SSH Key and 'sudo su'
- replace the sshd_config file with a new config
- change the SSH user to ssher
- delete any SSH Keys
- restart sshd
- set the ssher password to something you know
- quit ssh
- delete local SSH Key
- ssh to the instance and type the password

If you want to test the procedure manually, execute the following commands on a running instance you have 'ssh'ed to with a Key and done 'sudo su'. Alternatively, you can see the scripts in the next section which automate the process.

The new sshd_config file is as follows:

```
[chapter6/sshd_config_example]

# hardened sshd config file
# turns off Key access
# turns on Password access

# change the default ssh port
Port 38142

# use better security protocols
```

```
Protocol 2

# log to authriv
SyslogFacility AUTHPRIV
# log info messages
LogLevel INFO

# don't permit root login, or root forced commands
PermitRootLogin no

# TURNED OFF
# where the access keys can be found
#AuthorizedKeysFile    .ssh/authorized_keys

# turn off various things
HostbasedAuthentication no
IgnoreRhosts yes
X11Forwarding no

#' TURNED ON
# password authentication
PasswordAuthentication yes
ChallengeResponseAuthentication yes

# only ssher can sign in
AllowUsers ssher
# run user and session checks
UsePAM yes

# when last signed in
PrintLastLog yes

# more secure way to run the sshd
UsePrivilegeSeparation sandbox

# max seconds to sign in after connecting
LoginGraceTime 60

# max authentication attempts per connect
# setting this any lower can cause problems
MaxAuthTries 3

# max multiplexed ssh sessions
# to limit sessions add the following to
/etc/security/limits.conf:
#ssher - maxlogins 1
MaxSessions 1

# max concurrent unauthenticated sessions
MaxStartups 1

# check no world writeable files left in user home directory
StrictModes yes

# no empty passwords
PermitEmptyPasswords no

# allows scp
Subsystem     sftp     /usr/libexec/openssh/sftp-server
```

As you can see, I commented out the AuthorizedKeysFile directive and changed PasswordAuthentication and ChallengeResponseAuthentication to 'yes' from 'no'. I also used the hardened version of the config file. To install the new sshd config file, do:

```
# wipe the old file (but keep it and its permissions)
echo "" > /etc/ssh/sshd_config
# paste in with vi
# copy the sshd_config_example listing above
vi /etc/ssh/sshd_config
# in vi, press i, press command-V (paste), press Escape, then
type ":wq!"
```

The SSH keys are stored in two places: /home/ec2-user/.ssh/authorized_keys and /root/.ssh/authorized_keys. Delete both files:

```
rm -f /home/ec2-user/.ssh/authorized_keys
rm -f /root/.ssh/authorized_keys
```

Now let's make ssher:

```
groupadd ssher
useradd -g ssher ssher
```

Change ssher's password:

```
passwd ssher
[then type password twice]
```

Allow ssher to do 'sudo su':

```
vi /etc/sudoers.d/cloud-init
```

Then change the 3 occurrences of ec2-user to ssher: type i to insert, make the changes, press Escape and save with :wq!.

The file /etc/sudoers.d/cloud-init should look like this:

```
ssher ALL = NOPASSWD: ALL

# User rules for ssher
ssher ALL=(ALL) NOPASSWD:ALL
```

Now restart sshd with (note this doesn't affect your current SSH session):

```
/etc/init.d/sshd restart
```

And do a double 'exit' to leave sudo su and ssh.

AWS Scripted 2

Now SSH back in with the new command (note no -i specifying SSH Key, and using the new port):

```
ssh -p 38142 ssher@[Public IP]
```

You'll see a prompt 'Password:' - type the ssher password you set above. Bang! You're in. 'sudo su' still works with no password.

Building a Server with SSH Password

The procedure for automating the above process is documented in the following scripts. You can use the './make.sh' command from the chapter6 directory to launch a new instance and configure it to use an SSH password. Also remember a valid VPC needs to exist with VPC name set in vars.sh, see **Appendix A - VPC**.

```
[chapter6/make.sh]
```

```bash
#!/bin/bash

# makes an ec2 instance with SSH Password setup

# include chapter6 variables
. ./vars.sh

# show variables
echo AMI: $baseami
echo instance base name: $ibn
echo VPC name: $vpcname
echo new SSHD port: $sshport
echo logging to email address: $emailaddress
echo ssh user: $sshuser
echo ssher password: $ssherpassword

# get our ip from amazon
myip=$(curl http://checkip.amazonaws.com/)
echo myip=$myip

# make a new keypair
echo "making keypair"
rm "$ibn".pem
aws ec2 delete-key-pair --key-name "$ibn"
aws ec2 create-key-pair --key-name "$ibn" --query 'KeyMaterial'
--output text > "$ibn".pem
chmod 600 "$ibn".pem
echo "$ibn" keypair made

# get the vpc id
vpc_id=$(aws ec2 describe-vpcs --filters Name=tag-
key,Values=vpcname Name=tag-value,Values=$vpcname --output text
--query 'Vpcs[*].VpcId')
echo vpc_id=$vpc_id

# make a security group
```

```
    sgid=$(aws ec2 create-security-group --group-name "$ibn"sg
--description "$ibn security group" --vpc-id $vpc_id --output text
--query 'GroupId')
    # tag it
    aws ec2 create-tags --resources $sgid --tags
Key=sgname,Value="$ibn"sg
    # now get the security group id again by using the tag
    sgid=$(aws ec2 describe-security-groups --filters Name=tag-
key,Values=sgname Name=tag-value,Values="$ibn"sg --output text
--query 'SecurityGroups[*].GroupId')
    echo sgid=$sgid

    # allow ssh in on port 22 from our ip only
    aws ec2 authorize-security-group-ingress --group-id $sgid
--protocol tcp --port 22 --cidr $myip/32

    # get a vpc subnet
    subnet_id=$(aws ec2 describe-subnets --filters Name=vpc-
id,Values=$vpc_id Name=tag-key,Values=subnet Name=tag-
value,Values=1 --output text --query 'Subnets[*].SubnetId')
    echo subnet_id=$subnet_id

    # make the instance
    instance_id=$(aws ec2 run-instances --image $baseami --key "$ibn"
--security-group-ids $sgid --instance-type t2.micro --subnet-id
$subnet_id --associate-public-ip-address --output text --query
'Instances[*].InstanceId')
    echo instance_id=$instance_id

    # tag the instance (so we can get it later)
    aws ec2 create-tags --resources $instance_id --tags
Key=instancename,Value="$ibn"

    # wait for it
    echo -n "waiting for instance"
    while state=$(aws ec2 describe-instances --instance-ids
$instance_id --output text --query
'Reservations[*].Instances[*].State.Name'); test "$state" =
"pending"; do
      echo -n . ; sleep 3;
    done; echo " $state"

    # get the new instance's public ip address
    ip_address=$(aws ec2 describe-instances --instance-ids
$instance_id --output text --query
'Reservations[*].Instances[*].PublicIpAddress')
    echo ip_address=$ip_address

    # wait for ssh to work
    echo -n "waiting for ssh"
    while ! ssh -i "$ibn".pem -o ConnectTimeout=5 -o BatchMode=yes -o
StrictHostKeyChecking=no ec2-user@$ip_address > /dev/null 2>&1
true; do
      echo -n . ; sleep 5;
    done; echo " ssh ok"

    # remove old files
    rm -f install.sh
    rm -f emailsshlog.sh
    rm -f sshd_config

    # sed the install script
    sed -e "s/SEDsshuserSED/$sshuser/g" -e "s/SEDssherpasswordSED/
$ssherpassword/g" -e "s/SEDemailaddressSED/$emailaddress/g"
install_template.sh > install.sh

    # sed the email logging script
    sed -e "s/SEDemailaddressSED/$emailaddress/g"
```

```
emailsshlog_template.sh > emailsshlog.sh

    # sed the sshd_config file
    sed -e "s/SEDsshportSED/$sshport/g" -e "s/SEDsshuserSED/
$sshuser/g" sshd_config_template > sshd_config

    # make the scripts executable
    chmod +x install.sh
    chmod +x emailsshlog.sh

    # send required files
    echo "transferring files"
    scp -i "$ibn".pem install.sh ec2-user@$ip_address:
    scp -i "$ibn".pem sshd_config ec2-user@$ip_address:
    scp -i "$ibn".pem emailsshlog.sh ec2-user@$ip_address:
    echo "transferred files"

    # remove sent files
    rm -f install.sh
    rm -f emailsshlog.sh
    rm -f sshd_config

    # run the install script
    ssh -i "$ibn".pem -t -o ConnectTimeout=60 -o BatchMode=yes ec2-
user@$ip_address sudo ./install.sh

    # remove the local key (it won't work anyway)
    rm -f "$ibn".pem

    # drop the port 22 rule
    aws ec2 revoke-security-group-ingress --group-id $sgid --protocol
tcp --port 22 --cidr $myip/32

    # open up the new ssh port
    aws ec2 authorize-security-group-ingress --group-id $sgid
--protocol tcp --port $sshport --cidr $myip/32

    echo
    echo now ssh to the box with:
    echo ssh -p "$sshport" "$sshuser"@"$ip_address"
    echo "enter password ($ssherpassword)"
    echo 'sudo su' still works

    echo
    echo when finished, terminate the server or close the 22 inbound
port
    echo "eg aws ec2 revoke-security-group-ingress --group-id $sgid
--protocol tcp --port $sshport --cidr $myip/32"
```

The make.sh script relies on 4 files to finish its task. The first is a shared variables file - anything configurable is in this file, as is my 'global variables' convention. I like to stick to a system whereby variables are only defined once, or else as soon as things get complicated you always find you forgot to change that one definition in that one obscure file and it doesn't work. 'vars.sh' is also used for the SSH connect script in the next section.

[chapter6/vars.sh]

```
#!/bin/bash
```

```
# include globals
. ./../globals.sh

# shared variables for scripts in chapter6

# the base name for the instance
# this string is used for key name, instance and sg names and
tags
  ibn=sshpass

# password for ssher
ssherpassword=1234
```

The next three files follow my convention of suffixing '_template' to any files which have strings replaced in them using the bash command 'sed'. This is a vital step in automating complex scripts and to ensure original template files are never wiped by mistake (which is easy to do in bash...), I always sed a '*_template' file to its counterpart '*', for instance install_template.sh goes to install.sh.

The install script is run on the instance. It performs the tasks as described in the last section (update sshd, delete keys, update ec2-user password), sets up sending the sshd log via email and also limits ssh sessions to 1 by editing /etc/security/limits.conf.

[chapter6/install_template.sh]

```
#!/bin/bash

# this script needs to be run on the instance as root
# it changes the ssh user to ssher
# it configures sshd to use a password
# it sets up a daily email of the sshd log file

# the following strings are replaced:
# SEDsshuserSED
# SEDssherpasswordSED
# SEDemailaddressSED

# update yum
yum -y update

# add ssher user
groupadd SEDsshuserSED
useradd -g SEDsshuserSED SEDsshuserSED

# allow ssher to 'sudo su'
sed -e "s/ec2-user/SEDsshuserSED/g" /etc/sudoers.d/cloud-init
> /etc/sudoers.d/cloud-init2
cat /etc/sudoers.d/cloud-init2 > /etc/sudoers.d/cloud-init
rm /etc/sudoers.d/cloud-init2
cat /etc/sudoers.d/cloud-init

# update sshd config
mv sshd_config /etc/ssh/sshd_config
```

```
chown root:root /etc/ssh/sshd_config
chmod 600 /etc/ssh/sshd_config

# remove sshd keys so users can't sign in with a key
rm -f /home/ec2-user/.ssh/authorized_keys
rm -f /root/.ssh/authorized_keys

# set the max concurrent ssh sessions
echo "SEDsshuserSED - maxlogins 1" >> /etc/security/limits.conf

# restart sshd
# careful, sshd doesn't seem to like
# being restarted just as you end an ssh session
/etc/init.d/sshd restart

# change ssher's password with expect
# install expect
yum install -y expect
# make expect script
echo "#!/usr/bin/expect -f" > expect.sh
echo "set timeout -1" >> expect.sh
echo "spawn passwd SEDsshuserSED" >> expect.sh
echo "expect \"New password:\"" >> expect.sh
echo "send \"SEDssherpasswordSED\n\";" >> expect.sh
echo "expect \"new password:\"" >> expect.sh
echo "send \"SEDssherpasswordSED\n\";" >> expect.sh
echo "interact" >> expect.sh
# run it
chmod +x expect.sh
./expect.sh
# remove it
rm -f expect.sh
# erase expect
yum erase -y expect

# set up email logging
mv emailsshlog.sh /root/emailsshlog.sh
chown root:root /root/emailsshlog.sh
chmod 500 /root/emailsshlog.sh

# run daily at 12:05am
line="5 0 * * * /root/emailsshlog.sh"
(crontab -u root -1; echo "$line" ) | crontab -u root -

# send immediate email for sudo use
 echo 'Defaults mailto="SEDemailaddressSED",mail_always' >>
/etc/sudoers.d/cloud-init

# send immediate email for root signin
 echo "echo Subject: Root Access\$'\n'\$(who) | sendmail
SEDemailaddressSED" >> /root/.bashrc

# delete this script
rm -f install.sh
```

This is a template version of a hardened sshd_config file which allows the SSH port to be changed dynamically as defined in vars.sh:

[chapter6/sshd_config_template]

```
# hardened sshd config file
# turns off Key access
```

```
# turns on Password access

# the following strings are replaced:
# SEDsshportSED
# SEDsshuserSED

# change the default ssh port
Port SEDsshportSED

# use better security protocols
Protocol 2

# log to authriv
SyslogFacility AUTHPRIV
# log info messages
LogLevel INFO

# don't permit root login, or root forced commands
PermitRootLogin no

# TURNED OFF
# where the access keys can be found
#AuthorizedKeysFile    .ssh/authorized_keys

# turn off various things
HostbasedAuthentication no
IgnoreRhosts yes
X11Forwarding no

# TURNED ON
# password authentication
PasswordAuthentication yes
ChallengeResponseAuthentication yes

# only SEDsshuserSED can sign in
AllowUsers SEDsshuserSED
# run user and session checks
UsePAM yes

# when last signed in
PrintLastLog yes

# more secure way to run the sshd
UsePrivilegeSeparation sandbox

# max seconds to sign in after connecting
LoginGraceTime 60

# max authentication attempts per connect
# setting this any lower can cause problems
MaxAuthTries 3

# max multiplexed ssh sessions
# to limit sessions add the following to
/etc/security/limits.conf:
#ssher - maxlogins 1
MaxSessions 1

# max concurrent unauthenticated sessions
MaxStartups 1

# check no world writeable files left in user home directory
StrictModes yes

# no empty passwords
PermitEmptyPasswords no

# allows scp
```

```
Subsystem      sftp      /usr/libexec/openssh/sftp-server
```

This is the script which is run by cron to send the sshd logs via email. The email address is configurable in the globals.sh script.

`[chapter6/emailsshlog_template.sh]`

```
#!/bin/bash

# a script to send an email with the last days sshd log
# old log entries are moved to secureold

# the following strings are replaced:
# SEDemailaddressSED

echo  .   JJ  )var/log/uuuu.
/usr/sbin/sendmail SEDemailaddressSED < /var/log/secure
cat /var/log/secure >> /var/log/secureold
echo "" > /var/log/secure
chown root:root /var/log/secureold
chmod 600 /var/log/secureold
```

Automating SSH Password Access

Automating SSH access involves opening the ssh port, using expect to spawn the ssh command and enter the ssher password, then closing the port on exit from ssh:

`[chapter6/connectsshpass.sh]`

```
#!/bin/bash

# open an ssh session to a server
# which has keys disabled and password enabled
# as created by make.sh in this directory (chapter6)

# include chapter6 variables
. ./vars.sh

# show variables
echo instance base name: $ibn
echo new SSHD port: $sshport
echo ssh user: $sshuser
echo ssher password: $ssherpassword

# if you want to make this script standalone
# (ie not relying on vars.sh)
# comment out '. ./vars.sh' above and define the variables here,
eg:
#ibn=sshpass
#sshport=38142
#sshuser=ssher
#ssherpassword=1234

# if you wanted to have a typed password,
# ie you don't want to encode the password in this script,
```

```
# you could use:
#read -s -p "ssher password:" ssherpassword
# also remove the declaration above

echo "connecting to instance $ibn on $sshport with user $sshuser"

myip=$(curl http://checkip.amazonaws.com/)
echo myip=$myip

# get ip of server
ip_address=$(aws ec2 describe-instances --filters Name=tag-
key,Values=instancename Name=tag-value,Values="$ibn" --output text
--query 'Reservations[*].Instances[*].PublicIpAddress')
echo ip_address=$ip_address

# allow ssh in sg
sgid=$(aws ec2 describe-security-groups --filters Name=tag-
key,Values=sgname Name=tag-value,Values="$ibn"sg --output text
--query 'SecurityGroups[*].GroupId')
echo sgid=$sgid
aws ec2 authorize-security-group-ingress --group-id $sgid
--protocol tcp --port $sshport --cidr $myip/32

# make and run expect script
# use timeout -1 for no timeout
echo "#!/usr/bin/expect -f" > expect.sh
echo "set timeout -1" >> expect.sh
echo "spawn ssh -p $sshport $sshuser@$ip_address" >> expect.sh
echo "expect \"Password:\"" >> expect.sh
echo "send \"$ssherpassword\n\"" >> expect.sh
echo "interact" >> expect.sh
chmod +x expect.sh
./expect.sh
rm expect.sh

# script now waits for 'exit'
# or double 'exit' if you 'sudo su'

# remove ssh in sg
aws ec2 revoke-security-group-ingress --group-id $sgid --protocol
tcp --port $sshport --cidr $myip/32
echo "revoked sg access"
```

You can test the script with:

```
./connectsshpass.sh
```

And you can verify only one SSH session is allowed by running the script again in a new terminal (while still signed in on the first) - you'll get "Too many logins for 'ssher'." Unfortunately, the second call will also close your Security Group rule, thereby crippling the first connection...

It's worth mentioning that limiting sign ins to 1 in /etc/limits/security.conf *can* lock you out of your server if the connection is dropped and sshd still thinks you're signed in. This has happened several times to me when, for instance, the IP address of my Internet connection changed and my Security Group therefore locked me out (ssh hangs and then says 'broken pipe'). If you do get locked out, you need to restart the instance from AWS Console.

Chapter 7 - SSH with Password/MFA

Requiring an SSH MFA Code

You can setup SSH on an Amazon Linux AMI to require MFA authentication pretty easily. All the required software is available from 'yum' and trusted AWS repositories. Use the Google Authenticator PAM module. This means that when you sign in with ssh, first you need to enter the password and then an MFA code.

MFA makes your SSH setup very secure, because even if your client computer is breached or infected, hackers will need a code which comes, for example, from your smartphone. And it also helps against brute force attacks (should you accidentally leave your SSH port open) by decreasing the chance of a successful guess by a factor of several hundred thousand, as well as introducing rate-limiting (1 attempt per minute). MFA is further secured by setting 'no code reuse', so technically valid codes can't be reused if intercepted by a key logger.

The procedure for setting up MFA for SSH builds on Chapter 6 - SSH with Password. Instead of recopying out all the instructions found there, I will proceed from a working setup built in Chapter 6, either manually (in **Chapter 6 - Requiring an SSH Password**) or with scripts (in **Chapter 6 - Building a Server with SSH Password**). So go ahead and follow those instructions and come back here when you have a working server, have opened the port in the Security Group, have 'ssh'ed in and have done 'sudo su'. Or you can skip to the next section which builds the entire server from scratch with scripts.

First, install Google Authenticator and PAM with (this needs to be done as root so 'sudo su' first):

```
yum -y install google-authenticator.x86_64 pam.x86_64 pam-devel.x86_64
```

Next, enable Google Authenticator in the PAM config with:

```
echo "auth required pam_google_authenticator.so" >>
/etc/pam.d/sshd
```

which appends the line 'auth required pam_google_authenticator.so' to the file /etc/pam.d/sshd (which configures PAM for sshd).

You don't need to change the /etc/ssh/sshd_config file as it is the same as for SSH with Password - SSH with MFA is just an extension of this. Restarting sshd is always a good idea:

```
/etc/init.d/sshd restart
```

Last of all, configure the MFA key for ssher. To do this you need to be running as ssher, so type 'exit' to exit the 'sudo su'. Then use the following command:

```
google-authenticator --time-based --disallow-reuse --force
--rate-limit=1 --rate-time=60 --window-size=3 --quiet
```

You can just type 'google-authenticator' and answer the questions, but by specifying the options, you save yourself an expect script. '--time-based' means it's a time based algorithm (this is what you want). '--disallow-reuse' disallows reuse of MFA codes (even if valid). '--force' forces writing the generated key to file (/home/ssher/.google_authenticator) without confirmation. '--rate-limit=1' and '--rate-time=60' limit sign in attempts to 1 every 60 seconds. '--window-size=3' means the current code, the code before and the code after are all valid, so you could in theory have plus or minus about 45 seconds difference in your smartphone and server clocks. You can use 'date' on the server and compare to your smartphone (they should be at most a few seconds apart). You can increase this value to 5 if clock desynchronisation is an issue, but it will reduce your security. '--quiet' makes the command not print any output.

The 'google-authenticator' command generates your MFA key and creates the file /home/ssher/.google_authenticator which is used by PAM to authenticate your code. The last step is to read this code from the file and type it into your Google Authenticator App. You can get this code with these commands (from the /home/ssher directory, which you should already be in):

```
bits=($(cat .google_authenticator))
echo MFA KEY is ${bits[0]}
```

The first line above reads the file '.google_authenticator' with 'cat' and splits this up into an array (using '()'). The second line prints the first element of the array. Feel free to 'cat .google_authenticator' to see the entire file. It might be a good idea to write down some of the codes at the bottom, which are use-once safety codes if you loose your MFA device. Just write these codes down securely, using the suggestions and cypher in **Chapter 1 - Writing Down Passwords**.

Install the Google Authenticator App on your smartphone. Now type the MFA KEY into the App (you need to select 'New' or the plus sign, then select Manual Entry; use a decent name or you'll get confused later). Careful, I've done this many times and still get it wrong one in three times! Especially with the tiny iPhone keyboard... Rechecking the code is vital. Also, it isn't case sensitive. Ensure 'Time-Based' is checked. OR, see **Appendix C - OTP Manager for OSX**.

Now 'exit' to leave ssh. Make sure the Security Group port is still open (connectsshpass.sh from Chapter 6 will have closed it...) and then reconnect with:

```
ssh -p 38142 ssher@[Public IP]
```

This time you'll be prompted for Password (enter the ssher password) and then Verification Code (enter the MFA code from your smartphone). That's it, your SSH is now very, very secure with no expensive software, services or dongles.

Let's have a look at the file created by the 'google-authenticator' command (originally '.google_authenticator'):

```
[chapter7/google_authenticator.txt]
```

```
2DSSKWLB43YQFLYJ
"RATE_LIMIT 1 60
" WINDOW_SIZE 3
" DISALLOW_REUSE
" TOTP_AUTH
39224841
72000665
32242730
75793697
366137
```

As you can see, the first line is your MFA Key. Then come the configuration options (rate limiting, window size, no reuse and time-based OTP). Last of all, there are 5 codes - these are 'get out of jail free' codes in case you lose your MFA device. Test it out - sign out and ssh back in and use one of the 8 digit codes... it works! But then, once you're in again, do:

```
cat /home/ssher/.google_authenticator
```

The code you just used is gone! So they really are 'use once only' codes. Is it secure to have these codes? Well, they are 8 digits, so that's 1 in 100 million of guessing... but there are 5 codes so it comes down to 1 in 20 million. At 1 attempt per minute, that's probably about 10 million minutes (assuming they get it half way), or (10,000,000 / (60 minutes * 24 hours * 365 days)) = 19 years to guess one... and that's not taking account of the SSH password! Not bad, but you can do better.

Let's try another experiment. In 'vi', add 2 digits to the first code, say '11', then sign out and try to get back in with the new 10 digit code. Doesn't work! These special codes need to be 8 digits long. So, what I do is delete 4 of them and keep just one, which I also write down using a cypher. Then the probable time to crack this code is 5x19years, or 95 years, without considering the SSH password, which is acceptable. Probably quicker to crack the 6 digit code at this point.

Another thing to check out is the permissions on '.google_authenticator':

```
$ ls -l .google_authenticator
-r-------- 1 ssher ssher 124 Jun  4 03:50 .google_authenticator
```

This is interesting because when this process is automated, you don't want to be messing about with different users. Initially, you're signed in as ec2-user and so getting to ssher is tough (given password changes, 'sudo' updates, etc), from a scripted environment and because of permissions. What you really want is to be able to run the 'google-authenticator' command as root and then sort out file location and permissions.

Luckily, there's a last option for 'google-authenticator': the 'secret' option. With it, you can specify the location of the '.google_authenticator' file to be created. Let's try it with the following:

```
sudo su
cd /root
rm -f /home/ssher/.google_authenticator
google-authenticator --time-based --disallow-reuse --force
--rate-limit=1 --rate-time=60 --window-size=3 --quiet
--secret=/home/ssher/.google_authenticator
  chown ssher:ssher /home/ssher/.google_authenticator
  chmod 400 /home/ssher/.google_authenticator
  cat /home/ssher/.google_authenticator
```

Don't forget to use the new MFA Key! But it works, which is quite handy for the scripting purposes which follow. The other thing I will do is reduce the 8 digit use-once codes to 1. So I want to remove the last 4 lines or keep the first 6. This can be done with the following:

```
cd /home/ssher
head -n 6 .google_authenticator > .google_authenticator
chown ssher:ssher /home/ssher/.google_authenticator
chmod 400 /home/ssher/.google_authenticator
# print out the codes
bits=($(cat .google_authenticator))
echo MFA KEY is ${bits[0]}
echo MFA GOOJ is ${bits[11]}
```

The GOOJ is the 'Get Out Of Jail Code'. You'll need to store one or both of these codes in a secure way in case you lose your MFA generator. Or if your server is completely disposable, you don't. If you ever use your GOOJ code, you'll probably want to reset the MFA or at least add a new GOOJ.

Building a Server with SSH Password/MFA

The procedure for automating the above process is documented in the following scripts. You can use the './make.sh' command from the chapter7 directory to launch a new instance and configure it to use an SSH password and MFA. Also remember a valid VPC needs to exist with VPC name set in vars.sh, see **Appendix A - VPC.**

`[chapter7/make.sh]`

```
#!/bin/bash

# makes an ec2 instance with SSH MFA setup

# include chapter7 variables
. ./vars.sh

# show variables
echo AMI: $baseami
echo instance base name: $ibn
echo VPC name: $vpcname
echo new SSHD port: $sshport
echo logging to email address: $emailaddress
echo ssh user: $sshuser
echo ssher password: $ssherpassword

# get our ip from amazon
myip=$(curl http://checkip.amazonaws.com/)
echo myip=$myip

# make a new keypair
echo "making keypair"
rm "$ibn".pem
aws ec2 delete-key-pair --key-name "$ibn"
aws ec2 create-key-pair --key-name "$ibn" --query 'KeyMaterial'
--output text > "$ibn".pem
chmod 600 "$ibn".pem
echo "$ibn" keypair made

# get the vpc id
vpc_id=$(aws ec2 describe-vpcs --filters Name=tag-
key,Values=vpcname Name=tag-value,Values=$vpcname --output text
--query 'Vpcs[*].VpcId')
echo vpc_id=$vpc_id

# make a security group
sgid=$(aws ec2 create-security-group --group-name "$ibn"sg
--description "$ibn security group" --vpc-id $vpc_id --output text
--query 'GroupId')
# tag it
aws ec2 create-tags --resources $sgid --tags
Key=sgname,Value="$ibn"sg
# now get the security group id again by using the tag
sgid=$(aws ec2 describe-security-groups --filters Name=tag-
key,Values=sgname Name=tag-value,Values="$ibn"sg --output text
--query 'SecurityGroups[*].GroupId')
echo sgid=$sgid

# allow ssh in on port 22 from our ip only
```

```
  aws ec2 authorize-security-group-ingress --group-id $sgid
--protocol tcp --port 22 --cidr $myip/32

  # get a vpc subnet
  subnet_id=$(aws ec2 describe-subnets --filters Name=vpc-
id,Values=$vpc_id Name=tag-key,Values=subnet Name=tag-
value,Values=1 --output text --query 'Subnets[*].SubnetId')
  echo subnet_id=$subnet_id

  # make the instance
  instance_id=$(aws ec2 run-instances --image $baseami --key "$ibn"
--security-group-ids $sgid --instance-type t2.micro --subnet-id
$subnet_id --associate-public-ip-address --output text --query
'Instances[*].InstanceId')
  echo instance_id=$instance_id

  # tag the instance (so we can get it later)
  aws ec2 create-tags --resources $instance_id --tags
Key=instancename,Value="$ibn"

  # wait for it
  echo -n "waiting for instance"
  while state=$(aws ec2 describe-instances --instance-ids
$instance_id --output text --query
'Reservations[*].Instances[*].State.Name'); test "$state" =
"pending"; do
    echo -n . ; sleep 3;
  done; echo " $state"

  # get the new instance's public ip address
  ip_address=$(aws ec2 describe-instances --instance-ids
$instance_id --output text --query
'Reservations[*].Instances[*].PublicIpAddress')
  echo ip_address=$ip_address

  # wait for ssh to work
  echo -n "waiting for ssh"
  while ! ssh -i "$ibn".pem -o ConnectTimeout=5 -o BatchMode=yes -o
StrictHostKeyChecking=no ec2-user@$ip_address > /dev/null 2>&1
true; do
    echo -n . ; sleep 5;
  done; echo " ssh ok"

  # remove old files
  rm -f install.sh
  rm -f emailsshlog.sh
  rm -f sshd_config

  # sed the install script
  sed -e "s/SEDsshuserSED/$sshuser/g" -e "s/SEDssherpasswordSED/
$ssherpassword/g" -e "s/SEDemailaddressSED/$emailaddress/g"
install_template.sh > install.sh

  # sed the email logging script
  sed -e "s/SEDemailaddressSED/$emailaddress/g"
emailsshlog_template.sh > emailsshlog.sh

  # sed the sshd_config file
  sed -e "s/SEDsshportSED/$sshport/g" -e "s/SEDsshuserSED/
$sshuser/g" sshd_config_template > sshd_config

  # make the scripts executable
  chmod +x install.sh
  chmod +x emailsshlog.sh

  # send required files
  echo "transferring files"
  scp -i "$ibn".pem install.sh ec2-user@$ip_address:
```

```
scp -i "$ibn".pem sshd_config ec2-user@$ip_address:
scp -i "$ibn".pem emailsshlog.sh ec2-user@$ip_address:
echo "transferred files"

# remove sent files
rm -f install.sh
rm -f emailsshlog.sh
rm -f sshd_config

# run the install script
ssh -i "$ibn".pem -t -o ConnectTimeout=60 -o BatchMode=yes ec2-
user@$ip_address sudo ./install.sh

# remove the local key (it won't work anyway)
rm -f "$ibn".pem

# drop the port 22 rule
aws ec2 revoke-security-group-ingress --group-id $sgid --protocol
tcp --port 22 --cidr $myip/32

# open up the new ssh port
aws ec2 authorize-security-group-ingress --group-id $sgid
--protocol tcp --port $sshport --cidr $myip/32

echo
echo now install the Google Authenticator App on a smartphone
echo find the MFA KEY in the output above
echo and create an account on the App with Manual Entry

echo
echo then ssh to the box with:
echo ssh -p "$sshport" "$sshuser"@"$ip_address"
echo "enter password ($ssherpassword) and an MFA code to sign in"
echo 'sudo su' still works

echo
echo when finished, terminate the server or close the $sshport
inbound port
echo "eg aws ec2 revoke-security-group-ingress --group-id $sgid
--protocol tcp --port $sshport --cidr $myip/32"
```

The make.sh script relies on 4 files to finish its task. The first is a shared variables file - anything configurable is in this file, as is my 'global variables' convention. 'vars.sh' is also used for the SSH connect script in the next section.

[chapter7/vars.sh]

```
#!/bin/bash

# include globals
. ./../globals.sh

# shared variables for scripts in chapter7

# the base name for the instance
# this string is used for key name, instance and sg names and
tags
ibn=sshmfa

# password for ssher
ssherpassword=1234
```

This is the install script which needs to be run as root and is therefore called by install.sh above with sudo. It is similar to the Chapter 6 install script in that it performs the tasks as described in the last section (update sshd, delete keys, create ssher, update ssher password, set up sending the sshd log via email and also limit ssh sessions to 1 by editing /etc/security/limits.conf). But it also installs Google Authenticator and configures PAM. Then it runs 'google-authenticator' to set up MFA for ssher.

[chapter7/install_template.sh]

```
#!/bin/bash

# this script needs to be run on the instance as root
# it changes the ssh user to ssher
# it hardens ssh
# it configures sshd to use a password and MFA
# it sets up a daily email of the sshd log file

# the following strings are replaced:
# SEDsshuserSED
# SEDssherpasswordSED
# SEDemailaddressSED

# update yum
yum -y update

# add ssher user
groupadd SEDsshuserSED
useradd -g SEDsshuserSED SEDsshuserSED

# change ssher's password with expect
# install expect
yum install -y expect
# make expect script
echo "#!/usr/bin/expect -f" > expect.sh
echo "set timeout -1" >> expect.sh
echo "spawn passwd SEDsshuserSED" >> expect.sh
echo "expect \"New password:\"" >> expect.sh
echo "send \"SEDssherpasswordSED\n\";" >> expect.sh
echo "expect \"new password:\"" >> expect.sh
echo "send \"SEDssherpasswordSED\n\";" >> expect.sh
echo "interact" >> expect.sh
# run it
chmod +x expect.sh
./expect.sh
# remove it
rm -f expect.sh
# erase expect
yum erase -y expect

# allow ssher to 'sudo su'
sed -e "s/ec2-user/SEDsshuserSED/g" /etc/sudoers.d/cloud-init
> /etc/sudoers.d/cloud-init2
cat /etc/sudoers.d/cloud-init2 > /etc/sudoers.d/cloud-init
rm /etc/sudoers.d/cloud-init2

# update sshd config
mv sshd_config /etc/ssh/sshd_config
chown root:root /etc/ssh/sshd_config
```

```
chmod 600 /etc/ssh/sshd_config

# remove sshd keys so ssher can't sign in with a key
rm -f /home/ec2-user/.ssh/authorized_keys
rm -f /root/.ssh/authorized_keys

# set the max concurrent ssh sessions
echo "SEDsshuserSED - maxlogins 1" >> /etc/security/limits.conf

# install mfa and pam modules
yum -y install google-authenticator.x86_64 pam.x86_64 pam-
devel.x86_64

# update pam config
echo "auth required pam_google_authenticator.so" >>
/etc/pam.d/sshd

# run the google authenticator for ssher
cd /home/SEDsshuserSED
google-authenticator --time based   disallow-reuse --force
--rate-limit=1 --rate-time=60 --window-size=3 --quiet
--secret=/home/SEDsshuserSED/.google_authenticator
chown SEDsshuserSED:SEDsshuserSED .google_authenticator
chmod 400 .google_authenticator

# delete last 4 GOOJ codes
head -n 6 .google_authenticator > .google_authenticator2
mv -f .google_authenticator2 .google_authenticator
chown SEDsshuserSED:SEDsshuserSED .google_authenticator
chmod 400 .google_authenticator

# print out the codes
bits=($(cat .google_authenticator))
echo MFA KEY is ${bits[0]}
echo MFA GOOJ is ${bits[11]}

# restart sshd
# careful, sshd doesn't seem to like
# being restarted just as you end an ssh session
/etc/init.d/sshd restart
sleep 5

# set up email logging
cd /home/ec2-user/
mv emailsshlog.sh /root/emailsshlog.sh
chown root:root /root/emailsshlog.sh
chmod 500 /root/emailsshlog.sh

# run daily at 12:05am
line="5 0 * * * /root/emailsshlog.sh"
(crontab -u root -l; echo "$line" ) | crontab -u root -

# send immediate email for sudo use
echo 'Defaults mailto="SEDemailaddressSED",mail_always' >>
/etc/sudoers.d/cloud-init

# send immediate email for root signin
echo "echo Subject: Root Access\$'\n'\$(who) | sendmail
SEDemailaddressSED" >> /root/.bashrc

# delete this script
rm -f /home/ec2-user/install.sh
```

This is a template version of a hardened sshd_config file which allows the SSH port and user to be changed dynamically as defined in vars.sh:

`[chapter7/sshd_config_template]`

```
# hardened sshd config file
# turns off Key access
# turns on Password access
# can also be used with MFA

# the following strings are replaced:
# SEDsshportSED
# SEDsshuserSED

# change the default ssh port
Port SEDsshportSED

# use better security protocols
Protocol 2

# log to authriv
SyslogFacility AUTHPRIV
# log info messages
LogLevel INFO

# don't permit root login, or root forced commands
PermitRootLogin no

# TURNED OFF
# where the access keys can be found
#AuthorizedKeysFile   .ssh/authorized_keys

# turn off various things
HostbasedAuthentication no
IgnoreRhosts yes
X11Forwarding no

# TURNED ON
# password authentication
PasswordAuthentication yes
ChallengeResponseAuthentication yes

# only SEDsshuserSED can sign in
AllowUsers SEDsshuserSED
# run user and session checks
UsePAM yes

# when last signed in
PrintLastLog yes

# more secure way to run the sshd
UsePrivilegeSeparation sandbox

# max seconds to sign in after connecting
LoginGraceTime 60

# max authentication attempts per connect
# setting this any lower can cause problems
MaxAuthTries 3

# max multiplexed ssh sessions
# to limit sesions add to /etc/security/limits.conf
#ssher - maxlogins 1
MaxSessions 1

# max concurrent unauthenticated sessions
```

```
MaxStartups 1

# check no world writeable files left in user home directory
StrictModes yes

# no empty passwords
PermitEmptyPasswords no

# allows scp
Subsystem       sftp      /usr/libexec/openssh/sftp-server
```

This is the script which is run by cron to send the sshd logs via email. The email address is configurable in globals.sh (or vars.sh).

[chapter7/emailsshlog_template.sh]

```
#!/bin/bash

# a script to send an email with the last days sshd log
# old log entries are moved to secureold

# the following strings are replaced:
# SEDemailaddressSED

echo "." >> /var/log/secure
/usr/sbin/sendmail SEDemailaddressSED < /var/log/secure
cat /var/log/secure >> /var/log/secureold
echo "" > /var/log/secure
chown root:root /var/log/secureold
chmod 600 /var/log/secureold
```

Automating SSH Password/MFA Access

Automating SSH access involves opening the sshd port, prompting for an MFA code (this shouldn't be automated... but see **Appendix D - Automating MFA**), running expect to enter the ssher password and MFA code, then closing the port on exit from ssh:

[chapter7/connectsshmfa.sh]

```
#!/bin/bash

# open an ssh session to a server
# which has keys disabled and MFA enabled
# as created by make.sh in this directory (chapter7)

# include chapter7 variables
. ./vars.sh

# show variables
echo instance base name: $ibn
echo new SSHD port: $sshport
echo ssh user: $sshuser
echo ssher password: $ssherpassword
```

```
# if you want to make this script standalone
# (ie not relying on vars.sh)
# comment out '. ./vars.sh' above and define the variables here,
eg:
#ibn=sshpass
#sshport=38142
#sshuser=ssher
#ssherpassword=1234

# if you wanted to have a typed password,
# ie you don't want to encode the password in this script,
# you could use:
#read -s -p "ssher password:" ssherpassword
# also remove the declaration above

echo "connecting to instance $ibn on $sshport with user $sshuser"

myip=$(curl http://checkip.amazonaws.com/)
echo myip=$myip

# get ip of server
ip_address=$(aws ec2 describe-instances --filters Name=tag-
key,Values=instancename Name=tag-value,Values="$ibn" --output text
--query 'Reservations[*].Instances[*].PublicIpAddress')
echo ip_address=$ip_address

# allow ssh in sg
sgid=$(aws ec2 describe-security-groups --filters Name=tag-
key,Values=sgname Name=tag-value,Values="$ibn"sg --output text
--query 'SecurityGroups[*].GroupId')
echo sgid=$sgid
aws ec2 authorize-security-group-ingress --group-id $sgid
--protocol tcp --port $sshport --cidr $myip/32

# get an mfa code
read -s -p "mfa code:" mfacode

# make and run expect script
# use timeout -1 for no timeout
echo "#!/usr/bin/expect -f" > expect.sh
echo "set timeout -1" >> expect.sh
echo "spawn ssh -p $sshport $sshuser@$ip_address" >> expect.sh
echo "expect \"Password:\"" >> expect.sh
echo "send \"$ssherpassword\n\"" >> expect.sh
echo "expect \"Verification code:\"" >> expect.sh
echo "send \"$mfacode\n\"" >> expect.sh
echo "interact" >> expect.sh
chmod +x expect.sh
./expect.sh
rm -f expect.sh

# script now waits for 'exit'
# or double 'exit' if you 'sudo su'

# remove ssh in sg
aws ec2 revoke-security-group-ingress --group-id $sgid --protocol
tcp --port $sshport --cidr $myip/32
echo "revoked sg access"
```

You can test the script with:

```
./connectsshmfa.sh
```

Again, only one SSH session will be allowed.

Chapter 8 - SSH with Password/MFA/Sudo-Password

Requiring a Sudo Password

When you build a cloud server with AWS, Amazon have found a sensible way to avoid having to dish out passwords to you. What they do is provide you with a Key which you can use to ssh in. Once in, you're allowed to 'sudo' all commands (like 'sudo yum update'), which runs them with root privileges. Or you can 'sudo su' to get root privileges until you use 'exit'.

The only problem with this is that if somehow an attacker gets in via ssh, because they have breached you client computer and stolen your SSH Key, they can do whatever they want as root. It's basically impossible to brute force SSH Keys, so if you're sticking with this SSH setup the problem is only that they can infect the client with the SSH Key. But if you use some of the techniques above to change SSH to Password Authentication or MFA, you might still be vulnerable to brute force (given you leave the SSH port open).

Is it worth disabling password-less 'sudo su'? It depends on where you store the password.

Let's say you store the password electronically on the same machine with all your other credentials. This is security bloat, because you have not added a new security layer. Anyone who can steal your SSH Key or ssher password can also steal your 'sudo su' password, because the password is on the same machine! However, you do get some extra defence if someone gets onto your box some other way, that is, not by stealing your credentials.

If you store the 'sudo su' password elsewhere, like in your head or cyphered on paper, that *is* an extra layer of security. However, most people find it too cumbersome and annoying to store and enter *another* password. In addition, if you double protect yourself with MFA - once for AWS CLI and once for SSH Access - it doesn't matter if they steal your credentials, they still can't get in.

Which is why I prefer to disable password-less 'sudo su' but I keep the root password electronically and I automate access. I have no hassles getting in. If my laptop is compromised, MFA protects me. And if someone gets into my servers some other way, they can't 'sudo su' because they don't have the password. Anyway, any static authentication token which you have to type into a keyboard is potentially vulnerable, so the 'sudo su' password could probably be stolen should you ever use it.

Disabling the ability to 'sudo su' without password is extremely easy. You just use:

```
echo "ssher ALL = ALL" > /etc/sudoers.d/cloud-init
echo "Defaults targetpw" >> /etc/sudoers.d/cloud-init
```

which rewrites the /etc/sudoers.d/cloud-init file to disallow password-less access. Note that this is actually done by the first line. The second line stipulates that the required password for 'sudo su' is the *target user* (that is, root) and not the normal behaviour, which requires the password of the user calling 'sudo su'. If you only ran the first line above, a password would be requested when you 'sudo su' but you would enter the ssher password. It's better to have a separate password, hence 'Defaults targetpw'. This also means you need to set up a root password, as it is set but you don't know it.

The procedure for setting up SSH with Password/MFA/Sudo-Password builds on Chapter 7 - SSH with Password/MFA. Instead of recopying out all the instructions found there, I will proceed from a working setup built in Chapter 7, either manually (in **Chapter 7 - Requiring an SSH MFA Code**) or with scripts (in **Chapter 7 - Building a Server with SSH Password/MFA**). So go ahead and follow those instructions and come back here when you have a working server, have opened the port in the Security Group, have 'ssh'ed in with MFA and have done 'sudo su'. Or you can skip to the next section which builds the entire server from scratch with scripts.

Create a new root password:

```
passwd root
[type the new password twice]
```

Then execute:

```
echo "ssher ALL = ALL" > /etc/sudoers.d/cloud-init
echo "Defaults targetpw" >> /etc/sudoers.d/cloud-init
```

Now do an 'exit' to leave 'sudo su'. Do 'sudo su' again. You will need to enter the root password you just set.

One interesting thing I should mention is that the root password for 'sudo su' only needs to be entered once per session. Try it by 'exit'ing 'sudo su' and doing it again. The password is only required the first time. So what? Well, some commands need to be run as the authenticated SSH user, as you will see later with SSH Agent Forwarding, and some for the user they apply to, like 'google-authenticator'. It's very useful for scripting with expect as you can run commands with or without sudo by doing a 'sudo su' at the start of a session, entering the password via expect, then doing an 'exit', thus meaning for the remainder of the session you can use 'sudo' without a password.

Building a Server with SSH Password/MFA/Sudo-Password

The procedure for automating the above process is documented in the following scripts. It's similar to Chapter 7, except I run the extra commands above to disable 'sudo su' with no password and I set a root password. You can use the './make.sh' command from the chapter8 directory to launch a new instance and configure it to use an SSH password and MFA and to require a password for 'sudo su'. Also remember a valid VPC needs to exist with VPC name set in vars.sh, see **Appendix A - VPC**.

```
[chapter8/make.sh]
```

```bash
#!/bin/bash

# makes an ec2 instance with SSH MFA setup
# disable password-less sudo su
# and require root password to do it

# include chapter8 variables
. ./vars.sh

# show variables
echo AMI: $baseami
echo instance base name: $ibn
echo VPC name: $vpcname
echo new SSHD port: $sshport
echo logging to email address: $emailaddress
echo ssh user: $sshuser
echo ssher password: $ssherpassword
echo root password: $rootpassword

# get our ip from amazon
myip=$(curl http://checkip.amazonaws.com/)
echo myip=$myip

# make a new keypair
echo "making keypair"
rm "$ibn".pem
aws ec2 delete-key-pair --key-name "$ibn"
aws ec2 create-key-pair --key-name "$ibn" --query 'KeyMaterial'
--output text > "$ibn".pem
chmod 600 "$ibn".pem
echo "$ibn" keypair made

# get the vpc id
vpc_id=$(aws ec2 describe-vpcs --filters Name=tag-
key,Values=vpcname Name=tag-value,Values=$vpcname --output text
--query 'Vpcs[*].VpcId')
echo vpc_id=$vpc_id

# make a security group
sgid=$(aws ec2 create-security-group --group-name "$ibn"sg
--description "$ibn security group" --vpc-id $vpc_id --output text
--query 'GroupId')
# tag it
aws ec2 create-tags --resources $sgid --tags
Key=sgname,Value="$ibn"sg
# now get the security group id again by using the tag
sgid=$(aws ec2 describe-security-groups --filters Name=tag-
key,Values=sgname Name=tag-value,Values="$ibn"sg --output text
--query 'SecurityGroups[*].GroupId')
echo sgid=$sgid

# allow ssh in on port 22 from our ip only
aws ec2 authorize-security-group-ingress --group-id $sgid
--protocol tcp --port 22 --cidr $myip/32

# get a vpc subnet
subnet_id=$(aws ec2 describe-subnets --filters Name=vpc-
id,Values=$vpc_id Name=tag-key,Values=subnet Name=tag-
value,Values=1 --output text --query 'Subnets[*].SubnetId')
echo subnet_id=$subnet_id

# make the instance
instance_id=$(aws ec2 run-instances --image $baseami --key "$ibn"
--security-group-ids $sgid --instance-type t2.micro --subnet-id
$subnet_id --associate-public-ip-address --output text --query
'Instances[*].InstanceId')
echo instance_id=$instance_id
```

```
# tag the instance (so we can get it later)
aws ec2 create-tags --resources $instance_id --tags
Key=instancename,Value="$ibn"

# wait for it
echo -n "waiting for instance"
while state=$(aws ec2 describe-instances --instance-ids
$instance_id --output text --query
'Reservations[*].Instances[*].State.Name'); test "$state" =
"pending"; do
  echo -n . ; sleep 3;
done; echo " $state"

# get the new instance's public ip address
ip_address=$(aws ec2 describe-instances --instance-ids
$instance_id --output text --query
'Reservations[*].Instances[*].PublicIpAddress')
echo ip_address=$ip_address

# wait for ssh to work
echo -n "waiting for ssh"
while ! ssh -i "$ibn".pem -o ConnectTimeout=5 -o BatchMode=yes -o
StrictHostKeyChecking=no ec2-user@$ip_address > /dev/null 2>&1
true; do
  echo -n . ; sleep 5;
done; echo " ssh ok"

# remove old files
rm -f install.sh
rm -f emailsshlog.sh
rm -f sshd_config

# sed the install script
sed -e "s/SEDsshuserSED/$sshuser/g" -e "s/SEDssherpasswordSED/
$ssherpassword/g" -e "s/SEDrootpasswordSED/$rootpassword/g" -e
"s/SEDemailaddressSED/$emailaddress/g" install_template.sh >
install.sh

# sed the email logging script
sed -e "s/SEDemailaddressSED/$emailaddress/g"
emailsshlog_template.sh > emailsshlog.sh

# sed the sshd_config file
sed -e "s/SEDsshportSED/$sshport/g" -e "s/SEDsshuserSED/
$sshuser/g" sshd_config_template > sshd_config

# make the scripts executable
chmod +x install.sh
chmod +x emailsshlog.sh

# send required files
echo "transferring files"
scp -i "$ibn".pem install.sh ec2-user@$ip_address:
scp -i "$ibn".pem sshd_config ec2-user@$ip_address:
scp -i "$ibn".pem emailsshlog.sh ec2-user@$ip_address:
echo "transferred files"

# remove sent files
rm -f install.sh
rm -f emailsshlog.sh
rm -f sshd_config

# run the install script
ssh -i "$ibn".pem -t -o ConnectTimeout=60 -o BatchMode=yes ec2-
user@$ip_address sudo ./install.sh

# remove the local key (it won't work anyway)
rm -f "$ibn".pem
```

```
# drop the port 22 rule
aws ec2 revoke-security-group-ingress --group-id $sgid --protocol
tcp --port 22 --cidr $myip/32

# open up the new ssh port
aws ec2 authorize-security-group-ingress --group-id $sgid
--protocol tcp --port $sshport --cidr $myip/32

echo
echo now install the Google Authenticator App on a smartphone
echo find the MFA KEY in the output above
echo and create an account on the App with Manual Entry
read -n 1 -p "Press a key when done"

echo
echo then ssh to the box with:
echo ssh -p "$sshport" "$sshuser"@"$ip_address"
echo "enter password ($ssherpassword) and an MFA code to sign in"
echo "sudo su needs the root password ($rootpassword)"
echo
echo when finished, terminate the server or close the $sshport
inbound port
echo "eg aws ec2 revoke-security-group-ingress --group-id $sgid
--protocol tcp --port $sshport --cidr $myip/32"
```

The make.sh script relies on 4 files to finish its task. The first is a shared variables file - anything configurable is in this file, as is my 'global variables' convention. 'vars.sh' is also used for the SSH connect script in the next section.

[chapter8/vars.sh]

```
#!/bin/bash

# include globals
. ./../globals.sh

# shared variables for scripts in chapter8

# the base name for the instance
# this string is used for key name, instance and sg names and
tags
ibn=sshmfapss

# password for ssher
ssherpassword=1234

# password for root
rootpassword=123456
```

This is the template install script which needs to be run as root. It updates sshd, deletes keys, adds the ssher user, updates the ssher password, sets up sending the sshd log via email and also limits ssh sessions to 1 by editing /etc/security/limits.conf. It installs Google Authenticator and configures PAM. It also configures the requirement for a password for 'sudo su', which can be done

because it will only take effect when 'sudo' is next used. And it sets
a new root password.

[chapter8/install_template.sh]

```
#!/bin/bash

# this script needs to be run on the instance as root
# it changes the ssh user to ssher
# it hardens ssh
# it configures sshd to use a password and MFA
# it sets up a daily email of the sshd log file
# it disables password-less 'sudo su'
# and requires the root password to do so

# the following strings are replaced:
# SEDsshuserSED
# SEDssherpasswordSED
# SEDrootpasswordSED
# SEDemailaddressSED

# update yum
yum -y update

# add ssher user
groupadd SEDsshuserSED
useradd -g SEDsshuserSED SEDsshuserSED

# install expect
yum install -y expect

# change ssher's password with expect
echo "#!/usr/bin/expect -f" > expect.sh
echo "set timeout -1" >> expect.sh
echo "spawn passwd SEDsshuserSED" >> expect.sh
echo "expect \"New password:\"" >> expect.sh
echo "send \"SEDssherpasswordSED\n\";" >> expect.sh
echo "expect \"new password:\"" >> expect.sh
echo "send \"SEDssherpasswordSED\n\";" >> expect.sh
echo "interact" >> expect.sh
# run it
chmod +x expect.sh
./expect.sh
# remove it
rm -f expect.sh

# change root's password with expect
echo "#!/usr/bin/expect -f" > expect.sh
echo "set timeout -1" >> expect.sh
echo "spawn passwd root" >> expect.sh
echo "expect \"New password:\"" >> expect.sh
echo "send \"SEDrootpasswordSED\n\";" >> expect.sh
echo "expect \"new password:\"" >> expect.sh
echo "send \"SEDrootpasswordSED\n\";" >> expect.sh
echo "interact" >> expect.sh
# run it
chmod +x expect.sh
./expect.sh
# remove it
rm -f expect.sh

# erase expect
yum erase -y expect

# disable passwordless 'sudo su'
```

```
echo "SEDsshuserSED ALL = ALL" > /etc/sudoers.d/cloud-init

# require root password for 'sudo su' (not sshers's)
echo "Defaults targetpw" >> /etc/sudoers.d/cloud-init

# update sshd config
mv sshd_config /etc/ssh/sshd_config
chown root:root /etc/ssh/sshd_config
chmod 600 /etc/ssh/sshd_config

# remove sshd keys so ssher can't sign in with a key
rm -f /home/ec2-user/.ssh/authorized_keys
rm -f /root/.ssh/authorized_keys

# set the max concurrent ssh sessions
echo "SEDsshuserSED - maxlogins 1" >> /etc/security/limits.conf

# install mfa and pam modules
yum -y install google-authenticator.x86_64 pam.x86_64 pam-
devel.x86_64

# update pam config
echo "auth required pam_google_authenticator.so" >>
/etc/pam.d/sshd

# run the google authenticator for ssher
cd /home/SEDsshuserSED
google-authenticator --time-based --disallow-reuse --force
--rate-limit=1 --rate-time=60 --window-size=3 --quiet
--secret=/home/SEDsshuserSED/.google_authenticator
chown SEDsshuserSED:SEDsshuserSED .google_authenticator
chmod 400 .google_authenticator

# delete last 4 GOOJ codes
head -n 6 .google_authenticator > .google_authenticator2
mv -f .google_authenticator2 .google_authenticator
chown SEDsshuserSED:SEDsshuserSED .google_authenticator
chmod 400 .google_authenticator

# print out the codes
bits=($(cat .google_authenticator))
echo MFA KEY is ${bits[0]}
echo MFA GOOJ is ${bits[11]}

# restart sshd
# careful, sshd doesn't seem to like
# being restarted just as you end an ssh session
/etc/init.d/sshd restart
sleep 5

# set up email logging
cd /home/ec2-user/
mv emailsshlog.sh /root/emailsshlog.sh
chown root:root /root/emailsshlog.sh
chmod 500 /root/emailsshlog.sh

# run daily at 12:05am
line="5 0 * * * /root/emailsshlog.sh"
(crontab -u root -l; echo "$line" ) | crontab -u root -

# send immediate email for sudo use
echo 'Defaults mailto="SEDemailaddressSED",mail_always' >>
/etc/sudoers.d/cloud-init

# send immediate email for root signin
echo "echo Subject: Root Access\$'\n'\$(who) | sendmail
SEDemailaddressSED" >> /root/.bashrc
```

```
# delete this script
rm -f /home/ec2-user/install.sh
```

This is a template version of a hardened sshd_config file which allows the SSH port and user to be changed dynamically as defined in vars.sh:

[chapter8/sshd_config_template]

```
# hardened sshd config file
# turns off Key access
# turns on Password access
# can also be used with MFA

# the following strings are replaced:
# SEDsshportSED

# change the default ssh port
Port SEDsshportSED

# use better security protocols
Protocol 2

# log to authriv
SyslogFacility AUTHPRIV
# log info messages
LogLevel INFO

# don't permit root login, or root forced commands
PermitRootLogin no

# TURNED OFF
# where the access keys can be found
#AuthorizedKeysFile    .ssh/authorized_keys

# turn off various things
HostbasedAuthentication no
IgnoreRhosts yes
X11Forwarding no

# TURNED ON
# password authentication
PasswordAuthentication yes
ChallengeResponseAuthentication yes

# only SEDsshuserSED can sign in
AllowUsers SEDsshuserSED
# run user and session checks
UsePAM yes

# when last signed in
PrintLastLog yes

# more secure way to run the sshd
UsePrivilegeSeparation sandbox

# max seconds to sign in after connecting
LoginGraceTime 60

# max authentication attempts per connect
# setting this any lower can cause problems
MaxAuthTries 3
```

```
# max multiplexed ssh sessions
# to limit sesions add to /etc/security/limits.conf
#ssher - maxlogins 1
MaxSessions 1

# max concurrent unauthenticated sessions
MaxStartups 1

# check no world writeable files left in user home directory
StrictModes yes

# no empty passwords
PermitEmptyPasswords no

# allows scp
Subsystem       sftp       /usr/libexec/openssh/sftp-server
```

This is the script which is run by cron to send the sshd logs via email. The email address is configurable in the globals.sh script.

[chapter8/emailsshlog_template.sh]

```
#!/bin/bash

# a script to send an email with the last days sshd log
# old log entries are moved to secureold

# the following strings are replaced:
# SEDemailaddressSED

echo "." >> /var/log/secure
/usr/sbin/sendmail SEDemailaddressSED < /var/log/secure
cat /var/log/secure >> /var/log/secureold
echo "" > /var/log/secure
chown root:root /var/log/secureold
chmod 600 /var/log/secureold
```

Automating SSH Password/MFA/Sudo-Password Access

Automating SSH access involves opening the sshd port, prompting for an MFA code (this shouldn't be automated... but see **Appendix D - Automating MFA**), running expect to enter the ssher password and MFA code and running 'sudo su' and entering the root password, then closing the port on exit from ssh:

[chapter8/connectsshmfapss.sh]

```
#!/bin/bash

# open an ssh session to a server
# which has keys disabled and MFA enabled
# then automate the 'sudo su' password entry
```

```
# as created by make.sh in this directory (chapter8)

# include chapter8 variables
. ./vars.sh

# show variables
echo instance base name: $ibn
echo new SSHD port: $sshport
echo ssh user: $sshuser
echo ssher password: $ssherpassword
echo root password: $rootpassword

# if you want to make this script standalone
# (ie not relying on vars.sh)
# comment out '. ./vars.sh' above and define the variables here,
eg:
#ibn=sshpass
#sshport=38142
#sshuser=ssher
#ssherpassword=1234
#rootpassword=123456

# if you wanted to have a typed password,
# ie you don't want to encode the password in this script,
# you could use:
#read -s -p "ssher password:" ssherpassword
#read -s -p "root password:" rootpassword
# also remove the declarations above

echo "connecting to instance $ibn on $sshport with user $sshuser"

myip=$(curl http://checkip.amazonaws.com/)
echo myip=$myip

# get ip of server
ip_address=$(aws ec2 describe-instances --filters Name=tag-
key,Values=instancename Name=tag-value,Values="$ibn" --output text
--query 'Reservations[*].Instances[*].PublicIpAddress')
echo ip_address=$ip_address

# allow ssh in sg
sgid=$(aws ec2 describe-security-groups --filters Name=tag-
key,Values=sgname Name=tag-value,Values="$ibn"sg --output text
--query 'SecurityGroups[*].GroupId')
echo sgid=$sgid
aws ec2 authorize-security-group-ingress --group-id $sgid
--protocol tcp --port $sshport --cidr $myip/32

# get an mfa code
read -s -p "mfa code:" mfacode

# make and run expect script
# use timeout -1 for no timeout
echo "#!/usr/bin/expect -f" > expect.sh
echo "set timeout -1" >> expect.sh
echo "spawn ssh -p $sshport $sshuser@$ip_address" >> expect.sh
echo "expect \"Password:\"" >> expect.sh
echo "send \"$ssherpassword\n\"" >> expect.sh
echo "expect \"Verification code:\"" >> expect.sh
echo "send \"$mfacode\n\"" >> expect.sh
echo "expect \"]\"" >> expect.sh
echo "send \"sudo su\n\"" >> expect.sh
echo "expect \"password for root:\"" >> expect.sh
echo "send \"$rootpassword\n\"" >> expect.sh
echo "interact" >> expect.sh
chmod +x expect.sh
./expect.sh
rm expect.sh
```

```
# script now waits for double 'exit' (because it did 'sudo su')

# remove ssh in sg
aws ec2 revoke-security-group-ingress --group-id $sgid --protocol
tcp --port $sshport --cidr $myip/32
echo "revoked sg access"
```

You can test the script with:

```
./connectsshmfapss.sh
```

Because this is the method which I recommend you use to secure
SSH on your servers, I now include a version of the script which
also uses the AWS CLI MFA protection from **Chapter 4 - MFA
for AWS CLI**. This is about as good as it gets for AWS SSH
Security.

[chapter8/connectsshmfapss2.sh]

```
#!/bin/bash

# open an ssh session to a server
# which has keys disabled and MFA enabled
# then automate the 'sudo su' password entry
# as created by make.sh in this directory (chapter8)

# ALSO require MFA to activate AWS CLI

# for the sign in and sign out scripts below,
# you could move them to the same directory and
# leave out '../chapter4/output/'

# sign out
./../chapter4/output/signout.sh

# sign in as connect
# you'll need to enter an MFA code
./../chapter4/output/signin.sh connect

# now connect
./connectsshmfapss.sh

# sign out of aws cli
./../chapter4/output/signout.sh
```

Make sure you have setup AWS CLI MFA with the scripts in
Chapter 4. You can then test the script with:

```
./connectsshmfapss2.sh
```

You'll be prompted for 2 MFA codes, one for AWS CLI and one
for your server - use the right ones...

Chapter 9 - Using a Bastion Host

Security Considerations

A Bastion Host is a server in your cloud network which you use to connect to other servers in that network. The theory is that you build one hyper-secure box and use it to connect to all your internal boxes, that is, servers with no Public Internet IP address. Bear in mind that even in a standard installation, you will have servers that don't directly receive traffic from the Internet, such as a database server. Allowing access to these sorts of sensitive servers from the Internet is just asking for trouble, even if you deny all access with Security Groups. After all, you database is your core asset and the most valuable item for a hacker to steal.

Bastion Hosts have pros and cons. A big pro is that you can make almost all your other servers *intrinsically* not accessible directly from the Internet. With AWS, you can use the '--no-associate-public-ip-address' directive when you run the 'aws ec2 run-instances' command. If you make an instance in this way, *there's no way* to access it directly from the Internet because it doesn't have an Internet IP address. The is no Security Group rule possible which will allow access from the Internet. So, in one fell swoop, you protect yourself from the whole class of attacks which rely on 'leaving ports open' or 'opening ports too liberally' or 'connecting from a shared Internet IP address'.

Now you're thinking, "most of my servers need to be accessed from the Internet". But do they? In a classic web and database server installation, *none* of your servers need a direct connection to the Internet, if you use an ELB (Elastic Load Balancer) to connect to your web servers. Database servers are only accessed by the web servers. So, the only exposed part of your network is the ELB, and good luck trying to hack that!

The major 'con' of Bastion Hosts is that you are putting all your eggs in one basket. If a hacker gets into your Bastion, they've basically got into everything. There are, however, ways to mitigate this risk, as I shall discuss. They are also impractical for large installations which, for instance, use AWS tools like auto-scaling, because in these situations actually 'ssh'ing into a large number of boxes is far too time consuming.

So what is the ideal security configuration for the Bastion Host and Internal Servers? For the Bastion, it's easy: maximum security, so full Chapter 8 Password/MFA/Password-Sudo. It's tempting to say the same thing for internal servers... but there are issues. The Bastion is a gateway, and once set up you'll probably never need to actually do anything on it, like oop files. But your internal servers will probably require maintenance, so if you MFA them this means every ssh or scp will need a code. So how are you going to update your 20-box-strong web server farm? That's at least 2 MFA codes per server (one for an scp to send the update and one for an ssh to execute it). More likely it's three - one scp for a data zip, one scp for a script, one ssh to run the script. It becomes impossible and your update times will stretch into hours of mind-numbing MFA hell.

Should you forego MFA on internal servers? Or, more precisely, is MFA on the Bastion Host sufficient to protect internal servers? Yes, it is. And here's why: under normal circumstances, internal servers are protected by not being directly accessible from the Internet (no Public IP); the only way to allow access is to open up a port to the Bastion and open a port from the Bastion to the internal server; now there is a theoretical route to the internal server, but to use it you need to MFA the Bastion. Remember that the main point of MFA is to protect you *even if* your client computer is compromised, by storing required credentials on something else, like your smartphone. And by limiting the allowed SSH sessions to 1, you still are protected with MFA on the Bastion and no MFA on internal servers, because when you are connected, no-one else can get in.

If you only need shell access on internal servers and they don't need to have files uploaded, double MFA is a good idea as it is the ultimate protection. With AWS CLI MFA, that means you would need 3 MFA codes to access an internal server!

I should also mention that there is a lot of discussion on the Internet about Bastion Hosts being 'old-fashioned'. To a certain extent this is true if you are running large pools of auto-scaling servers spread across various AWS regions. Practically speaking, you would never actually ssh into these sorts of boxes and you certainly wouldn't be in a position to install MFA on them. However, my experience is that, especially during the early days of a production system, there are always little issues which pop up. A little debugging or tuning is always required, so there will no doubt be *some* servers that you will need to ssh to. After a settling in period, ssh visits will probably dwindle to zero. Services such as a Centralised Rsyslog, whereby all your worker servers log to a central server, and emailing of security sensitive occurrences also cut down on the need to ssh. On the other hand, if you're updating websites often, you would need to continue using ssh.

Finally, bear in mind that everything that follows is about SSH security. If you have web servers behind an ELB, even if they have no Public IP address they are just as vulnerable to Application Level hacks, like PHP Session Hijacking or SQL Injections. SSH is actually easy to secure compared to Applications. However, there is a standard way to secure SSH, so you should! For more on securing Applications like PHP and MySQL, you should see my first book, "AWS Scripted: How to Automate the Deployment of Secure and Resilient Websites with Amazon Web Services VPC, ELB, EC2, RDS, IAM, SES and SNS".

Installation and Maintenance

This brings us to the next issue: if you create an instance which has no Internet or Public IP address, how do you configure it at launch and how do you maintain it? You've basically got three options here.

The first one is to run all 'aws' commands from your client, upload the configuration scripts and SSH Keys for the internal instances to the Bastion Host, then connect to internal servers and run the uploaded scripts. The advantage here is that your AWS CLI credentials don't go to the Cloud. But the downside is that your SSH Keys do, so now they are stored in two places, and therefore they are more likely to be stolen.

The second is to configure the Bastion to run 'aws' commands, upload all scripts to it and run everything from the Bastion. When instances are created, the corresponding SSH Keys are downloaded to the Bastion. This means the SSH Keys for internal servers never leave the Bastion, but your AWS credentials are in the Cloud. It is possible to attach a Role to an EC2 instance thereby granting AWS CLI privileges, but the fact remains that there is a server out there in the Cloud with power to build or destroy your network.

The last option is similar to the first but you avoid copying Keys to the Bastion Host by implementing SSH Agent Forwarding. So, you build everything with the 'aws' command on the client, then run commands on internal servers through the Bastion with Agent Forwarding. SSH Keys for internal servers never leave the client. AWS CLI is not installed on the Bastion.

Agent Forwarding

Let's take an in-depth look at SSH Agent Forwarding because it's really interesting and very cool.

SSH Agent Forwarding allows you to forward keys from your client computer through SSH sessions. So, if you are on box A and you ssh to box B, then from that shell you ssh to box C, you can use key credentials stored on A to authenticate on C. SSH Agent Forwarding is implemented by adding keys to a key-store, and this is achieved with the the 'ssh-agent' daemon and the 'ssh-add' command. Both Linux and OSX have these installed out of the box. On OSX, ssh-agent is already running and you can use ssh-add right away. On some Linuxes, you need to start it first for every session with:

```
eval `ssh-agent -s`
```

The Linux behaviour is slightly awkward. On Amazon Linux, you need to start the shh-agent *for each session*. This means that if you start it, sign out of ssh, then ssh back in, you need to start it again. Otherwise, when you try the 'ssh-add' commands below, you get:

```
Could not open a connection to your authentication agent.
```

But it's untidy because you get lingering 'ssh-agent' processes, so you can kill the ssh-agent when you've finished with:

```
kill $(pgrep ssh-agent)
```

In the scripts that follow, and which use ssh-agent, I kill any running ssh-agents at the start. Then I start a new ssh-agent. At the end of the script, I kill it again.

To add an SSH Key (test.pem) to your store, cd to the directory containing the key and type:

```
ssh-add test.pem
```

To list keys in the store, type:

```
ssh-add -L
```

To delete keys from the store:

```
ssh-add -D
```

There's a bug which stops 'ssh-add -d test.pem' working, which would delete only the key 'test.pem'. You need the Public Key, but it's not a big issue as you still have the original .pem file so you can add and remove as you like.

Let's assume you've made a Bastion Host with SSH secured with MFA and no SSH Key (it's a server created with the procedures in Chapter 8). You've made a new internal server which has no Public IP and you have its SSH Key (internal.pem) on your client computer. Let's say the IP for the Bastion host is 100.100.100.100 and the private IP for the internal server is 10.0.0.10. There's a Security Group (called bastionsg) attached to the Bastion allowing

SSH access on port 38142 from your IP. There's a Security Group on the new internal server allowing access on port 22 from the bastionsg Security Group.

Now you can ssh to the Bastion with:

```
ssh -p 38142 -o PubkeyAuthentication=no -A ec2-
user@100.100.100.100
```

Note that you need the '-o PubkeyAuthentication=no' now, otherwise authentication will fail since ssh will try keys in your key store first and I have set 'MaxAuthTries' to 3 in the sshd_config file on the Bastion (which is quite low). You can verify this by running ssh with the '-v' flag (verbose mode) and leaving out '-o PubkeyAuthentication=no'. The '-A' flag enables Agent Forwarding.

Once on the Bastion, you can reach the new server with:

```
ssh -i test.pem ec2-user@10.0.0.10
```

Note, there is no 'test.pem' file on the Bastion. An error is printed because the file cannot be found locally, but then it works. The '-A' flag in the original ssh command allows the second ssh command to authenticate via your key-store on your client computer. If you set 'MaxAuthTries' to something like 3 in the internal server's sshd_config and have several keys in your key-store and don't specify which key to use, ssh will try them in order, resulting in authentication failure, so you need to use '-i test.pem', which will request test.pem from your key-store.

To ssh through to the internal server in one command:

```
ssh -p 38142 -o PubkeyAuthentication=no -A ec2-
user@100.100.100.100 ssh -t -t -i test.pem ec2-user@10.0.0.10
```

The '-t -t' flags in the second ssh force an interactive terminal. I have, however, found the resulting shell to be a bit funny (your commands are reprinted and the cursor keys don't work). If you need an interactive shell, split the commands up. If you need to run a command or a script on the internal server, the one command version is fine. For the connect scripts later in this chapter, I use 'expect' to run split ssh commands.

Note that now scp has also changed. You need the '-o PubkeyAuthentication=no' option. Also, you'll need to authenticate with Password and MFA each time you use scp, which is a real pain. On the other hand, I've found it's pretty rare to need to upload or download files to servers after installation and configuration (except of course updating web roots on multiple web servers). Normally, for logs and similar things, you just shunt everything off to an S3 bucket. For more complex things, you use a script anyway, so automating with expect is possible. And, of course, to cut down on the MFA codes needed, you zip everything up, send one file and unzip on the server.

So, to send a file to the Bastion Host after you have added Keys to your key-store with ssh-add:

```
scp -P 38142 -o PubkeyAuthentication=no afile ec2-
user@100.100.100.100:
```

To send a file to an internal server, you need to send it to the Bastion first and then use:

```
scp -P 38142 -o PubkeyAuthentication=no -o ForwardAgent=yes ec2-
user@100.100.100.100:afile ec2-user@10.0.0.10:
```

An important note: SSH Agent Forwarding does not work if you run the same command as a different user, for instance if you have done 'sudo su'. The nested ssh command needs to be executed as the user who authenticated in the original ssh session.

There are some security issues associated with SSH Agent Forwarding. While you are connected to the Bastion, any process or user with enough privileges on the Bastion will be able to *use* all the keys stored on your client machine. Note 'use' - they can't download or read them. You mitigate this risk by ensuring the Bastion is very secure (as I have done above with SSH MFA, limiting SSH sessions to 1 etc). The situation is still much better than permanently storing SSH Keys on the Bastion, or even 'copying, using, deleting' them, since they can't be stolen, only used. If anyone can get into your Bastion Host, that is.

I would also point out that if both your client computer and your Bastion are secure, that is not infected, it is actually perfectly acceptable to copy SSH Keys temporarily to the Bastion. For a start, if your client computer is compromised, you've lost the Keys anyway. And your Bastion is secured with MFA and all the other measures discussed in Chapter 8, the highest level of SSH security. And if your client computer is infected, Agent Forwarding won't save you. Also, the keys can't be intercepted in-transit because everything is encrypted (unless you've been man-in-the-middled, although Host Key Checking will warn you about this). So, the above Agent Forwarding procedure is much more useful when dealing with less secure SSH installations, such as ones that are permanently open to the Internet, or which allow many users to sign in. However, it is the *proper way* to do things so I have included it - you might also find it useful for other situations.

Bear in mind also that I am using SSH Keys because this is how AWS initially sets up instances. So you need to use SSH Keys at the very least for Initial Configuration. But if you secure internal servers with MFA, Agent Forwarding will become redundant, as there are no keys. Instead, you would use expect to ssh in and type any required passwords, then ssh again and enter the next set of passwords.

SSH Tunnelling to Bypass Multiple MFA

There is still a big problem with sending files to a large set of internal servers. One way to fix this is to use SSH Tunnelling to link a new port on the Bastion (for instance 38143) to an internal server. So if you SSH to 100.100.100.100:38143, you get a shell on 10.0.0.10.

The first thing you need to do is open port 38143 in the Bastion's Security Group to your IP.

Now, copy test.pem to the Bastion (an MFA code will be required) and on the Bastion open a tunnel. This can be done with:

```
# copy test.pem to bastion (password/mfa required)
scp -P 38142 test.pem ec2-user@100.100.100.100
# get a shell on bastion (password/mfa required)
ssh -p 38142 ec2-user@100.100.100.100
# now you're on the Bastion
ssh -f -N -L 100.100.100.100:38143:10.0.0.10:22 -i test.pem ec2-
user@10.0.0.10
```

This opens a tunnel to 10.0.0.10:22 and and SSH connects to 38143 on the Bastion go direct to 10.0.0.10. So the following from your client will get you a shell on 10.0.0.10 WITHOUT asking for passwords or MFA:

```
ssh -p 38143 ec2-user@100.100.100.100
```

Note that you can also concatenate the tunnel commands above with:

```
ssh -p 38142 -o PubkeyAuthentication=no ec2-user@100.100.100.100
ssh -f -N -L *:38143:10.0.0.10:22 -i test.pem ec2-user@10.0.0.10
```

OK, the above procedure is not very good because the SSH Key was copied to the Bastion but more importantly, your internal server is now accessible to anyone who shares your IP address and has your SSH Key (for example if your client computer is infected). Limiting SSH session to 1 doesn't help because there is only 1 session to the Bastion - you can open as many as you want to the internal server 10.0.0.10. So if your client computer is infected, you've just lost all the protection MFA was providing.

Can you use Tunnelling with Agent Forwarding to improve the situation? First, ssh to the Bastion and delete the test.pem file. Now with no Keys on the Bastion, run the following on your client:

```
ssh -p 38142 -o PubkeyAuthentication=no -A ec2-user@52.74.220.151
ssh -L *:38143:10.0.0.10:22 -i test.pem ec2-user@10.0.0.10
```

You can connect to 10.0.0.10 with the following in a different Terminal (no Password or MFA):

```
ssh -p 38143 ec2-user@100.100.100.100
```

At least now you haven't copied the Key to the Bastion, but you have still lost MFA protection. Another thing that worried me was whether Agent Forwarding would allow any computer sharing your Public IP address to connect without credentials, but thankfully this is not the case. You can test it by trying the above ssh command from another laptop on your WiFi network or internal LAN - it doesn't work.

So you have a choice: MFA hell or allowing multiple ssh/scp commands with only one MFA code needed. As I said above, if you only need shell access on internal servers, go with the method above. But if you need to script updates or have many servers, you'll need to use the Tunnelling + Agent Forwarding method. And you'll still have to use an MFA code per tunnel you create, but at least it won't be an MFA code per ssh/scp command!

"Wait a minute!", I hear you exclaim. "I still have 50 servers... which means 50 MFA codes!" I understand you and I agree, which is why I would only use SSH Tunnelling and Agent Forwarding if I wanted a quick way to get a shell on an internal server.

What is really needed is a tunnel from the client to the Bastion which temporarily 'turns off' MFA. Unfortunately, this isn't possible. Every time you authenticate to the Bastion, an MFA code will be required. You don't need one when tunnelling via the Bastion to an internal server because you aren't opening a session on the Bastion - you're using an existing tunnel (which needed MFA to be created). So there's no way to get round 'one MFA per tunnel'.

A Solution

For a 'big' job, there is a better way, which reduces MFA requests to 2 *whatever* you need to do. And no credentials are copied to the Cloud. What you do is this: build a zip with everything you will need; send it to the Bastion with scp (first MFA code needed); then run an expect script which connects to the Bastion with ssh with Agent Forwarding enabled (second MFA needed); then, via expect which is now automating commands on the Bastion, unzip your package and run a script from it which manages the whole process; any ssh commands from that script to internal servers will be able to authenticate with Agent Forwarding; and you won't need any more MFA codes. Security is completely preserved. No tunnels are created. No new ports are opened to the Internet. MFA is intact on the Bastion so no-one can get in without your smartphone.

If you decide to go with a Bastion Host, I would recommend that for your network you use Key Based SSH for servers which require periodic updates (like web servers) and SSH MFA for more sensitive servers like databases. This means you can update all your SSH Key based servers with just two MFA codes. The point is that first layer servers which receive traffic from the Internet, even if they have no Public IP address, are still much more vulnerable to Application level hacks, and this will be the preferred route in for hackers. Second layer servers, like databases, which never receive traffic from the Internet, but rather respond to requests from first layer servers, are generally more sensitive, so SSH MFA is appropriate. Also, you hardly ever ssh into a database instance - it's more normal to access the database via the usual connect ports (like 3306 for MySQL) with something like PHPMyAdmin. Most maintenance involves things like doing database backups, and these are perfectly doable from a connected first layer host, like an Admin Server which handles an Admin Website and Centralised Logging. Again, see my first book for more on this. I would recommend SSH MFA for an Admin Server.

It sounds complicated and it is - but then *real* security comes at a price. I hope you've enjoyed our brief meander through some of the grittier parts of SSH. In the next sections, I'll build a Bastion Host, some internal servers and then use the technique from the last paragraph both to set an initial configuration and also to perform maintenance updates.

Internet Access from Internal Servers

Internal Servers have no Public IP Address, which not only means that they can't be reached directly from the Internet, but also that they can't connect to the Internet, because there's no IP address to send data back to.

For many servers, for normal operations, this is not a problem. For instance, a MySQL database server doesn't normally need to talk to the Internet, whether inbound or outbound. For web servers with no Public IP address, you would use an ELB (Elastic Load Balancer) to forward traffic in and out. But, you will need the ability to connect out for things like 'yum', or you may need to 'curl' from a PHP website.

You have 2 options here: a) temporarily connect an Elastic IP (EIP) to the internal server or b) set up a proxy on your Bastion Host and let 'yum' (or any other service) use that proxy.

I prefer the second option (the Squid proxy) because it preserves the 'No Public IP' ethos of the internal servers. But there is a little more configuration to be done on the servers. Adding and removing an Elastic IP is done on the client computer and then 'yum' on an internal server just works. One more reason to use a proxy is if you have many servers: adding and removing Elastic IPs isn't practical if you're running a long expect script which configures 50 servers.

Using Elastic IPs

To allocate an EIP (which means get hold of one from Amazon):

```
eip=$(aws ec2 allocate-address --domain vpc --output text --query
'AllocationId')
```

Then associate the EIP with an instance:

```
assid=$(aws ec2 associate-address --instance-id $instance_id
--allocation-id $eip --output text --query 'AssociationId')
```

Once you're finished, disassociate the address with:

```
aws ec2 disassociate-address --association-id $assid
```

You can now reuse the EIP for other servers. Once you're done, release it with:

```
aws ec2 release-address --allocation-id $eip
```

Note that Amazon charges if you have allocated but disassociated EIPs.

Using a Proxy

I'll use Squid on the Bastion Host and then configure 'yum' on the internal servers to connect via the proxy.

On the Bastion Host:

```
sudo yum -y install squid
service squid start
```

The Squid configuration file is /etc/squid/squid.conf which looks like this when Squid is first installed:

[chapter9/bastion/squid_default.conf]

```
# cat /etc/squid/squid.conf
#
# Recommended minimum configuration:
#
acl manager proto cache_object
acl localhost src 127.0.0.1/32 ::1
acl to_localhost dst 127.0.0.0/8 0.0.0.0/32 ::1

# Example rule allowing access from your local networks.
# Adapt to list your (internal) IP networks from where browsing
# should be allowed
acl localnet src 10.0.0.0/8    # RFC1918 possible internal network
acl localnet src 172.16.0.0/12      # RFC1918 possible internal
network
acl localnet src 192.168.0.0/16     # RFC1918 possible internal
network
acl localnet src fc00::/7     # RFC 4193 local private network
range
acl localnet src fe80::/10      # RFC 4291 link-local (directly
plugged) machines

acl SSL_ports port 443
acl Safe_ports port 80          # http
acl Safe_ports port 21          # ftp
acl Safe_ports port 443         # https
acl Safe_ports port 70          # gopher
acl Safe_ports port 210         # wais
acl Safe_ports port 1025-65535  # unregistered ports
acl Safe_ports port 280         # http-mgmt
```

```
acl Safe_ports port 488          # gss-http
acl Safe_ports port 591          # filemaker
acl Safe_ports port 777          # multiling http
acl CONNECT method CONNECT

#
# Recommended minimum Access Permission configuration:
#
# Only allow cachemgr access from localhost
http_access allow manager localhost
http_access deny manager

# Deny requests to certain unsafe ports
http_access deny !Safe_ports

# Deny CONNECT to other than secure SSL ports
http_access deny CONNECT !SSL_ports

# We strongly recommend the following be uncommented to protect
innocent
# web applications running on the proxy server who think the only
# one who can access services on "localhost" is a local user
#http_access deny to_localhost

#
# INSERT YOUR OWN RULE(S) HERE TO ALLOW ACCESS FROM YOUR CLIENTS
#

# Example rule allowing access from your local networks.
# Adapt localnet in the ACL section to list your (internal) IP
networks
# from where browsing should be allowed
http_access allow localnet
http_access allow localhost

# And finally deny all other access to this proxy
http_access deny all

# Squid normally listens to port 3128
http_port 3128

# We recommend you to use at least the following line.
hierarchy_stoplist cgi-bin ?

# Uncomment and adjust the following to add a disk cache
directory.
#cache_dir ufs /var/spool/squid 100 16 256

# Leave coredumps in the first cache dir
coredump_dir /var/spool/squid

# Add any of your own refresh_pattern entries above these.
refresh_pattern ^ftp:              1440           20%
10080
refresh_pattern ^gopher:           1440           0%
1440
refresh_pattern -i (/cgi-bin/|\?) 0     0%      0
refresh_pattern .                       0       20%
4320
```

In that file you will find the following two lines:

```
acl localnet src 10.0.0.0/8
http_access allow localnet
```

which will allow any traffic from 10.*.*.* to use the proxy for HTTP. The servers are on a 10. subnet so it will work out of the box, otherwise you'll need to change the Squid configuration file. A more secure version of the Squid configuration file is as follows:

[chapter9/bastion/squid.conf]

```
#
# Recommended minimum configuration:
#
acl manager proto cache_object
acl localhost src 127.0.0.1/32 ::1
acl to_localhost dst 127.0.0.0/8 0.0.0.0/32 ::1

# Example rule allowing access from your local networks.
# Adapt to list your (internal) IP networks from where browsing
# should be allowed

# allow any 10.0.0.x IPs
acl localnet src 10.0.0.0/24

# allow only http and https
acl SSL_ports port 443
acl Safe_ports port 80                    # http
acl CONNECT method CONNECT

#
# Recommended minimum Access Permission configuration:
#
# Only allow cachemgr access from localhost
http_access allow manager localhost
http_access deny manager

# Deny requests to certain unsafe ports
http_access deny !Safe_ports

# Deny CONNECT to other than secure SSL ports
http_access deny CONNECT !SSL_ports

# We strongly recommend the following be uncommented to protect
innocent
# web applications running on the proxy server who think the only
# one who can access services on "localhost" is a local user
#http_access deny to_localhost

#
# INSERT YOUR OWN RULE(S) HERE TO ALLOW ACCESS FROM YOUR CLIENTS
#

# Example rule allowing access from your local networks.
# Adapt localnet in the ACL section to list your (internal) IP
networks
# from where browsing should be allowed
http_access allow localnet
http_access allow localhost

# And finally deny all other access to this proxy
http_access deny all

# Squid normally listens to port 3128
http_port 3128

# We recommend you to use at least the following line.
```

```
hierarchy_stoplist cgi-bin ?

# Uncomment and adjust the following to add a disk cache
directory.
#cache_dir ufs /var/spool/squid 100 16 256

# Leave coredumps in the first cache dir
coredump_dir /var/spool/squid

# Add any of your own refresh_pattern entries above these.
refresh_pattern ^ftp:             1440           20%
10080
refresh_pattern ^gopher:                 1440          0%
1440
refresh_pattern -i (/cgi-bin/|\?) 0        0%            0
refresh_pattern .                          0            20%
4320
```

which is copied to the Bastion and installed in the scripts that
follow. As you can see, I've removed some 'acl localnet'
declarations and cut down on the safe ports. You can copy and
paste it in to /etc/squid/squid.conf, if you're doing this by hand.

On the internal server, all you need to do is update /etc/yum.conf -
the yum configuration file. At the end, paste in:

```
proxy=http://10.0.0.10:3128
```

Last, open port 3128 to traffic from the internal server, with
something like:

```
aws ec2 authorize-security-group-ingress --group-id $bastionsgid
--source-group $internal1sgid --protocol tcp --port 3128
```

Now 'yum' commands will work. Obviously, even though there are
no Security Groups linking Squid to the outside world, it's a
potential security hazard so turn it off when you don't need it and
don't set it to start at boot. On the Bastion Host:

```
service squid stop
```

For similar reasons, close the Security Group port as well:

```
aws ec2 revoke-security-group-ingress --group-id $bastionsgid
--source-group $internal1sgid --protocol tcp --port 3128
```

If you need continuous outbound connectivity, keep Squid running,
or even consider a dedicated server for the task depending on

traffic. You might need this for using 'curl' for PHP websites for a 3rd party service or similar.

If you need to use 'wget' from an internal server via Squid, you can use something like:

```
wget -e use_proxy=yes -e http_proxy=10.0.0.10:3128
http://www.google.com
```

Obviously, Squid needs to be running on the Bastion and the Bastion Security Group needs to accept Inbound 3128 from the internal server.

Last, the lack of Outbound connectivity also means you can't send emails from internal servers. So sending the SSH logs daily via email is out. This is easily fixed: use rsyslog to forward the logs to the Bastion, which *can* send emails. The rsyslog setup doesn't expose any network ports to the Internet, so it doesn't compromise security. It's sensible to use the Bastion Host as the collector for all SSH logs because it is, so to say, *in charge* of SSH for the network. But you could also use another server - you probably combine web server logs in the same way so that would be another option. In the scripts that follow, I'll configure rsyslog on all servers to implement this.

Building a Bastion and Internal Servers

I shall now script the build of a Bastion Host and then two Internal Servers. I'll configure the internal servers with hardened SSH and forwarding of SSH logs via rsyslog. I'll keep SSH with Keys for the first internal server, because for any large installation this is the only practical way. You can then see how to manage updates to such a server. But the second internal server I shall configure with SSH MFA so you can see how that also can be updated. For small installations of 2 to 10 servers, MFA might be practical, and it does provide the absolute highest security.

I'll also use Squid on the Bastion Hosts to allow outbound HTTP internet access for the internal servers. Code for the Elastic IP alternative is not included because, as stated above, you can't allocate an unlimited number of EIPs. So you would need to associate and disassociate between every call to a script on internal servers... but you need an MFA code for this as you are disconnecting and then reconnecting to the Bastion. So using EIP for a large number of servers is impractical.

If you've read my first book, "AWS Scripted: How to Automate the Deployment of Secure and Resilient Websites with Amazon Web Services VPC, ELB, EC2, RDS, IAM, SES and SNS", you'll be familiar with a 'mammoth script'. What follows is not as long, but I must admit much harder because you're building scripts to be run on the Bastion and then on internal servers. There's a lot of indirection, *Oratio Obliqua* if you know what I mean, but I hope the following pages facilitate the process for your own Cloud installation.

Building a Bastion Host

The Bastion Host is almost exactly the same as the server created in Chapter 8, except the base instance name has changed to 'bastion'. All the files are in the chapter9/bastion folder and they are mostly the same as Chapter 8. The make.sh script which makes the instance, prepares scripts, uploads and runs them is:

[chapter9/bastion/make.sh]

```
#!/bin/bash

# makes an ec2 instance with SSH MFA setup
# disable password-less sudo su
# and require root password to do it

# include chapter9 variables
cd ..
. ./vars.sh
cd bastion

# show variables
echo AMI: $baseami
echo instance base name: $ibn
echo VPC name: $vpcname
echo new SSHD port: $sshport
echo logging to email address: $emailaddress
echo ssh user: $sshuser
echo ssher password: $bastion_ssherpassword
echo root password: $bastion_rootpassword
```

```
# get our ip from amazon
myip=$(curl http://checkip.amazonaws.com/)
echo myip=$myip

# make a new keypair
echo "making keypair"
rm "$ibn".pem
aws ec2 delete-key-pair --key-name "$ibn"
aws ec2 create-key-pair --key-name "$ibn" --query 'KeyMaterial'
--output text > "$ibn".pem
chmod 600 "$ibn".pem
echo "$ibn" keypair made

# get the vpc id
vpc_id=$(aws ec2 describe-vpcs --filters Name=tag-
key,Values=vpcname Name=tag-value,Values=$vpcname --output text
--query 'Vpcs[*].VpcId')
echo vpc_id=$vpc_id

# make a security group
sgid=$(aws ec2 create-security-group --group-name "$ibn"sg
--description "$ibn security group" --vpc-id $vpc_id --output text
--query 'GroupId')
# tag it
aws ec2 create-tags --resources $sgid --tags
Key=sgname,Value="$ibn"sg
# now get the security group id again by using the tag
sgid=$(aws ec2 describe-security-groups --filters Name=tag-
key,Values=sgname Name=tag-value,Values="$ibn"sg --output text
--query 'SecurityGroups[*].GroupId')
echo sgid=$sgid

# allow ssh in on port 22 from our ip only
aws ec2 authorize-security-group-ingress --group-id $sgid
--protocol tcp --port 22 --cidr $myip/32

# get a vpc subnet
subnet_id=$(aws ec2 describe-subnets --filters Name=vpc-
id,Values=$vpc_id Name=tag-key,Values=subnet Name=tag-
value,Values=1 --output text --query 'Subnets[*].SubnetId')
echo subnet_id=$subnet_id

# make the instance
instance_id=$(aws ec2 run-instances --image $baseami --key "$ibn"
--security-group-ids $sgid --instance-type t2.micro --subnet-id
$subnet_id --associate-public-ip-address --private-ip-address
10.0.0.10 --output text --query 'Instances[*].InstanceId')
echo instance_id=$instance_id

# tag the instance (so we can get it later)
aws ec2 create-tags --resources $instance_id --tags
Key=instancename,Value="$ibn"

# wait for it
echo -n "waiting for instance"
while state=$(aws ec2 describe-instances --instance-ids
$instance_id --output text --query
'Reservations[*].Instances[*].State.Name'); test "$state" =
"pending"; do
  echo -n . ; sleep 3;
done; echo " $state"

# get the new instance's public ip address
ip_address=$(aws ec2 describe-instances --instance-ids
$instance_id --output text --query
'Reservations[*].Instances[*].PublicIpAddress')
echo ip_address=$ip_address
```

```
# wait for ssh to work
echo -n "waiting for ssh"
while ! ssh -i "$ibn".pem -o ConnectTimeout=5 -o BatchMode=yes -o
StrictHostKeyChecking=no ec2-user@$ip_address > /dev/null 2>&1
true; do
  echo -n . ; sleep 5;
done; echo " ssh ok"

# remove old files
rm -f install.sh
rm -f emailsshlog.sh
rm -f sshd_config

# sed the install script
sed -e "s/SEDsshuserSED/$sshuser/g" -e "s/SEDssherpasswordSED/
$bastion_ssherpassword/g" -e "s/SEDrootpasswordSED/
$bastion_rootpassword/g" -e "s/SEDemailaddressSED/$emailaddress/g"
install_template.sh > install.sh

# sed the email logging script
sed -e "s/SEDemailaddressSED/$emailaddress/g"
emailsshlog_template.sh > emailsshlog.sh

# sed the sshd_config file
sed -e "s/SEDsshportSED/$sshport/g" -e "s/SEDsshuserSED/
$sshuser/g" sshd_config_template > sshd_config

# make the scripts executable
chmod +x install.sh
chmod +x emailsshlog.sh

# send required files
echo "transferring files"
scp -i "$ibn".pem install.sh ec2-user@$ip_address:
scp -i "$ibn".pem sshd_config ec2-user@$ip_address:
scp -i "$ibn".pem emailsshlog.sh ec2-user@$ip_address:
scp -i "$ibn".pem rsyslog.conf ec2-user@$ip_address:
scp -i "$ibn".pem squid.conf ec2-user@$ip_address:
echo "transferred files"

# remove sent files
rm -f install.sh
rm -f emailsshlog.sh
rm -f sshd_config

# run the install script
ssh -i "$ibn".pem -t -o ConnectTimeout=60 -o BatchMode=yes ec2-
user@$ip_address sudo ./install.sh

# remove the local key (it won't work anyway)
rm -f "$ibn".pem

# drop the port 22 rule
aws ec2 revoke-security-group-ingress --group-id $sgid --protocol
tcp --port 22 --cidr $myip/32

# open up the new ssh port
aws ec2 authorize-security-group-ingress --group-id $sgid
--protocol tcp --port $sshport --cidr $myip/32

echo
echo now install the Google Authenticator App on a smartphone
echo find the MFA KEY in the output above
echo and create an account on the App with Manual Entry
echo call it BASTION
read -n 1 -p "Press a key when done"
echo
```

AWS Scripted 2

```
# delete ec2-user from the box
# you'll need an mfa code
echo deleting ec2-user
read -s -p "mfa code for BASTION:" mfacode
# make and run expect script
echo "#!/usr/bin/expect -f" > expect.sh
echo "set timeout -1" >> expect.sh
echo "spawn ssh -p $sshport $sshuser@$ip_address" >> expect.sh
echo "expect \"Password:\"" >> expect.sh
echo "send \"$bastion_ssherpassword\n\"" >> expect.sh
echo "expect \"Verification code:\"" >> expect.sh
echo "send \"$mfacode\n\"" >> expect.sh
echo "expect \"]\"" >> expect.sh
echo "send \"sudo su\n\"" >> expect.sh
echo "expect \"password for root:\"" >> expect.sh
echo "send \"$bastion_rootpassword\n\"" >> expect.sh
echo "expect \"]\"" >> expect.sh
echo "send \"userdel -r ec2-user\n\"" >> expect.sh
echo "expect \"]\"" >> expect.sh
echo "send \"exit\n\"" >> expect.sh
echo "expect \"]\"" >> expect.sh
echo "send \"exit\n\"" >> expect.sh
echo "interact" >> expect.sh
chmod +x expect.sh
./expect.sh
rm expect.sh

echo
echo then ssh to the Bastion with:
echo ssh -p "$sshport" "$sshuser"@"$ip_address"
echo "enter password ($bastion_ssherpassword) and a BASTION MFA
code to sign in"
echo "'sudo su' needs the root password ($bastion_rootpassword)"
echo
echo when finished, terminate the server or close the $sshport
inbound port
echo "eg aws ec2 revoke-security-group-ingress --group-id $sgid
--protocol tcp --port $sshport --cidr $myip/32"
```

The only changes are that I include the vars.sh definition file from the chapter9 directory (it's shared between all scripts in Chapter 9). Also, because I am now launching several instances, I assign a private IP to the Bastion of 10.0.0.10. This is achieved by including '--private-ip-address 10.0.0.10' in the 'aws ec2 run-instances' command which launches the Bastion. There is also code for automating the deletion of the ec2-user with expect.

This is the variables definition file for all scripts in Chapter 9 (it includes globals.sh):

[chapter9/vars.sh]

```
#!/bin/bash

# include globals
. ./../globals.sh
```

```
# shared variables for scripts in chapter9

# the base name for the bastion instance
# this string is used for key name, instance and sg names and
tags
  ibn=bastion

# the base name for internal instances
# this string is used for key name, instance and sg names and
tags
  iibn=internal

# bastion password for ssher
bastion_ssherpassword=1234

# bastion password for root
bastion_rootpassword=123456

# password for ssher on internal1
internal1_ssherpassword=1111

# password for root on internal1
internal1_rootpassword=111111

# password for ssher on internal2
internal2_ssherpassword=2222

# password for root on internal2
internal2_rootpassword=222222
```

This is the template for the script I run on the instance to configure
it, note the addition of rsyslog and the Squid installation and
configuration:

[chapter9/bastion/install_template.sh]

```
#!/bin/bash

# this script needs to be run on the instance as root
# it changes the ssh user to ssher
# it hardens ssh
# it configures sshd to use a password and MFA
# it sets up a daily email of the sshd log file
# it disables password-less 'sudo su'
# and requires the root password to do so

# the following strings are replaced
# SEDsshuserSED
# SEDssherpasswordSED
# SEDrootpasswordSED
# SEDemailaddressSED

# update yum
yum -y update

# install squid
# works out of the box for 10.0.0.0/8 subnets
# but we use a hardened conf file
sudo yum -y install squid
mv squid.conf /etc/squid/squid.conf
chown root:root /etc/squid/squid.conf
chmod 600 /etc/squid/squid.conf
```

```
# add ssher user
groupadd SEDsshuserSED
useradd -g SEDsshuserSED SEDsshuserSED

# install expect
yum install -y expect

# change ssher's password with expect
echo "#!/usr/bin/expect -f" > expect.sh
echo "set timeout -1" >> expect.sh
echo "spawn passwd SEDsshuserSED" >> expect.sh
echo "expect \"New password:\"" >> expect.sh
echo "send \"SEDssherpasswordSED\n\";" >> expect.sh
echo "expect \"new password:\"" >> expect.sh
echo "send \"SEDssherpasswordSED\n\";" >> expect.sh
echo "interact" >> expect.sh
# run it
chmod +x expect.sh
./expect.sh
# remove it
rm -f expect.sh

# change root's password with expect
echo "#!/usr/bin/expect -f" > expect.sh
echo "set timeout -1" >> expect.sh
echo "spawn passwd root" >> expect.sh
echo "expect \"New password:\"" >> expect.sh
echo "send \"SEDrootpasswordSED\n\";" >> expect.sh
echo "expect \"new password:\"" >> expect.sh
echo "send \"SEDrootpasswordSED\n\";" >> expect.sh
echo "interact" >> expect.sh
# run it
chmod +x expect.sh
./expect.sh
# remove it
rm -f expect.sh

# erase expect
yum erase -y expect

# disable passwordless 'sudo su'
echo "SEDsshuserSED ALL = ALL" > /etc/sudoers.d/cloud-init

# require root password for 'sudo su' (not sshers's)
echo "Defaults targetpw" >> /etc/sudoers.d/cloud-init

# update sshd config
mv sshd_config /etc/ssh/sshd_config
chown root:root /etc/ssh/sshd_config
chmod 600 /etc/ssh/sshd_config

# remove sshd keys so ssher can't sign in with a key
rm -f /home/ec2-user/.ssh/authorized_keys
rm -f /root/.ssh/authorized_keys

# set the max concurrent ssh sessions
echo "SEDsshuserSED - maxlogins 1" >> /etc/security/limits.conf

# install mfa and pam modules
yum -y install google-authenticator.x86_64 pam.x86_64 pam-devel.x86_64

# update pam config
echo "auth required pam_google_authenticator.so" >> /etc/pam.d/sshd

# run the google authenticator for ssher
cd /home/SEDsshuserSED
```

```
      google-authenticator --time-based --disallow-reuse --force
--rate-limit=1 --rate-time=60 --window-size=3 --quiet
--secret=/home/SEDsshuserSED/.google_authenticator
      chown SEDsshuserSED:SEDsshuserSED .google_authenticator
      chmod 400 .google_authenticator

      # delete last 4 GOOJ codes
      head -n 6 .google_authenticator > .google_authenticator2
      mv -f .google_authenticator2 .google_authenticator
      chown SEDsshuserSED:SEDsshuserSED .google_authenticator
      chmod 400 .google_authenticator

      # print out the codes
      bits=($(cat .google_authenticator))
      echo MFA KEY is ${bits[0]}
      echo MFA GOOJ is ${bits[11]}

      # restart sshd
      # Curiously, sshd doesn't seem to like
      # being restarted just as you end an ssh session
      /etc/init.d/sshd restart
      sleep 5

      # set up email logging
      cd /home/ec2-user/
      mv emailsshlog.sh /root/emailsshlog.sh
      chown root:root /root/emailsshlog.sh
      chmod 500 /root/emailsshlog.sh

      # run daily at 12:05am
      line="5 0 * * * /root/emailsshlog.sh"
      (crontab -u root -l; echo "$line" ) | crontab -u root -

      # send immediate email for sudo use
      echo 'Defaults mailto="SEDemailaddressSED",mail_always' >>
/etc/sudoers.d/cloud-init

      # send immediate email for root signin
      echo "echo Subject: Root Access\$'\n'\$(who) | sendmail
SEDemailaddressSED" >> /root/.bashrc

      # configure rsyslog
      cd /home/ec2-user
      mv -f rsyslog.conf /etc/rsyslog.conf
      chown root:root /etc/rsyslog.conf
      chmod 400 /etc/rsyslog.conf

      # delete this script
      rm -f /home/ec2-user/install.sh
```

You can find the squid.conf file in the last section.

This is the new rsyslog.conf file (which is mainly the same but turns on the ability to receive logs via tcp/udp):

[chapter9/bastion/rsyslog.conf]

```
      # rsyslog for bastion server

      $ModLoad imuxsock
      $ModLoad imklog
      $ModLoad imudp
```

```
$UDPServerRun 514
$ModLoad imtcp
$InputTCPServerRun 514

$ActionFileDefaultTemplate RSYSLOG_TraditionalFileFormat

$umask 0000
$FileCreateMode 0666

  *.info;mail.none;authpriv.none;cron.none
/var/log/messages

  authpriv.*
/var/log/secure

  mail.*
-/var/log/maillog

  cron.*
/var/log/cron

  *.emerg                                          *

  uucp,news.crit
/var/log/spooler

  local7.*
/var/log/boot.log

  $IncludeConfig /etc/rsyslog.d/*.conf
```

To make a Bastion Host, cd to 'chapter9/bastion' and use:

```
./make.sh
```

You'll need to set up MFA with the MFA KEY which is printed out as in Chapter 8. When you're all done, verify access by doing an ssh and authenticating (instructions are echoed out at the end of the script).

Note that if you get 'Too many authentication failures for ec2-user' you probably still have identities in your SSH Agent. Try ssh again after you have removed them with:

```
ssh-add -D
```

Then move to the next section.

Building Internal Servers

You need two internal servers for the scripts which follow. cd to 'chapter9/internal' and use:

```
./make.sh internal1 10.0.0.11
./make.sh internal2 10.0.0.12
```

This builds two boxes with no configuration and no Public IP addresses.

The script which accomplishes this is quite short:

[chapter9/internal/make.sh]

```
#!/bin/bash

# makes an ec2 instance with no Public IP Address
# attaches a security group
# does no configuration

# call from chapter9/internal directory
# expects 2 arguments:
# basename for the server (used for names and tags)
# internal ip address
# eg ./make.sh internal1 10.0.0.11

# include chapter9 variables
cd ..
. ./vars.sh
cd internal

# show variables
echo AMI: $baseami
echo VPC name: $vpcname

# make a new keypair
echo "making keypair"
rm credentials/"$1".pem
aws ec2 delete-key-pair --key-name "$1"
aws ec2 create-key-pair --key-name "$1" --query 'KeyMaterial'
--output text > credentials/"$1".pem
chmod 600 credentials/"$1".pem
echo "$1" keypair made

# get the vpc id
vpc_id=$(aws ec2 describe-vpcs --filters Name=tag-
key,Values=vpcname Name=tag-value,Values=$vpcname --output text
--query 'Vpcs[*].VpcId')
echo vpc_id=$vpc_id

# make a security group
sgid=$(aws ec2 create-security-group --group-name "$1"sg
--description "$1 security group" --vpc-id $vpc_id --output text
--query 'GroupId')
# tag it
aws ec2 create-tags --resources $sgid --tags
Key=sgname,Value="$1"sg
# now get the security group id again by using the tag
sgid=$(aws ec2 describe-security-groups --filters Name=tag-
key,Values=sgname Name=tag-value,Values="$1"sg --output text
--query 'SecurityGroups[*].GroupId')
echo sgid=$sgid
```

```
# get a vpc subnet
subnet_id=$(aws ec2 describe-subnets --filters Name=vpc-
id,Values=$vpc_id Name=tag-key,Values=subnet Name=tag-
value,Values=1 --output text --query 'Subnets[*].SubnetId')
  echo subnet_id=$subnet_id

# make the instance
instance_id=$(aws ec2 run-instances --image $baseami --key "$1"
--security-group-ids $sgid --instance-type t2.micro --subnet-id
$subnet_id --no-associate-public-ip-address --private-ip-address $2
--output text --query 'Instances[*].InstanceId')
  echo instance_id=$instance_id

# tag the instance (so we can get it later)
aws ec2 create-tags --resources $instance_id --tags
Key=instancename,Value="$1"

# wait for it
echo -n "waiting for instance"
while state=$(aws ec2 describe-instances --instance-ids
$instance_id --output text --query
'Reservations[*].Instances[*].State.Name'); test "$state" =
"pending"; do
  echo -n . ; sleep 3;
done; echo " $state"

echo created internal server $1 with private ip $2
```

Configuring Internal Servers

Once your internal servers are built, you'll need to do a once-only configuration. This means setting up SSH how you like it, adding cron jobs and things like installing a web server or a database server.

I'll show you how to configure both new internal servers with only 2 Bastion MFA codes. This would also work for many more internal servers and would still only need 2 Bastion MFA codes. I am going to harden the sshd config for internal1 and keep authentication with SSH Keys. I will set up MFA and a password for 'sudo su' for internal2 (for a bit of variety). Both servers will have SSH logs emailed daily via rsyslog and sendmail on the Bastion.

To run the whole process, cd to chapter9/configure and use:

```
./configure.sh
```

This will zip up chapter9/vars.sh, chapter9/data/install.sh and all the internal* folders in chapter9/configure/data, send the zip to the

Bastion Host (which costs 1 MFA Code) and then run install.sh on the Bastion (which costs another MFA code). I use expect to manage the process, hence only one MFA code to unzip and run the install.sh script.

In order to save time and work, I try to change the install scripts as little as possible from what I would use if I were doing a direct installation to a server with a Public IP Address. You might say: But you are uploading vars.sh type files to the Bastion which have sensitive data like user passwords. This is true, however, you also upload that data in expect scripts to servers with Public IP addresses, and also remember that user passwords are not a security layer. They are either required (for SSH with MFA you need an ssher password) or additional protection (such as the root password for password-less 'sudo su'). But the main protection comes from SSH Keys (which are not uploaded to the Bastion) or SSH MFA (which is a distinct layer mediated by a smartphone).

The main configure script is as follows:

[chapter9/configure/configure.sh]

```
#!/bin/bash

# this script configures the 2 internal servers

# it will zip up all the configure/internal* folders
# eg internal1, internal2, ..., internalN
# and install.sh and a generated vars.sh
# then send this zip to the bastion with scp
# then install.sh will be run on the bastion

# this script needs to be called from chapter9/configure
directory
# with ./configure.sh

# include chapter9 variables
cd ..
. ./vars.sh
cd configure

# get my ip
myip=$(curl http://checkip.amazonaws.com/)
echo myip=$myip

# get ip of bastion
bastionip=$(aws ec2 describe-instances --filters Name=tag-
key,Values=instancename Name=tag-value,Values=bastion --output text
--query 'Reservations[*].Instances[*].PublicIpAddress')
echo bastionip=$bastionip

# * TEMPORARY RULES
```

```
# allow ssh in sg
bastionsgid=$(aws ec2 describe-security-groups --filters
Name=tag-key,Values=sgname Name=tag-value,Values=bastionsg --output
text --query 'SecurityGroups[*].GroupId')
echo bastionsgid=$bastionsgid
aws ec2 authorize-security-group-ingress --group-id $bastionsgid
--protocol tcp --port $sshport --cidr $myip/32

# allow ssh access from bastion to internal1
internal1sgid=$(aws ec2 describe-security-groups --filters
Name=tag-key,Values=sgname Name=tag-value,Values=internal1sg
--output text --query 'SecurityGroups[*].GroupId')
echo internal1sgid=$internal1sgid
aws ec2 authorize-security-group-ingress --group-id
$internal1sgid --source-group $bastionsgid --protocol tcp --port 22

# allow ssh access from bastion to internal2
internal2sgid=$(aws ec2 describe-security-groups --filters
Name=tag-key,Values=sgname Name=tag-value,Values=internal2sg
--output text --query 'SecurityGroups[*].GroupId')
echo internal2sgid=$internal2sgid
aws ec2 authorize-security-group-ingress --group-id
$internal2sgid --source-group $bastionsgid --protocol tcp --port 22

# allow squid access from internal1 to bastion
aws ec2 authorize-security-group-ingress --group-id $bastionsgid
--source-group $internal1sgid --protocol tcp --port 3128

# allow squid access from internal2 to bastion
aws ec2 authorize-security-group-ingress --group-id $bastionsgid
--source-group $internal2sgid --protocol tcp --port 3128

# * PERMANENT RULES

# allow access on 514 (rsyslog) from internal1 to bastion
aws ec2 authorize-security-group-ingress --group-id $bastionsgid
--source-group $internal1sgid --protocol tcp --port 514

# allow access on 514 (rsyslog) from internal2 to bastion
aws ec2 authorize-security-group-ingress --group-id $bastionsgid
--source-group $internal2sgid --protocol tcp --port 514

# make a vars.sh file from globals.sh and chapter9/vars.sh
# we are in chapter9/configure directory
cat ../../globals.sh > data/vars.sh
tail -n +5 ../vars.sh >> data/vars.sh
chmod +x data/vars.sh

# make the zip
cd data
zip -r upload.zip vars.sh install.sh internal*
cd ..

# remove temporary vars.sh file
rm -f data/vars.sh

# get an mfa code
read -s -p "MFA code for Bastion:" mfacode

# make and run expect script to upload zip
echo "#!/usr/bin/expect -f" > expect.sh
echo "set timeout -1" >> expect.sh
echo "spawn scp -P $sshport -o PubkeyAuthentication=no
data/upload.zip $sshuser@$bastionip:" >> expect.sh
echo "expect \"Password:\"" >> expect.sh
echo "send \"$bastion_ssherpassword\n\"" >> expect.sh
echo "expect \"Verification code:\"" >> expect.sh
```

```
echo "send \"$mfacode\n\"" >> expect.sh
echo "interact" >> expect.sh
chmod +x expect.sh
./expect.sh
rm expect.sh

# remove zip
rm -f data/upload.zip

# kill any ssh agents and start a new one
kill $(pgrep ssh-agent)
eval `ssh-agent -s`

# add internal keys to ssh agent
cd ../internal/credentials
ssh-add -D
ssh-add internal1.pem
ssh-add internal2.pem
cd ../../configure

# get an mfa code
read -s -p "MFA code for Bastion:" mfacode

# make and run expect script to run zip
# the ssh -A option enables agent forwarding
# note agent forwarding does not work if you're in 'sudo su'
echo "#!/usr/bin/expect -f" > expect.sh
echo "set timeout -1" >> expect.sh
echo "spawn ssh -p $sshport -A -o PubkeyAuthentication=no
$sshuser@$bastionip" >> expect.sh
echo "expect \"Password:\"" >> expect.sh
echo "send \"$bastion_ssherpassword\n\"" >> expect.sh
echo "expect \"Verification code:\"" >> expect.sh
echo "send \"$mfacode\n\"" >> expect.sh

# we use a little trick to sudo su and then exit
# so we can use it later with no password
echo "expect \"]\"" >> expect.sh
echo "send \"sudo su\n\"" >> expect.sh
echo "expect \"password for root:\"" >> expect.sh
echo "send \"$bastion_rootpassword\n\"" >> expect.sh
echo "expect \"]\"" >> expect.sh
echo "send \"exit\n\"" >> expect.sh

echo "expect \"]\"" >> expect.sh
echo "send \"rm -f -r upload\n\"" >> expect.sh
echo "expect \"]\"" >> expect.sh
echo "send \"mkdir upload\n\"" >> expect.sh
echo "expect \"]\"" >> expect.sh
echo "send \"mv upload.zip upload\n\"" >> expect.sh
echo "expect \"]\"" >> expect.sh
echo "send \"cd upload\n\"" >> expect.sh
echo "expect \"]\"" >> expect.sh
echo "send \"unzip upload.zip\n\"" >> expect.sh

echo "expect \"]\"" >> expect.sh
echo "send \"ls -al\n\"" >> expect.sh
echo "expect \"]\"" >> expect.sh
echo "send \"chmod +x install.sh\n\"" >> expect.sh
echo "expect \"]\"" >> expect.sh
echo "send \"./install.sh\n\"" >> expect.sh

echo "expect \"finished install.sh on bastion\"" >> expect.sh
echo "send \"cd ..\n\"" >> expect.sh
echo "expect \"]\"" >> expect.sh
echo "send \"rm -f -r *\n\"" >> expect.sh
echo "expect \"]\"" >> expect.sh
echo "send \"exit\n\"" >> expect.sh
```

```
echo "interact" >> expect.sh

chmod +x expect.sh
./expect.sh
rm expect.sh

# remove internal keys from ssh agent
ssh-add -D

# kill it
kill $(pgrep ssh-agent)

# delete internal2.pem (MFA now installed)
cd ../internal/credentials
rm -f internal2.pem
cd ../../configure

# revoke ssh to bastion
aws ec2 revoke-security-group-ingress --group-id $bastionsgid
--protocol tcp --port $sshport --cidr $myip/32

# revoke ssh between bastion and internal1
aws ec2 revoke-security-group-ingress --group-id $internal1sgid
--source-group $bastionsgid --protocol tcp --port 22

# revoke ssh between bastion and internal2
aws ec2 revoke-security-group-ingress --group-id $internal2sgid
--source-group $bastionsgid --protocol tcp --port 22

# revoke squid access from internal1 to bastion
aws ec2 revoke-security-group-ingress --group-id $bastionsgid
--source-group $internal1sgid --protocol tcp --port 3128

# revoke access from internal2 to bastion
aws ec2 revoke-security-group-ingress --group-id $bastionsgid
--source-group $internal2sgid --protocol tcp --port 3128

echo revoked sg access

echo configuration done
```

The data zip I send to the Bastion which performs the configuration of both internal servers contains an install script (chapter9/configure/data/install.sh) and two folders, internal1 and internal2. The install script is executed on the Bastion and runs make.sh in each internal* folder. The folder internal1 contains all the files required to configure the internal1 server and similarly for the internal2 folder. In each internal* folder, make.sh prepares files, sends them to the appropriate internal server and then runs the install scripts on those servers.

This is the install.sh file run on the Bastion to orchestrate running make.sh in each internal* folder. It's generic and would work for any number of internal* folders.

[chapter9/configure/data/install.sh]

```
#!/bin/bash

# this script is run on the bastion with expect
# it starts squid
# it lists all folders beginning with 'internal'
# then runs make.sh from each folder
# would work for any number of folders

# start squid
sudo service squid start

# make vars.sh executable just in case
chmod +x vars.sh

# list internal* folders and loop
folders=$(ls -d internal*)
bits=($folders)
for i in "${bits[@]}"
do
  echo running $i/make.sh
  cd $i
  chmod +x make.sh
  ./make.sh
  cd ..
  echo finished $i/make.sh
done

# stop squid
sudo service squid stop

echo finished install.sh on bastion
```

Looking at the configuration of internal1, there are 4 files. 'make.sh' is run to prepare scripts, send them to internal1, and then run them:

[chapter9/configure/data/internal1/make.sh]

```
#!/bin/bash

# this script is run on the Bastion
# it prepares the scripts to be run on internal1
# which will harden SSH
# change the ssh user to ssher
# set passwords

# include variables
. ./../vars.sh

# name and ipaddress for internal1
ibn=internal1
ip_address=10.0.0.11

# show variables
echo internal1 variables
echo ibn: $ibn
echo ip address: $ip_address
echo new SSHD port: $sshport
echo ssh user: $sshuser
echo ssher password: $internal1_ssherpassword
echo root password: $internal1_rootpassword

# wait for ssh to work
```

```
  # we are using agent forwarding (so the key is on the client)
  echo -n "waiting for ssh"
  while ! ssh -i "$ibn".pem -o ConnectTimeout=5 -o BatchMode=yes -o
StrictHostKeyChecking=no ec2-user@$ip_address > /dev/null 2>&1
true; do
    echo -n . ; sleep 5;
  done; echo " ssh ok"

  # remove old files
  rm -f install.sh
  rm -f sshd_config

  # sed the install script
  sed -e "s/SEDsshuserSED/$sshuser/g" -e "s/SEDssherpasswordSED/
$internal1_ssherpassword/g" -e "s/SEDrootpasswordSED/
$internal1_rootpassword/g" install_template.sh > install.sh

  # sed the sshd_config file
  sed -e "s/SEDsshportSED/$sshport/g" -e "s/SEDsshuserSED/
$sshuser/g" sshd_config_template > sshd_config

  # make the script executable
  chmod +x install.sh

  # send required files
  echo "transferring files"
  scp -i "$ibn".pem install.sh ec2-user@$ip_address:
  scp -i "$ibn".pem sshd_config ec2-user@$ip_address:
  scp -i "$ibn".pem rsyslog.conf ec2-user@$ip_address:
  echo "transferred files"

  # remove sent files
  rm -f install.sh
  rm -f sshd_config

  # run the install script
  ssh -i "$ibn".pem -t -o ConnectTimeout=60 -o BatchMode=yes ec2-
user@$ip_address sudo ./install.sh

  echo make.sh for internal1 finished
```

The second internal1 file is 'install_template.sh' which is 'sed'ed, sent to internal1 and run there:

```
[chapter9/configure/data/internal1/install_template.s
h]
```

```
  #!/bin/bash

  # this script changes the ssh user to ssher
  # it hardens ssh, but keeps key based auth
  # it disables password-less 'sudo su'
  # and requires the root password to do so
  # it sets up rsyslog forwarding for authpriv.* to bastion
  # it sets up yum to use squid on bastion

  # the following strings are replaced:
  # SEDsshuserSED
  # SEDssherpasswordSED
  # SEDrootpasswordSED

  # configure and update yum
  echo "proxy=http://10.0.0.10:3128" >> /etc/yum.conf
  yum -y update
```

```
# add ssher user
groupadd SEDsshuserSED
useradd -g SEDsshuserSED SEDsshuserSED

# install expect
yum install -y expect

# change ssher's password with expect
echo "#!/usr/bin/expect -f" > expect.sh
echo "set timeout -1" >> expect.sh
echo "spawn passwd SEDsshuserSED" >> expect.sh
echo "expect \"New password:\"" >> expect.sh
echo "send \"SEDssherpasswordSED\n\";" >> expect.sh
echo "expect \"new password:\"" >> expect.sh
echo "send \"SEDssherpasswordSED\n\";" >> expect.sh
echo "interact" >> expect.sh
# run it
chmod +x expect.sh
./expect.sh
# remove it
rm -f expect.sh

# change root's password with expect
echo "#!/usr/bin/expect -f" > expect.sh
echo "set timeout -1" >> expect.sh
echo "spawn passwd root" >> expect.sh
echo "expect \"New password:\"" >> expect.sh
echo "send \"SEDrootpasswordSED\n\";" >> expect.sh
echo "expect \"new password:\"" >> expect.sh
echo "send \"SEDrootpasswordSED\n\";" >> expect.sh
echo "interact" >> expect.sh
# run it
chmod +x expect.sh
./expect.sh
# remove it
rm -f expect.sh

# erase expect
yum erase -y expect

# disable passwordless 'sudo su'
echo "SEDsshuserSED ALL = ALL" > /etc/sudoers.d/cloud-init

# require root password for 'sudo su' (not sshers's)
echo "Defaults targetpw" >> /etc/sudoers.d/cloud-init

# update sshd config
mv sshd_config /etc/ssh/sshd_config
chown root:root /etc/ssh/sshd_config
chmod 600 /etc/ssh/sshd_config

# move the ssh key
cd /home/SEDsshuserSED
mkdir .ssh
chown SEDsshuserSED:SEDsshuserSED .ssh
chmod 700 .ssh
ls -al
mv /home/ec2-user/.ssh/authorized_keys .ssh
chown SEDsshuserSED:SEDsshuserSED .ssh/authorized_keys
chmod 600 .ssh/authorized_keys
ls -al .ssh

# set the max concurrent ssh sessions
echo "SEDsshuserSED - maxlogins 1" >> /etc/security/limits.conf

# restart sshd
# careful, sshd doesn't seem to like
```

```
# being restarted just as you end an ssh session
/etc/init.d/sshd restart
sleep 5

# configure rsyslog
cd /home/ec2-user
mv -f rsyslog.conf /etc/rsyslog.conf
chown root:root /etc/rsyslog.conf
chmod 400 /etc/rsyslog.conf
```

The internal1 folder also contains the sshd_config file:

```
[chapter9/configure/data/internal1/sshd_config_templa
te]
```

```
# hardened sshd config file
# turns off Key access
# turns on Password access

# the following strings are replaced:
# SEDsshportSED

# change the default ssh port
Port SEDsshportSED

# use better security protocols
Protocol 2

# log to authpriv
SyslogFacility AUTHPRIV
# log info messages
LogLevel INFO

# don't permit root login, or root forced commands
PermitRootLogin no

# where the access keys can be found
AuthorizedKeysFile    .ssh/authorized_keys

# turn off various things
HostbasedAuthentication no
IgnoreRhosts yes
X11Forwarding no

# password authentication
PasswordAuthentication no
ChallengeResponseAuthentication no

# only SEDsshuserSED can sign in
AllowUsers SEDsshuserSED
# run user and session checks
UsePAM yes

# when last signed in
PrintLastLog yes

# more secure way to run the sshd
UsePrivilegeSeparation sandbox

# max seconds to sign in after connecting
LoginGraceTime 60

# max authentication attempts per connect
# setting this any lower can cause problems
```

```
MaxAuthTries 3

# max multiplexed ssh sessions
# to limit sesions add to /etc/security/limits.conf
#ssher - maxlogins 1
MaxSessions 1

# max concurrent unauthenticated sessions
MaxStartups 1

# check no world writeable files left in user home directory
StrictModes yes

# no empty passwords
PermitEmptyPasswords no

# allows scp
Subsystem      sftp     /usr/libexec/openssh/sftp-server
```

And the rsyslog configuration:

`[chapter9/configure/data/internal1/rsyslog.conf]`

```
# rsyslog for webphp

$ModLoad imuxsock # provides support for local system logging
(e.g. via logger command)
$ModLoad imklog   # provides kernel logging support (previously
done by rklogd)
#$ModLoad immark  # provides --MARK-- message capability

$ActionFileDefaultTemplate RSYSLOG_TraditionalFileFormat

mail.*
-/var/log/maillog
  cron.*
/var/log/cron
  *.emerg                                              *
  uucp,news.crit
/var/log/spooler
  local7.*
/var/log/boot.log

# send authpriv logs to the Bastion
$WorkDirectory /var/lib/rsyslog # where to place spool files
$ActionQueueFileName fwdRule1 # unique name prefix for spool
files
$ActionQueueMaxDiskSpace 1g   # 1gb space limit (use as much as
possible)
$ActionQueueSaveOnShutdown on # save messages to disk on shutdown
$ActionQueueType LinkedList   # run asynchronously
$ActionResumeRetryCount -1    # infinite retries if host is down
authpriv.* @@10.0.0.10:514    .

$IncludeConfig /etc/rsyslog.d/*.conf
```

Moving to the slightly more complex configuration of internal2
(because I am setting up SSH MFA and a password for 'sudo su'),
there are 5 files to handle this. The 'make.sh' again handles
preparing the scripts, sending them to internal2 and then running

AWS Scripted 2   178

them there.

[chapter9/configure/data/internal2/make.sh]

```bash
#!/bin/bash

# this script is run on the Bastion
# it prepares the scripts to be run on internal2
# which will harden SSH, set up SSH daily logging,
# set up SSH MFA and disable password-less sudo su

# include variables
. ./../vars.sh

# name and ipaddress for internal2
ibn=internal2
ip_address=10.0.0.12

# show variables
echo internal2 variables
echo ibn: $ibn
echo ip address: $ip_address
echo new SSHD port: $sshport
echo ssh user: $sshuser
echo ssher password: $internal2_ssherpassword
echo root password: $internal2_rootpassword

# wait for ssh to work
echo -n "waiting for ssh"
while ! ssh -i "$ibn".pem -o ConnectTimeout=5 -o BatchMode=yes -o
StrictHostKeyChecking=no ec2-user@$ip_address > /dev/null 2>&1
true; do
  echo -n . ; sleep 5;
done; echo " ssh ok"

# remove old files
rm -f install.sh
rm -f sshd_config

# sed the root install script
sed -e "s/SEDsshuserSED/$sshuser/g" -e "s/SEDssherpasswordSED/
$internal2_ssherpassword/g" -e "s/SEDrootpasswordSED/
$internal2_rootpassword/g" install_template.sh > install.sh

# sed the sshd_config file
sed -e "s/SEDsshportSED/$sshport/g" -e "s/SEDsshuserSED/
$sshuser/g" sshd_config_template > sshd_config

# make the script executable
chmod +x install.sh

# send required files
echo "transferring files"
scp -i "$ibn".pem install.sh ec2-user@$ip_address:
scp -i "$ibn".pem sshd_config ec2-user@$ip_address:
scp -i "$ibn".pem rsyslog.conf ec2-user@$ip_address:
echo "transferred files"

# remove sent files
rm -f install.sh
rm -f sshd_config

# run the install script
ssh -i "$ibn".pem -t -o ConnectTimeout=60 -o BatchMode=yes ec2-
user@$ip_address sudo ./install.sh
```

```
echo
echo now install the Google Authenticator App on a smartphone
echo find the MFA KEY in the output above
echo and create an account on the App with Manual Entry
echo call it INTERNAL2
echo

echo make.sh for internal2 finished
```

This is the template for the install script which is run on internal2:

[chapter9/configure/data/internal2/install_template.sh]

```
#!/bin/bash

# this script changes the ssh user to ssher
# it hardens ssh
# it configures sshd to use a password and MFA
# it disables password-less 'sudo su'
# and requires the root password to do so
# it sets up rsyslog forwarding for authpriv.* to bastion
# it sets up yum to use squid on bastion

# the following strings are replaced:
# SEDsshuserSED
# SEDssherpasswordSED
# SEDrootpasswordSED

# configure and update yum
echo "proxy=http://10.0.0.10:3128" >> /etc/yum.conf
yum -y update

# add ssher user
groupadd SEDsshuserSED
useradd -g SEDsshuserSED SEDsshuserSED

# install expect
yum install -y expect

# change ssher's password with expect
echo "#!/usr/bin/expect -f" > expect.sh
echo "set timeout -1" >> expect.sh
echo "spawn passwd SEDsshuserSED" >> expect.sh
echo "expect \"New password:\"" >> expect.sh
echo "send \"SEDssherpasswordSED\n\";" >> expect.sh
echo "expect \"new password:\"" >> expect.sh
echo "send \"SEDssherpasswordSED\n\";" >> expect.sh
echo "interact" >> expect.sh
# run it
chmod +x expect.sh
./expect.sh
# remove it
rm -f expect.sh

# change root's password with expect
echo "#!/usr/bin/expect -f" > expect.sh
echo "set timeout -1" >> expect.sh
echo "spawn passwd root" >> expect.sh
echo "expect \"New password:\"" >> expect.sh
echo "send \"SEDrootpasswordSED\n\";" >> expect.sh
echo "expect \"new password:\"" >> expect.sh
echo "send \"SEDrootpasswordSED\n\";" >> expect.sh
```

```
echo "interact" >> expect.sh
# run it
chmod +x expect.sh
./expect.sh
# remove it
rm -f expect.sh

# erase expect
yum erase -y expect

# disable passwordless 'sudo su'
echo "SEDsshuserSED ALL = ALL" > /etc/sudoers.d/cloud-init

# require root password for 'sudo su' (not sshers's)
echo "Defaults targetpw" >> /etc/sudoers.d/cloud-init

# update sshd config
mv sshd_config /etc/ssh/sshd_config
chown root:root /etc/ssh/sshd_config
chmod 600 /etc/ssh/sshd_config

# remove sshd keys so ssher can't sign in with a key
rm -f /home/ec2-user/.ssh/authorized_keys
rm -f /root/.ssh/authorized_keys

# set the max concurrent ssh sessions
echo "SEDsshuserSED - maxlogins 1" >> /etc/security/limits.conf

# install mfa and pam modules
yum -y install google-authenticator.x86_64 pam.x86_64 pam-
devel.x86_64

# update pam config
echo "auth required pam_google_authenticator.so" >>
/etc/pam.d/sshd

# run the google authenticator for ssher
cd /home/SEDsshuserSED
google-authenticator --time-based --disallow-reuse --force
--rate-limit=1 --rate-time=60 --window-size=3 --quiet
--secret=/home/SEDsshuserSED/.google_authenticator
chown SEDsshuserSED:SEDsshuserSED .google_authenticator
chmod 400 .google_authenticator

# delete last 4 GOOJ codes
head -n 6 .google_authenticator > .google_authenticator2
mv -f .google_authenticator2 .google_authenticator
chown SEDsshuserSED:SEDsshuserSED .google_authenticator
chmod 400 .google_authenticator

# print out the codes
bits=($(cat .google_authenticator))
echo MFA KEY is ${bits[0]}
echo MFA GOOJ is ${bits[11]}

# restart sshd
# careful, sshd doesn't seem to like
# being restarted just as you end an ssh session
/etc/init.d/sshd restart
sleep 5

# configure rsyslog
cd /home/ec2-user
mv -f rsyslog.conf /etc/rsyslog.conf
chown root:root /etc/rsyslog.conf
chmod 400 /etc/rsyslog.conf

# delete this script
```

```
rm -f /home/ec2-user/install.sh
```

Again, I need the sshd_config file. The sshd_config file enforces
SSH MFA:

```
[chapter9/configure/data/internal2/sshd_config_templa
te]

    # hardened sshd config file
    # turns off Key access
    # turns on Password access
    # can also be used with MFA

    # the following strings are replaced:
    # SEDsshportSED

    # change the default ssh port
    Port SEDsshportSED

    # use better security protocols
    Protocol 2

    # log to authpriv
    SyslogFacility AUTHPRIV
    # log info messages
    LogLevel INFO

    # don't permit root login, or root forced commands
    PermitRootLogin no

    # TURNED OFF
    # where the access keys can be found
    #AuthorizedKeysFile   .ssh/authorized_keys

    # turn off various things
    HostbasedAuthentication no
    IgnoreRhosts yes
    X11Forwarding no

    # TURNED ON
    # password authentication
    PasswordAuthentication yes
    ChallengeResponseAuthentication yes

    # only SEDsshuserSED can sign in
    AllowUsers SEDsshuserSED
    # run user and session checks
    UsePAM yes

    # when last signed in
    PrintLastLog yes

    # more secure way to run the sshd
    UsePrivilegeSeparation sandbox

    # max seconds to sign in after connecting
    LoginGraceTime 60

    # max authentication attempts per connect
    # setting this any lower can cause problems
    MaxAuthTries 3

    # max multiplexed ssh sessions
    # to limit sesions add to /etc/security/limits.conf
```

```
#ssher - maxlogins 1
MaxSessions 1

# max concurrent unauthenticated sessions
MaxStartups 1

# check no world writeable files left in user home directory
StrictModes yes

# no empty passwords
PermitEmptyPasswords no

# allows scp
Subsystem       sftp      /usr/libexec/openssh/sftp-server
```

The rsyslog configuration is the same as for internal1:

[chapter9/configure/data/internal1/rsyslog.conf]

```
# rsyslog for webphp

$ModLoad imuxsock # provides support for local system logging
(e.g. via logger command)
$ModLoad imklog   # provides kernel logging support (previously
done by rklogd)
#$ModLoad immark  # provides --MARK-- message capability

$ActionFileDefaultTemplate RSYSLOG_TraditionalFileFormat

mail.*
-/var/log/maillog
cron.*
/var/log/cron
*.emerg                                                     *
uucp,news.crit
/var/log/spooler
local7.*
/var/log/boot.log

# send authpriv logs to the Bastion
$WorkDirectory /var/lib/rsyslog # where to place spool files
$ActionQueueFileName fwdRule1 # unique name prefix for spool
files
$ActionQueueMaxDiskSpace 1g   # 1gb space limit (use as much as
possible)
$ActionQueueSaveOnShutdown on # save messages to disk on shutdown
$ActionQueueType LinkedList   # run asynchronously
$ActionResumeRetryCount -1    # infinite retries if host is down
authpriv.* @@10.0.0.10:514

$IncludeConfig /etc/rsyslog.d/*.conf
```

This may seem complicated, but it is the nature of advanced scripting. It might take a while to get your tailored scripts working, but once it's done it works and it's 'documented'. And just imagine doing all that by hand! Then it breaks so you have to redo it a few months later - sure you've remembered everything? The scripts have.

So with configure.sh, you have a generic way to upload to the Bastion a main script (install.sh) and associated data files per internal server. If you're launching a farm with one or two 'types' of server, the folders will be mainly the same, except changing a few things like IP addresses and passwords. And even that could be automated.

Updating Internal Servers

Updating internal servers is different from configuring them. It's likely you'll need to update them often, whether to refresh yum software, update your website, perhaps take a database backup or any of the other one million things we like to do to our servers.

I'll show you how to update both new internal servers. To send the zip with required scripts to the Bastion and run it, you'll need 2 MFA codes. This would also work for many more internal servers using SSH Keys and would still only need 2 Bastion MFA codes. Because I set up SSH MFA on internal2, you'll need another 2 MFA codes to send to it and run on it. For simplicity, I'll just run a yum update and delete the ec2-user on each internal server. For your scripts, add files to the appropriate internal* folder, prepare them in make.sh, then send them to the internal server from make.sh and finally use them with install.sh. If you're using MFA on the internal server, you'll need to zip everything up to save on codes, so you'll be running a similar procedure to the one I used to upload to and run on the Bastion, but this time it will be from Bastion to internal server.

To run the whole process, cd to chapter9/update and use:

```
./update.sh
```

Don't forget, when you enter successive MFA codes for the same resource, they need to be different - no code reuse!

The update script is as follows:

```
[chapter9/update/update.sh]
```

```bash
#!/bin/bash

# this script updates the 2 internal servers

# it will zip up all the update/internal* folders
# eg internal1, internal2, ..., internalN
# and install.sh and a generated vars.sh
# then send this zip to the bastion with scp
# then install.sh will be run on the bastion

# this script needs to be called from chapter9/update directory
# with ./update.sh

# include chapter9 variables
cd ..
. ./vars.sh
cd update

# get my ip
myip=$(curl http://checkip.amazonaws.com/)
echo myip=$myip

# get ip of bastion
bastionip=$(aws ec2 describe-instances --filters Name=tag-
key,Values=instancename Name=tag-value,Values=bastion --output text
--query 'Reservations[*].Instances[*].PublicIpAddress')
echo bastionip=$bastionip

# allow ssh in sg
bastionsgid=$(aws ec2 describe-security-groups --filters
Name=tag-key,Values=sgname Name=tag-value,Values=bastionsg --output
text --query 'SecurityGroups[*].GroupId')
echo bastionsgid=$bastionsgid
aws ec2 authorize-security-group-ingress --group-id $bastionsgid
--protocol tcp --port $sshport --cidr $myip/32

# allow ssh access from bastion to internal1
internal1sgid=$(aws ec2 describe-security-groups --filters
Name=tag-key,Values=sgname Name=tag-value,Values=internal1sg
--output text --query 'SecurityGroups[*].GroupId')
echo internal1sgid=$internal1sgid
aws ec2 authorize-security-group-ingress --group-id
$internal1sgid --source-group $bastionsgid --protocol tcp --port
$sshport

# allow ssh access from bastion to internal2
internal2sgid=$(aws ec2 describe-security-groups --filters
Name=tag-key,Values=sgname Name=tag-value,Values=internal2sg
--output text --query 'SecurityGroups[*].GroupId')
echo internal2sgid=$internal2sgid
aws ec2 authorize-security-group-ingress --group-id
$internal2sgid --source-group $bastionsgid --protocol tcp --port
$sshport

# allow squid access from internal1 to bastion
aws ec2 authorize-security-group-ingress --group-id $bastionsgid
--source-group $internal1sgid --protocol tcp --port 3128

# allow squid access from internal2 to bastion
aws ec2 authorize-security-group-ingress --group-id $bastionsgid
--source-group $internal2sgid --protocol tcp --port 3128

# make a vars.sh file from globals.sh and chapter9/vars.sh
# we are in chapter9/update directory
cat ../../globals.sh > data/vars.sh
tail -n +5 ../vars.sh >> data/vars.sh
chmod +x data/vars.sh
```

```
# make the zip
cd data
zip -r upload.zip vars.sh install.sh internal*
cd ..

# remove temporary vars.sh file
rm -f data/vars.sh

# get an mfa code
read -s -p "MFA code for Bastion:" mfacode

# make and run expect script to upload zip
echo "#!/usr/bin/expect -f" > expect.sh
echo "set timeout -1" >> expect.sh
echo "spawn scp -P $sshport -o PubkeyAuthentication=no
data/upload.zip $sshuser@$bastionip:" >> expect.sh
echo "expect \"Password:\"" >> expect.sh
echo "send \"$bastion_ssherpassword\n\"" >> expect.sh
echo "expect \"Verification code:\"" >> expect.sh
echo "send \"$mfacode\n\"" >> expect.sh
echo "interact" >> expect.sh
#cat expect.sh
chmod +x expect.sh
./expect.sh
rm expect.sh

# remove zip
rm -f data/upload.zip

# kill any ssh agents and start a new one
kill $(pgrep ssh-agent)
eval `ssh-agent -s`

# add internal1 key to ssh agent
# internal2 is now on MFA
cd ../internal/credentials
ssh-add -D
ssh-add internal1.pem
cd ../../configure

# get an mfa code
read -s -p "MFA code for Bastion:" mfacode

# make and run expect script to run zip
# the ssh -A option enables agent forwarding
# note agent forwarding does not work if you 'sudo su'
echo "#!/usr/bin/expect -f" > expect.sh
echo "set timeout -1" >> expect.sh
echo "spawn ssh -p $sshport -A -o PubkeyAuthentication=no
$sshuser@$bastionip" >> expect.sh
echo "expect \"Password:\"" >> expect.sh
echo "send \"$bastion_ssherpassword\n\"" >> expect.sh
echo "expect \"Verification code:\"" >> expect.sh
echo "send \"$mfacode\n\"" >> expect.sh

# we use a little trick to sudo su and then exit
# so we can use it later with no password
echo "expect \"]\"" >> expect.sh
echo "send \"sudo su\n\"" >> expect.sh
echo "expect \"password for root:\"" >> expect.sh
echo "send \"$bastion_rootpassword\n\"" >> expect.sh
echo "expect \"]\"" >> expect.sh
echo "send \"exit\n\"" >> expect.sh

echo "expect \"]\"" >> expect.sh
echo "send \"rm -f -r upload\n\"" >> expect.sh
echo "expect \"]\"" >> expect.sh
echo "send \"mkdir upload\n\"" >> expect.sh
```

```
echo "expect \"]\"" >> expect.sh
echo "send \"mv upload.zip upload\n\"" >> expect.sh
echo "expect \"]\"" >> expect.sh
echo "send \"cd upload\n\"" >> expect.sh
echo "expect \"]\"" >> expect.sh
echo "send \"unzip upload.zip\n\"" >> expect.sh

echo "expect \"]\"" >> expect.sh
echo "send \"ls -al\n\"" >> expect.sh
echo "expect \"]\"" >> expect.sh
echo "send \"chmod +x install.sh\n\"" >> expect.sh
echo "expect \"]\"" >> expect.sh
echo "send \". ./install.sh\n\"" >> expect.sh

# by using 'interact' here and not 'expect'ing anything
# install.sh can use expect normally and get user input for mfa
codes
echo "interact" >> expect.sh

# however, any further expects or send won't now work
# eg you can't do this:
#echo "expect \"]\"" >> expect.sh
#echo "send \"exit\n\"" >> expect.sh
#echo "interact" >> expect.sh

# this is why we call install.sh with
# . ./install.sh (not ./install.sh)
# so that it can 'exit' ssh

chmod +x expect.sh
./expect.sh
rm expect.sh

# remove internal keys from ssh agent
ssh-add -D

# kill it
kill $(pgrep ssh-agent)

# revoke ssh to bastion
aws ec2 revoke-security-group-ingress --group-id $bastionsgid
--protocol tcp --port $sshport --cidr $myip/32

# revoke ssh between bastion and internal1
aws ec2 revoke-security-group-ingress --group-id $internal1sgid
--source-group $bastionsgid --protocol tcp --port $sshport

# revoke ssh between bastion and internal2
aws ec2 revoke-security-group-ingress --group-id $internal2sgid
--source-group $bastionsgid --protocol tcp --port $sshport

# revoke squid access from internal1 to bastion
aws ec2 revoke-security-group-ingress --group-id $bastionsgid
--source-group $internal1sgid --protocol tcp --port 3128

# revoke access from internal2 to bastion
aws ec2 revoke-security-group-ingress --group-id $bastionsgid
--source-group $internal2sgid --protocol tcp --port 3128

echo revoked sg access

echo configuration done
```

The data folder used by the update script contains (as with the configure data folder) a generic install.sh script and a folder for each internal server. The data folder, along with chapter9/vars.sh, is zipped and sent to the Bastion. After unpacking, install.sh is executed, which does some housekeeping and executes make.sh in each internal* folder.

Here is 'install.sh' which is uploaded to and run on the Bastion:

[chapter9/update/data/install.sh]

```
#!/bin/bash

# this script is run on the bastion with expect
# it lists all folders beginning with 'internal'
# then runs make.sh from each folder
# would work for any number of folders

# squid already installed
sudo service squid start

# install expect (it's needed by the make.sh scripts that follow)
sudo yum -y install expect

# list internal* folders and loop
folders=$(ls -d internal*)
bits=($folders)
for i in "${bits[@]}"
do
 echo running $i/make.sh
 cd $i
 chmod +x make.sh
 ./make.sh
 cd ..
 echo finished $i/make.sh
done

# stop squid
sudo service squid stop

# remove expect
sudo yum -y erase expect

# cleanup
cd ~
rm -f -r *

echo finished install.sh on bastion

# exits from ssh
# because this script was called with '. ./install.sh'
exit
```

The internal1 folder contains a make.sh script, run to prepare and send files to internal1, then execute them.

[chapter9/update/data/internal1/make.sh]

```
#!/bin/bash
```

```
# this script is run on the Bastion
# it prepares the scripts to be run on internal1
# which will do a yum update
# and delete the ec2-user

# include variables
. ./../vars.sh

# name and ipaddress for internal1
ibn=internal1
ip_address=10.0.0.11

# show variables
echo internal1 variables
echo ibn: $ibn
echo ip address: $ip_address
echo new SSHD port: $sshport
echo ssh user: $sshuser
echo ssher password: $internal1_ssherpassword
echo root password: $internal1_rootpassword

# make the script executable
chmod +x install.sh

# send required files
echo "transferring files"
scp -i "$ibn".pem -P $sshport -o StrictHostKeyChecking=no
install.sh $sshuser@$ip_address:
echo "transferred files"

# use expect to run the script
echo "#!/usr/bin/expect -f" > expect.sh
echo "set timeout -1" >> expect.sh
echo "spawn ssh -i $ibn.pem -p $sshport $sshuser@$ip_address" >>
expect.sh
echo "expect \"]\"" >> expect.sh
echo "send \"sudo su\n\"" >> expect.sh
echo "expect \"password for root:\"" >> expect.sh
echo "send \"$internal1_rootpassword\n\"" >> expect.sh
echo "expect \"]\"" >> expect.sh
echo "send \"./install.sh\n\"" >> expect.sh
echo "expect \"finished install.sh on internal 1\"" >> expect.sh
echo "send \"exit\n\"" >> expect.sh
echo "expect \"]\"" >> expect.sh
echo "send \"exit\n\"" >> expect.sh
echo "interact" >> expect.sh
chmod +x expect.sh
./expect.sh
rm expect.sh

echo make.sh for internal1 finished
```

The 'install.sh' script, to be run on internal1 is also in update/data/internal1:

`[chapter9/update/data/internal1/install.sh]`

```
#!/bin/bash

# this script needs to be run on the instance
# simple demonstration of how to run a script to update an
internal server

echo running install.sh on internal 1
```

```
yum -y update

userdel -r ec2-user

echo finished install.sh on internal 1
```

The internal2 folder contains a make.sh script, run to prepare and send files to internal2, then execute them.

[chapter9/update/data/internal2/make.sh]

```
#!/bin/bash

# this script is run on the Bastion
# it prepares the scripts to be run on internal2
# which will do a yum update
# and delete the ec2-user
# internal2 now has SSH MFA and 'sudo su' password

# include variables
. ./../vars.sh

# name and ipaddress for internal2
ibn=internal2
ip_address=10.0.0.12

# show variables
echo internal2 variables
echo ibn: $ibn
echo ip address: $ip_address
echo new SSHD port: $sshport
echo ssh user: $sshuser
echo ssher password: $internal2_ssherpassword
echo root password: $internal2_rootpassword

# make the script executable
chmod +x install.sh

# make and run expect script to upload install.sh
echo "#!/usr/bin/expect -f" > expect.sh
echo "set timeout -1" >> expect.sh
echo "send_user \"MFA code for internal2: \"" >> expect.sh
echo "expect_user -re \"(.*)\n\"" >> expect.sh
echo "spawn scp -P $sshport -o PubkeyAuthentication=no -o
StrictHostKeyChecking=no install.sh $sshuser@$ip_address:" >>
expect.sh
echo "expect \"Password:\"" >> expect.sh
echo "send \"$internal2_ssherpassword\n\"" >> expect.sh
echo "expect \"Verification code:\"" >> expect.sh
echo 'send $expect_out(1,string)\n' >> expect.sh
echo "interact" >> expect.sh
chmod +x expect.sh
./expect.sh
rm expect.sh

# make and run expect script to run install.sh
echo "#!/usr/bin/expect -f" > expect.sh
echo "set timeout -1" >> expect.sh
echo "send_user \"MFA code for internal2: \"" >> expect.sh
echo "expect_user -re \"(.*)\n\"" >> expect.sh
echo "spawn ssh -p $sshport -o PubkeyAuthentication=no
$sshuser@$ip_address" >> expect.sh
echo "expect \"Password:\"" >> expect.sh
```

```
echo "send \"$internal2_ssherpassword\n\"" >> expect.sh
echo "expect \"Verification code:\"" >> expect.sh
echo 'send $expect_out(1,string)\n' >> expect.sh
echo "expect \"]\"" >> expect.sh
echo "send \"sudo su\n\"" >> expect.sh
echo "expect \"password for root:\"" >> expect.sh
echo "send \"$internal2_rootpassword\n\"" >> expect.sh
echo "expect \"]\"" >> expect.sh
echo "send \"./install.sh\n\"" >> expect.sh
echo "expect \"finished install.sh on internal 2\"" >> expect.sh
echo "send \"exit\n\"" >> expect.sh
echo "expect \"]\"" >> expect.sh
echo "send \"exit\n\"" >> expect.sh
echo "interact" >> expect.sh
chmod +x expect.sh
./expect.sh
rm expect.sh

echo make.sh for internal2 finished
```

The 'install.sh' script, to be run on internal2 is also in
update/data/internal2:

`[chapter9/update/data/internal2/install.sh]`

```
#!/bin/bash

# this script needs to be run on the instance as ec2-user
# simple demonstration of how to run a script to update an
internal server

echo running install.sh on internal 2

yum -y update

userdel -r ec2-user

echo finished install.sh on internal 2
```

Updating Internal Servers Part 2

OK, so I can tell you're a little disappointed by the simplicity of the
update scripts in the last section...

So in chapter9/update2 you can find more complicated ones which
simulate updating a web root on both internal servers.

The files chapter9/update2/update.sh and
chapter9/update2/data/install.sh are exactly the same as their
counterparts in the chapter9/update folder. So I won't list them in
an effort to save paper or bytes.

What has changed is that in the chapter9/update2/data/internal1 and chapter9/update2/data/internal2 folders, you'll find updated scripts and 'webroot' folders which contain dummy files for a web root update. The webroot folder is actually the same for both internal* folders, so if you wanted to be cool, you could rewrite the scripts to use a single copy of the 'webroot' folder...

The new internal1 make.sh script, run to prepare and send files to internal1, then execute them, is as follows:

[chapter9/update2/data/internal1/make.sh]

```bash
#!/bin/bash

# this script is run on the Bastion
# it prepares the scripts to be run on internal1
# which will do a yum update and update a phantom webroot

# include variables
. ./../vars.sh

# name and ipaddress for internal1
ibn=internal1
ip_address=10.0.0.11

# show variables
echo internal1 variables
echo ibn: $ibn
echo ip address: $ip_address
echo new SSHD port: $sshport
echo ssh user: $sshuser
echo ssher password: $internal1_ssherpassword
echo root password: $internal1_rootpassword

# make the script executable
chmod +x install.sh

# make the zip
zip -r upload.zip install.sh webroot

# send the zip
echo "transferring files"
scp -i "$ibn".pem -P $sshport -o StrictHostKeyChecking=no
upload.zip $sshuser@$ip_address:
echo "transferred files"

# delete the zip
rm -f upload.zip

# expect to unzip and run install.sh
echo "#!/usr/bin/expect -f" > expect.sh
echo "set timeout -1" >> expect.sh
echo "spawn ssh -i $ibn.pem -p $sshport $sshuser@$ip_address" >>
expect.sh
echo "expect \"]\"" >> expect.sh

echo "send \"rm -f -r upload\n\"" >> expect.sh
echo "expect \"]\"" >> expect.sh
echo "send \"mkdir upload\n\"" >> expect.sh
echo "expect \"]\"" >> expect.sh
```

```
echo "send \"mv upload.zip upload\n\"" >> expect.sh
echo "expect \"]\"" >> expect.sh
echo "send \"cd upload\n\"" >> expect.sh
echo "expect \"]\"" >> expect.sh
echo "send \"unzip upload.zip\n\"" >> expect.sh
echo "expect \"]\"" >> expect.sh
echo "send \"ls -al\n\"" >> expect.sh
echo "expect \"]\"" >> expect.sh
echo "send \"chmod +x install.sh\n\"" >> expect.sh
echo "expect \"]\"" >> expect.sh

# we can run install.sh and expect output
# because install.sh doesn't need user input
echo "send \"sudo su\n\"" >> expect.sh
echo "expect \"password for root:\"" >> expect.sh
echo "send \"$internal1_rootpassword\n\"" >> expect.sh
echo "expect \"]\"" >> expect.sh
echo "send \"./install.sh\n\"" >> expect.sh
echo "expect \"finished install.sh on internal 1\"" >> expect.sh
echo "send \"exit\n\"" >> expect.sh
echo "expect \"]\"" >> expect.sh
echo "send \"exit\n\"" >> expect.sh

echo "interact" >> expect.sh

chmod +x expect.sh
./expect.sh
rm expect.sh

echo make.sh for internal1 finished
```

The new 'install.sh' script, to be run on internal1 is as follows:

[chapter9/update2/data/internal1/install.sh]

```
#!/bin/bash

# this script needs to be run on the instance
# simple demonstration of how to run a script to update an
internal server

echo running install.sh on internal 1

yum -y update

rm -f -r /var/www/html
mkdir -p /var/www/html
mv webroot/* /var/www/html
ls /var/www/html

echo finished install.sh on internal 1
```

The new internal2 make.sh script, run to prepare and send files to internal2, then execute them, is as follows:

[chapter9/update2/data/internal2/make.sh]

```
#!/bin/bash

# this script is run on the Bastion
# it prepares the scripts to be run on internal2
```

```
# which will do a yum update and update a phantom webroot
# internal2 now has SSH MFA and 'sudo su' password

# include variables
. ./../vars.sh

# name and ipaddress for internal2
ibn=internal2
ip_address=10.0.0.12

# show variables
echo internal2 variables
echo ibn: $ibn
echo ip address: $ip_address
echo new SSHD port: $sshport
echo ssh user: $sshuser
echo ssher password: $internal2_ssherpassword
echo root password: $internal2_rootpassword

# make the script executable
chmod +x install.sh

# make the zip
zip -r upload.zip install.sh webroot

# make and run expect script to upload zip
echo "#!/usr/bin/expect -f" > expect.sh
echo "set timeout -1" >> expect.sh
echo "send_user \"MFA code for internal2: \"" >> expect.sh
echo "expect_user -re \"(.*)\n\"" >> expect.sh
echo "spawn scp -P $sshport -o PubkeyAuthentication=no -o
StrictHostKeyChecking=no upload.zip $sshuser@$ip_address:" >>
expect.sh
echo "expect \"Password:\"" >> expect.sh
echo "send \"$internal2_ssherpassword\n\"" >> expect.sh
echo "expect \"Verification code:\"" >> expect.sh
echo 'send $expect_out(1,string)\n' >> expect.sh
echo "interact" >> expect.sh
chmod +x expect.sh
./expect.sh
rm expect.sh

# delete the zip
rm -f upload.zip

# use expect to unzip and run install.sh
echo "#!/usr/bin/expect -f" > expect.sh
echo "set timeout -1" >> expect.sh
echo "send_user \"MFA code for internal2: \"" >> expect.sh
echo "expect_user -re \"(.*)\n\"" >> expect.sh
echo "spawn ssh -p $sshport -o PubkeyAuthentication=no
$sshuser@$ip_address" >> expect.sh
echo "expect \"Password:\"" >> expect.sh
echo "send \"$internal2_ssherpassword\n\"" >> expect.sh
echo "expect \"Verification code:\"" >> expect.sh
echo 'send $expect_out(1,string)\n' >> expect.sh
echo "expect \"]\"" >> expect.sh
echo "send \"sudo su\n\"" >> expect.sh
echo "expect \"password for root:\"" >> expect.sh
echo "send \"$internal2_rootpassword\n\"" >> expect.sh
echo "expect \"]\"" >> expect.sh

echo "send \"rm -f -r upload\n\"" >> expect.sh
echo "expect \"]\"" >> expect.sh
echo "send \"mkdir upload\n\"" >> expect.sh
echo "expect \"]\"" >> expect.sh
echo "send \"mv upload.zip upload\n\"" >> expect.sh
echo "expect \"]\"" >> expect.sh
```

```
echo "send \"cd upload\n\"" >> expect.sh
echo "expect \"]\"" >> expect.sh
echo "send \"unzip upload.zip\n\"" >> expect.sh
echo "expect \"]\"" >> expect.sh
echo "send \"ls -al\n\"" >> expect.sh
echo "expect \"]\"" >> expect.sh
echo "send \"chmod +x install.sh\n\"" >> expect.sh
echo "expect \"]\"" >> expect.sh

# we can run install.sh and expect output
# because install.sh doesn't need user input
echo "send \"./install.sh\n\"" >> expect.sh
echo "expect \"finished install.sh on internal 2\"" >> expect.sh
echo "send \"exit\n\"" >> expect.sh
echo "expect \"]\"" >> expect.sh
echo "send \"exit\n\"" >> expect.sh
echo "interact" >> expect.sh

chmod +x expect.sh
./expect.sh
rm expect.sh

echo make.sh for internal2 finished
```

The new 'install.sh' script, to be run on internal2 is as follows:

[chapter9/update2/data/internal2/install.sh]

```
#!/bin/bash

# this script needs to be run on the instance
# simple demonstration of how to run a script to update an
internal server

echo running install.sh on internal 2

yum -y update

rm -f -r /var/www/html
mkdir -p /var/www/html
mv webroot/* /var/www/html
ls /var/www/html

echo finished install.sh on internal 2
```

All the files in both 'webroot' folders are dummies.

The Master Script

If you've got this far, well done! For your convenience, here's a master script which brings it all together. It builds a Bastion, builds 2 internal servers, configures the internal servers via the Bastion and then updates the internal servers via the Bastion. To test it out, delete any instances, Security Groups and Keys created in Chapter 9, then from the chapter9 directory use:

```
./master.sh
```

This is the file listing:

```
[chapter9/master.sh]

  #!/bin/bash

  # this is the chapter 9 master script
  # it builds a bastion (from chapter 8 scripts)
  # then 2 internal servers
  # next, it configures the 2 internal servers
  # next, it updates the 2 internal servers
  # next, it updates the 2 internal servers more substantially

  # this script needs to be called from chapter9 directory

  echo $'\n\n*****\n CHAPTER 9 MASTER SCRIPT\n*****\n\n'

  # build a bastion
  cd bastion
  echo $'\n\n*****\n BUILDING BASTION\n*****\n\n'
  ./make.sh
  echo $'\n\n*****\n BUILT BASTION\n*****\n\n'
  cd ..

  # build internal servers
  cd internal
  echo $'\n\n*****\n BUILDING INTERNAL1\n*****\n\n'
  ./make.sh internal1 10.0.0.11
  echo $'\n\n*****\n BUILT INTERNAL1\n*****\n\n'
  echo $'\n\n*****\n BUILDING INTERNAL2\n*****\n\n'
  ./make.sh internal2 10.0.0.12
  echo $'\n\n*****\n BUILT INTERNAL2\n*****\n\n'
  cd ..

  # configure internal servers
  cd configure
  echo $'\n\n*****\n CONFIGURING\n*****\n\n'
  ./configure.sh
  echo $'\n\n*****\n CONFIGURED\n*****\n\n'
  cd ..

  echo Sort out Internal2 MFA Code
  echo THEN press a key
  read -n 1 -s

  # update internal servers
  cd update
  echo $'\n\n*****\n UPDATING\n*****\n\n'
  ./update.sh
  echo $'\n\n*****\n UPDATED\n*****\n\n'
  cd ..

  # update internal servers more substantially
  cd update2
  echo $'\n\n*****\n UPDATING PART 2\n*****\n\n'
  ./update.sh
  echo $'\n\n*****\n UPDATED PART 2\n*****\n\n'
  cd ..

  echo $'\n\n*****\n CHAPTER 9 MASTER SCRIPT FINISHED\n*****\n\n'
```

Automating Access

When you've built all the servers above, you can connect directly to each server with the following scripts.

This is the connect script to get a shell on the Bastion Host. It's mainly similar to other connect scripts earlier in the book which automate MFA and the 'sudo su' password with expect.

[chapter9/connect/connect_bastion.sh]

```
#!/bin/bash

# open an ssh session to the chapter 9 bastion
# which has keys disabled and MFA enabled
# then automate the 'sudo su' password entry

# include chapter9 variables
cd ..
. ./vars.sh
cd connect

# show variables
echo bastion base name: $ibn
echo new SSHD port: $sshport
echo ssh user: $sshuser
echo ssher password: $bastion_ssherpassword
echo root password: $bastion_rootpassword

# if you want to make this script standalone
# (ie not relying on vars.sh)
# comment out '. ./vars.sh' above and define the variables here,
eg:
#ibn=sshpass
#sshport=38142
#sshuser=ssher
#bastion_ssherpassword=1234
#bastion_rootpassword=123456

# if you wanted to have a typed password,
# ie you don't want to encode the password in this script,
# you could use:
#read -s -p "ssher password:" bastion_ssherpassword
#read -s -p "root password:" bastion_rootpassword
# also remove the declarations above

echo "connecting to instance $ibn on $sshport with user $sshuser"

# get my ip
myip=$(curl http://checkip.amazonaws.com/)
echo myip=$myip

# get ip of server
ip_address=$(aws ec2 describe-instances --filters Name=tag-key,Values=instancename Name=tag-value,Values="$ibn" --output text --query 'Reservations[*].Instances[*].PublicIpAddress')
echo ip_address=$ip_address

# allow ssh in sg
sgid=$(aws ec2 describe-security-groups --filters Name=tag-
```

```
key,Values=sgname Name=tag-value,Values="$ibn"sg --output text
--query 'SecurityGroups[*].GroupId')
  echo sgid=$sgid
  aws ec2 authorize-security-group-ingress --group-id $sgid
--protocol tcp --port $sshport --cidr $myip/32

  # get an mfa code
  read -s -p "mfa code:" mfacode

  # make and run expect script
  # use timeout -1 for no timeout
  echo "#!/usr/bin/expect -f" > expect.sh
  echo "set timeout -1" >> expect.sh
  echo "spawn ssh -p $sshport $sshuser@$ip_address" >> expect.sh
  echo "expect \"Password:\"" >> expect.sh
  echo "send \"$bastion_ssherpassword\n\"" >> expect.sh
  echo "expect \"Verification code:\"" >> expect.sh
  echo "send \"$mfacode\n\"" >> expect.sh
  echo "expect \"]\"" >> expect.sh
  echo "send \"sudo su\n\"" >> expect.sh
  echo "expect \"password for root:\"" >> expect.sh
  echo "send \"$bastion_rootpassword\n\"" >> expect.sh
  echo "interact" >> expect.sh
  chmod +x expect.sh
  ./expect.sh
  rm expect.sh

  # script now waits for double 'exit' (because it did 'sudo su')

  # remove ssh in sg
  aws ec2 revoke-security-group-ingress --group-id $sgid --protocol
tcp --port $sshport --cidr $myip/32
  echo "revoked sg access"
```

This is the connect script to get a shell on internal1. internal1 uses
SSH Keys and needs the root password for 'sudo su'. I use SSH
Agent Forwarding to open a connection to Bastion and then
forward the internal1.pem key in order to ssh to internal1. With
expect, this is automated, as is the 'sudo su' password on internal1.

[chapter9/connect/connect_internal1.sh]

```
#!/bin/bash

# open an ssh session to the chapter 9 internal1
# which has keys enabled
# using agent forwarding
# then automate the 'sudo su' password entry

# include chapter9 variables
cd ..
. ./vars.sh
cd connect

# set internal1 base name
iibn+=1

# show variables
echo bastion base name: $ibn
echo internal1 base name: $iibn
echo new SSHD port: $sshport
echo ssh user: $sshuser
```

```
echo bastion ssher password: $bastion_ssherpassword
echo bastion root password: $bastion_rootpassword
echo internal1 ssher password: $internal1_ssherpassword
echo internal1 root password: $internal1_rootpassword

echo "connecting to instance $iibn via $ibn on $sshport with user
$sshuser"

# kill any ssh agents and start a new one
kill $(pgrep ssh-agent)
eval `ssh-agent -s`

# add internal keys to ssh agent
cd ../internal/credentials
ssh-add -D
ssh-add internal1.pem
cd ../../connect

# get my ip
myip=$(curl http://checkip.amazonaws.com/)
echo myip=$myip

# get ip of server
ip_address=$(aws ec2 describe-instances --filters Name=tag-
key,Values=instancename Name=tag-value,Values="$ibn" --output text
--query 'Reservations[*].Instances[*].PublicIpAddress')
echo ip_address=$ip_address

# allow ssh in bastion sg
bastionsgid=$(aws ec2 describe-security-groups --filters
Name=tag-key,Values=sgname Name=tag-value,Values="$ibn"sg --output
text --query 'SecurityGroups[*].GroupId')
echo bastionsgid=$bastionsgid
aws ec2 authorize-security-group-ingress --group-id $bastionsgid
--protocol tcp --port $sshport --cidr $myip/32

# allow ssh access from bastion to internal1
internal1sgid=$(aws ec2 describe-security-groups --filters
Name=tag-key,Values=sgname Name=tag-value,Values="$iibn"sg --output
text --query 'SecurityGroups[*].GroupId')
echo internal1sgid=$internal1sgid
aws ec2 authorize-security-group-ingress --group-id
$internal1sgid --source-group $bastionsgid --protocol tcp --port
$sshport

# get an mfa code
read -s -p "mfa code:" mfacode

# make and run expect script
# use timeout -1 for no timeout
echo "#!/usr/bin/expect -f" > expect.sh
echo "set timeout -1" >> expect.sh
echo "spawn ssh -p $sshport -A $sshuser@$ip_address" >> expect.sh
echo "expect \"Password:\"" >> expect.sh
echo "send \"$bastion_ssherpassword\n\"" >> expect.sh
echo "expect \"Verification code:\"" >> expect.sh
echo "send \"$mfacode\n\"" >> expect.sh
echo "expect \"]\"" >> expect.sh
echo "send \"ssh -p $sshport -i internal1.pem
$sshuser@10.0.0.11\n\"" >> expect.sh
echo "expect \"]\"" >> expect.sh
echo "send \"sudo su\n\"" >> expect.sh
echo "expect \"password for root:\"" >> expect.sh
echo "send \"$internal1_rootpassword\n\"" >> expect.sh
echo "interact" >> expect.sh
chmod +x expect.sh
./expect.sh
rm expect.sh
```

```
# script now waits for triple 'exit'
# one for internal1 'sudo su', one for internal1 ssh, one for
bastion ssh

# remove internal keys from ssh agent
ssh-add -D

# kill it
kill $(pgrep ssh-agent)

# remove bastion ssh in sg
aws ec2 revoke-security-group-ingress --group-id $bastionsgid
--protocol tcp --port $sshport --cidr $myip/32

# remove internal1 ssh access from bastion
aws ec2 revoke-security-group-ingress --group-id $internal1sgid
--source-group $bastionsgid --protocol tcp --port $sshport

echo "revoked sg access"
```

This is the connect script to get a shell on internal2. internal2 is
configured with MFA for SSH and needs the root password for
'sudo su'. With expect, I automate the first ssh to the Bastion (with
MFA code) and then automate a second ssh command and
authentication (with the second MFA code). The 'sudo su'
password on internal2 is also automated in.

[chapter9/connect/connect_internal2.sh]

```
#!/bin/bash

# open an ssh session to the chapter 9 internal2
# which is using ssh MFA
# then automate the 'sudo su' password entry

# include chapter9 variables
cd ..
. ./vars.sh
cd connect

# set internal2 base name
iibn+=2

# show variables
echo bastion base name: $ibn
echo internal2 base name: $iibn
echo new SSHD port: $sshport
echo ssh user: $sshuser
echo bastion ssher password: $bastion_ssherpassword
echo bastion root password: $bastion_rootpassword
echo internal2 ssher password: $internal2_ssherpassword
echo internal2 root password: $internal2_rootpassword

echo "connecting to instance $iibn via $ibn on $sshport with user
$sshuser"

# remove any ssh agent keys
ssh-add -D

# get my ip
```

```
myip=$(curl http://checkip.amazonaws.com/)
echo myip=$myip

# get ip of server
ip_address=$(aws ec2 describe-instances --filters Name=tag-
key,Values=instancename Name=tag-value,Values="$ibn" --output text
--query 'Reservations[*].Instances[*].PublicIpAddress')
echo ip_address=$ip_address

# allow ssh in bastion sg
bastionsgid=$(aws ec2 describe-security-groups --filters
Name=tag-key,Values=sgname Name=tag-value,Values="$ibn"sg --output
text --query 'SecurityGroups[*].GroupId')
echo bastionsgid=$bastionsgid
aws ec2 authorize-security-group-ingress --group-id $bastionsgid
--protocol tcp --port $sshport --cidr $myip/32

# allow ssh access from bastion to internal2
internal2sgid=$(aws ec2 describe-security-groups --filters
Name=tag-key,Values=sgname Name=tag-value,Values="$iibn"sg --output
text --query 'SecurityGroups[*].GroupId')
echo internal2sgid=$internal2sgid
aws ec2 authorize-security-group-ingress --group-id
$internal2sgid --source-group $bastionsgid --protocol tcp --port
$sshport

# get mfa codes
read -s -p "bastion mfa code:" mfacode1
echo
read -s -p "internal2 mfa code:" mfacode2

# make and run expect script
# use timeout -1 for no timeout
echo "#!/usr/bin/expect -f" > expect.sh
echo "set timeout -1" >> expect.sh
echo "spawn ssh -p $sshport $sshuser@$ip_address" >> expect.sh
echo "expect \"Password:\"" >> expect.sh
echo "send \"$bastion_ssherpassword\n\"" >> expect.sh
echo "expect \"Verification code:\"" >> expect.sh
echo "send \"$mfacode1\n\"" >> expect.sh
echo "expect \"]\"" >> expect.sh
echo "send \"ssh -p $sshport $sshuser@10.0.0.12\n\"" >> expect.sh
echo "expect \"Password:\"" >> expect.sh
echo "send \"$internal2_ssherpassword\n\"" >> expect.sh
echo "expect \"Verification code:\"" >> expect.sh
echo "send \"$mfacode2\n\"" >> expect.sh
echo "expect \"]\"" >> expect.sh
echo "send \"sudo su\n\"" >> expect.sh
echo "expect \"password for root:\"" >> expect.sh
echo "send \"$internal2_rootpassword\n\"" >> expect.sh
echo "interact" >> expect.sh
chmod +x expect.sh
./expect.sh
rm expect.sh

# script now waits for triple 'exit'
# one for internal2 'sudo su', one for internal2 ssh, one for
bastion ssh

# remove bastion ssh in sg
aws ec2 revoke-security-group-ingress --group-id $bastionsgid
--protocol tcp --port $sshport --cidr $myip/32

# remove internal2 ssh access from bastion
aws ec2 revoke-security-group-ingress --group-id $internal2sgid
--source-group $bastionsgid --protocol tcp --port $sshport

echo "revoked sg access"
```

Note that you can't ssh connect simultaneously to more than one server (whether it be Bastion, internal1 or internal2), because on the Bastion, in /etc/security/limits.conf, maxlogins for the ssher user is set to 1. For development and testing, feel free to change this setting on the Bastion to 2 or 3. However, for maximum security, it should be set to 1 on a Production System.

Well, that about does it for the 2 level network build. I hope the above scripts and setups prove useful in your own networks.

Appendix A - VPC

All the scripts in this book rely on a VPC which has been made with the following script:

[appendixa/vpc.sh]

```
#!/bin/bash

# makes a vpc

# include gobal variables like vpc name and deploy zones
. ./../globals.sh

# make a new vpc with a master 10.0.0.0/16 subnet
vpc_id=$(aws ec2 create-vpc --cidr-block 10.0.0.0/16 --output
text --query 'Vpc.VpcId')
echo vpc_id=$vpc_id

# enable dns support
aws ec2 modify-vpc-attribute --vpc-id $vpc_id --enable-dns-
support
aws ec2 modify-vpc-attribute --vpc-id $vpc_id --enable-dns-
hostnames

# tag the vpc
aws ec2 create-tags --resources $vpc_id --tags
Key=vpcname,Value=$vpcname

# wait for the vpc
echo -n "waiting for vpc..."
while state=$(aws ec2 describe-vpcs --filters Name=tag-
key,Values=vpcname --filters Name=tag-value,Values=$vpcname
--output text --query 'Vpcs[*].State'); test "$state" = "pending";
do
    echo -n . ; sleep 3;
    done; echo " $state"

# create an internet gateway (to allow access out to the
internet)
igw=$(aws ec2 create-internet-gateway --output text --query
'InternetGateway.InternetGatewayId')
echo igw=$igw

# attach the igw to the vpc
echo attaching igw
aws ec2 attach-internet-gateway --internet-gateway-id $igw --vpc-
id $vpc_id

# get the route table id for the vpc (we need it later)
rtb_id=$(aws ec2 describe-route-tables --filters Name=vpc-
id,Values=$vpc_id --output text --query
'RouteTables[*].RouteTableId')
echo rtb_id=$rtb_id

# create our main subnets
# we use 10.0.0.0/24 as our main subnet and 10.0.10.0/24 as a
backup for multi-az rds
subnet_id=$(aws ec2 create-subnet --vpc-id $vpc_id --cidr-block
10.0.0.0/24 --availability-zone $deployzone --output text --query
'Subnet.SubnetId')
```

```
echo subnet_id=$subnet_id
# tag this subnet
aws ec2 create-tags --resources $subnet_id --tags
Key=subnet,Value=1
# associate this subnet with our route table
aws ec2 associate-route-table --subnet-id $subnet_id --route-
table-id $rtb_id
# now the 10.0.10.0/24 subnet in our secondary deployment zone
subnet_id=$(aws ec2 create-subnet --vpc-id $vpc_id --cidr-block
10.0.10.0/24 --availability-zone $deployzone2 --output text --query
'Subnet.SubnetId')
echo subnet_id=$subnet_id
# tag this subnet
aws ec2 create-tags --resources $subnet_id --tags
Key=subnet,Value=2
# associate this subnet with our route table
aws ec2 associate-route-table --subnet-id $subnet_id --route-
table-id $rtb_id

# create a route out from our route table to the igw
echo creating route from igw
aws ec2 create-route --route-table-id $rtb_id --gateway-id $igw
--destination-cidr-block 0.0.0.0/0

# done
echo vpc setup done
```

You should run the script by 'cd'ing to 'appendixa' and using:

```
./vpc.sh
```

For this script to work, you will need to edit global.sh and make sure the VPC name is unique and that the deployment zones are valid and match the region you used in 'aws configure'. So, if you used 'us-west-1' as you region with 'aws configure', in globals.sh you would use:

```
deployzone=us-west-1a
deployzone2=us-west-1c
```

Note that 'us-west-1b' was unavailable at the time of publishing. Run the command and if you get an error, try a different zone. Just remember to delete the failed VPC first. It is possible to do this with AWS CLI, but it's an involved process. Deleting VPCs or partial VPCs is much easier from the AWS Console, which deletes everything in one go. You can find more on regions and zones at **http://docs.aws.amazon.com/AWSEC2/latest/UserGuide/using-regions-availability-zones.html**.

The reason I set up 2 subnets in different Availability Zones is that this is needed by things like Multi-AZ RDS deployments, so best to do it properly from the start.

I think it's a good idea to work with a new VPC rather than the default VPC because you might have more than one VPC. In that case, code written to operate in the default VPC will need substantial adaptation to make it work for a different VPC. VPCs are free so make your own and use it. Then if you need to operate in a different VPC, all you need to do is change the VPC name variable and make the new VPC.

Appendix B - Fun with Expect

In Chapter 9, I took the use of the very handy 'expect' command to a new level by using nested expect scripts. It's worthwhile to spend a little time to understand expect fully as it is one of the most useful tools for the advanced automator.

There follow a series of scripts which show what you can do with expect. To use them, cd to the 'appendixb' directory and use './expectN.sh' where N is the number of the example. 'expect' is installed by default on OSX, and on linux you can use:

```
sudo yum -y install expect
```

Normally, because expect would be quite useful to a hacker, when I've finished with it, I deinstall it with:

```
sudo yum -y erase expect
```

Here is the first example which shows how to get user input from within an expect script:

[appendixb/expect1.sh]

```
#!/usr/bin/expect -f

# this script demos how to use expect
# to get user input and print it

set timeout -1
send_user "code: "
expect_user -re "(.*)\n"
send_user "you typed code: $expect_out(1,string)\n"
```

Output:

[appendixb/expect1.txt]

```
$ ./expect1.sh
code: 111
you typed code: 111
```

Example 2 creates 2 expect scripts. The first prompts for input, then calls the second which also prompts for input. What is interesting is that you can nest expect scripts perfectly well.

[appendixb/expect2.sh]

```
#!/bin/bash

# this script demos nested expects
# ex1.sh prompts for a string
# then spawns ex2.sh
# ex2.sh also prompts for a string

echo "#!/usr/bin/expect -f" > ex1.sh
echo "set timeout -1" >> ex1.sh
echo "send_user \"code1: \"" >> ex1.sh
echo "expect_user -re \"(.*)\n\"" >> ex1.sh
echo 'send_user "you typed code1: $expect_out(1,string)\n"' >>
ex1.sh
echo "spawn ./ex2.sh" >> ex1.sh
echo "interact" >> ex1.sh

echo
echo ex1.sh file:
cat ex1.sh
echo

echo "#!/usr/bin/expect -f" > ex2.sh
echo "set timeout -1" >> ex2.sh
echo "send_user \"code2: \"" >> ex2.sh
echo "expect_user -re \"(.*)\n\"" >> ex2.sh
echo 'send_user "you typed code2: $expect_out(1,string)\n"' >>
ex2.sh

echo
echo ex2.sh file:
cat ex2.sh
echo

chmod +x ex1.sh
chmod +x ex2.sh
./ex1.sh
rm ex1.sh
rm ex2.sh

echo expect2.sh finished
```

Output:

[appendixb/expect2.txt]

```
$ ./expect2.sh

ex1.sh file:
#!/usr/bin/expect -f
set timeout -1
send_user "code1: "
expect_user -re "(.*)\n"
send_user "you typed code1: $expect_out(1,string)\n"
spawn ./ex2.sh
interact

ex2.sh file:
```

```
#!/usr/bin/expect -f
set timeout -1
send_user "code2: "
expect_user -re "(.*)\n"
send_user "you typed code2: $expect_out(1,string)\n"

code1: 1111
you typed code1: 1111
spawn ./ex2.sh
code2: 2222
you typed code2: 2222
expect2.sh finished
```

Example 3 again creates 2 expect scripts. The first prompts for input, then calls the second which also prompts for input. However, this time the first script fills out the prompt in the second script.

[appendixb/expect3.sh]

```
#!/bin/bash

# this script demos nested expects
# ex1.sh prompts for a string
# then spawns ex2.sh
# ex2.sh also prompts for a string
# but ex1.sh auto fills it out

echo "#!/usr/bin/expect -f" > ex1.sh
echo "set timeout -1" >> ex1.sh
echo "send_user \"code1: \"" >> ex1.sh
echo "expect_user -re \"(.*)\n\"" >> ex1.sh
echo 'send_user "you typed code1: $expect_out(1,string)\n"' >>
ex1.sh
echo "spawn ./ex2.sh" >> ex1.sh
echo "expect \"code2: \"" >> ex1.sh
echo 'send $expect_out(1,string)\n' >> ex1.sh
echo "interact" >> ex1.sh

echo
echo ex1.sh file:
cat ex1.sh
echo

echo "#!/usr/bin/expect -f" > ex2.sh
echo "set timeout -1" >> ex2.sh
echo "send_user \"code2: \"" >> ex2.sh
echo "expect_user -re \"(.*)\n\"" >> ex2.sh
echo 'send_user "ex1.sh typed code2: $expect_out(1,string)\n"' >>
ex2.sh

echo
echo ex2.sh file:
cat ex2.sh
echo

chmod +x ex1.sh
chmod +x ex2.sh
./ex1.sh
rm ex1.sh
rm ex2.sh
```

```
echo expect3.sh finished
```

Output:

[appendixb/expect3.txt]

```
$ ./expect3.sh

ex1.sh file:
#!/usr/bin/expect -f
set timeout -1
send_user "code1: "
expect_user -re "(.*)\n"
send_user "you typed code1: $expect_out(1,string)\n"
spawn ./ex2.sh
expect "code2:
send $expect_out(1,string)\n
interact

ex2.sh file:
#!/usr/bin/expect -f
set timeout -1
send_user "code2: "
expect_user -re "(.*)\n"
send_user "ex1.sh typed code2: $expect_out(1,string)\n"

code1: 1111
you typed code1: 1111
spawn ./ex2.sh
code2: 1111
ex1.sh typed code2: 1111
expect3.sh finish
```

Now things get interesting. Example 4 runs the third example twice. The first time, it works because I 'spawn' and then 'interact'. The second time, it hangs, because I 'spawn' then 'expect' then 'interact'. The use of the 'expect' command means getting user input in the nested script won't work.

[appendixb/expect4.sh]

```
#!/usr/bin/expect -f

# this script demos how to use nested expect
# by calling expect3.sh with expect

set timeout -1

# this works

spawn ./expect3.sh
interact

send_user "\nsecond run\n"

# this hangs because the expect here interferes
# with nested expect_user
```

AWS Scripted 2   210

```
spawn ./expect3.sh
expect "expect3.sh finished"
interact
```

Output:

```
[appendixb/expect4.txt]

$ ./expect4.sh
spawn ./expect3.sh

ex1.sh file:
#!/usr/bin/expect -f
set timeout -1
send_user "code1: "
expect_user -re "(.*)\n"
send_user "you typed code1: $expect_out(1,string)\n"
spawn ./ex2.sh
expect "code2: "
send $expect_out(1,string)\n
interact


ex2.sh file:
#!/usr/bin/expect -f
set timeout -1
send_user "code2: "
expect_user -re "(.*)\n"
send_user "ex1.sh typed code2: $expect_out(1,string)\n"

code1: 1111
you typed code1: 1111
spawn ./ex2.sh
code2: 1111
ex1.sh typed code2: 1111
expect3.sh finished

second run
spawn ./expect3.sh

ex1.sh file:
#!/usr/bin/expect -f
set timeout -1
send_user "code1: "
expect_user -re "(.*)\n"
send_user "you typed code1: $expect_out(1,string)\n"
spawn ./ex2.sh
expect "code2: "
send $expect_out(1,string)\n
interact


ex2.sh file:
#!/usr/bin/expect -f
set timeout -1
send_user "code2: "
expect_user -re "(.*)\n"
send_user "ex1.sh typed code2: $expect_out(1,string)\n"

code1: 2222
^C
```

It's vital to understand this point when dealing with MFA. The reason is you often need to get user input from within a nested expect script. For example: you obtained a Bastion MFA code and 'expect'ed your way in with shh; now you want to ssh to an internal server with MFA, so you need to prompt for another MFA code (for the internal server); but this will fail if you are 'expect'ing output with the top level expect script.

The last example uses 2 scripts to show how this works with the bash 'read' command. expect5.sh calls expect6.sh twice, once correctly and then incorrectly. The second call hangs.

[appendixb/expect5.sh]

```
#!/usr/bin/expect -f

# this script demos how to use 'read' in subscripts
# by calling expect6.sh with expect

set timeout -1

# this works

spawn ./expect6.sh
interact

send_user "\nsecond run\n"

# this hangs because the expect here interferes
# with nested read

spawn ./expect6.sh
expect "done connecting"
interact
```

And:

[appendixb/expect6.sh]

```
#!/bin/bash

# this script demos nested expects
# it simulates a bash script which is
# requesting input with 'read'

echo "connecting to server..."

read -s -p "MFA code for required:" mfacode
echo
echo mfacode=$mfacode

echo "done connecting"
```

Output:

```
[appendixb/expect5.txt]

    $ ./expect5.sh
    spawn ./expect6.sh
    connecting to server...
    MFA code for required:
    mfacode=123456
    done connecting

    second run
    spawn ./expect6.sh
    connecting to server...
    MFA code for required:123456
    ^C
```

So, to conclude, if you are running an expect script which will then call another script (say on the box you 'ssh'ed to) and that script needs user input or calls an expect script which needs user input, you need to call the initial script without expecting any output from it, else it won't be able to read user input.

A good way to handle this is to call the initial script with:

```
    . ./install.sh
```

instead of:

```
    ./install.sh
```

because then you can do any cleanup in install.sh, such as 'exit' from the ssh session. In the first example ('. ./install.sh'), 'exit' in the script will 'exit' the ssh session. In the second example ('./install.sh'), exit will exit from the script, not ssh.

Appendix C - OTP Manager

If you are on OSX and working through the examples in the book or doing any development with Multi-Factor Authentication, an absolute MUST is a great little App called 'OTP Manager'. Just open App Store and search 'OTP Manager'. It's Free, although it saved me so much time I would have happily paid a few dollars for it.

Basically, it's just a MFA code generator for your Mac. It means you don't need to get you phone out every 2 minutes. But the greatest thing about it is that you can copy and paste MFA Keys so no more typing random letters into your smartphone. You can also copy and paste MFA codes from the App or from the menu bar. Very handy!

Obviously, you shouldn't use it for a production system as it's vital MFA Keys are not on your client computer.

Many Thanks to the developer Carlos de Boer Ver Voorn and his company Sticky Bit.

Cheers, mate!

Appendix D - Automating MFA

I really shouldn't put this here because it is *exceedingly bad* security to automate MFA codes. You destroy all the security benefits by keeping the MFA key on the same computer as you other credentials. However, for testing and development purposes, this might be of use.

Normally, when you need an MFA code, you prompt for it with:

```
read -s -p "mfa code:" mfacode
echo you typed: $mfacode
```

The '-s' option makes input silent (not really a priority with MFA as the code can't be reused anyway) and the '-p' prints the string which follows as a prompt. 'mfacode' at the end puts the entered string into the bash variable 'mfacode'.

PHP works out of the box in Terminal in OSX. Here's a PHP script which calculates the current MFA code given an MFA Key:

[appendixd/mfa.php]

```
<?
/**
 * This program is free software: you can redistribute it and/or modify
 * it under the terms of the GNU General Public License as published by
 * the Free Software Foundation, either version 3 of the License, or
 * (at your option) any later version.
 *
 * This program is distributed in the hope that it will be useful,
 * but WITHOUT ANY WARRANTY; without even the implied warranty of
 * MERCHANTABILITY or FITNESS FOR A PARTICULAR PURPOSE.  See the
 * GNU General Public License for more details.
 *
 * You should have received a copy of the GNU General Public License
 * along with this program.  If not, see
 * <http://www.gnu.org/licenses/>.
 *
 * PHP Google two-factor authentication module.
 *
 * See http://www.idontplaydarts.com/2011/07/google-totp-two-factor-authentication-for-php/
 * for more details
 *
```

```
 * originnally from
https://www.idontplaydarts.com/static/ga.php_.txt
 *
 * @author Phil
 **/

class Google2FA {

    const keyRegeneration    = 30;   // Interval between key
regeneration
    const otpLength          = 6;    // Length of the Token
generated

    private static $lut = array(    // Lookup needed for Base32
encoding
            "A" => 0,        "B" => 1,
            "C" => 2,        "D" => 3,
            "E" => 4,        "F" => 5,
            "G" => 6,        "H" => 7,
            "I" => 8,        "J" => 9,
            "K" => 10,       "L" => 11,
            "M" => 12,       "N" => 13,
            "O" => 14,       "P" => 15,
            "Q" => 16,       "R" => 17,
            "S" => 18,       "T" => 19,
            "U" => 20,       "V" => 21,
            "W" => 22,       "X" => 23,
            "Y" => 24,       "Z" => 25,
            "2" => 26,       "3" => 27,
            "4" => 28,       "5" => 29,
            "6" => 30,       "7" => 31
    );

    /**
     * Generates a 16 digit secret key in base32 format
     * @return string
     **/
    public static function generate_secret_key($length = 16) {
            $b32    = "234567QWERTYUIOPASDFGHJKLZXCVBNM";
            $s      = "";

            for ($i = 0; $i < $length; $i++)
                    $s .= $b32[rand(0,31)];

            return $s;
            }

    /**
     * Returns the current Unix Timestamp devided by the
keyRegeneration
     * period.
     * @return integer
     **/
    public static function get_timestamp() {
            return
floor(microtime(true)/self::keyRegeneration);
            }

    /**
     * Decodes a base32 string into a binary string.
     **/
    public static function base32_decode($b32) {

            $b32    = strtoupper($b32);

            if (!
preg_match('/^[ABCDEFGHIJKLMNOPQRSTUVWXYZ234567]+$/', $b32,
$match))
```

```
                              throw new Exception('Invalid characters in
the base32 string.');

                    $l        = strlen($b32);
                    $n        = 0;
                    $j        = 0;
                    $binary = "";

                    for ($i = 0; $i < $l; $i++) {

                        $n = $n << 5;                            //
Move buffer left by 5 to make room
                        $n = $n + self::$lut[$b32[$i]];          //
Add value into buffer
                        $j = $j + 5;                             //
Keep track of number of bits in buffer

                        if ($j >= 8) {
                            $j = $j - 8;
                            $binary .= chr(($n & (0xFF << $j))
>> $j);
                        }
                    }

                    return $binary;
                }

        /**
         * Takes the secret key and the timestamp and returns the
one time
         * password.
         *
         * @param binary $key - Secret key in binary form.
         * @param integer $counter - Timestamp as returned by
get_timestamp.
         * @return string
         **/
        public static function oath_hotp($key, $counter) {
                if (strlen($key) < 8)
                    throw new Exception('Secret key is too short. Must
be at least 16 base 32 characters');

                    $bin_counter = pack('N*', 0) . pack('N*', $counter);
// Counter must be 64-bit int
                    $hash        = hash_hmac ('sha1', $bin_counter, $key,
true);

                    return str_pad(self::oath_truncate($hash),
self::otpLength, '0', STR_PAD_LEFT);
                }

        /**
         * Verifys a user inputted key against the current
timestamp. Checks $window
         * keys either side of the timestamp.
         *
         * @param string $b32seed
         * @param string $key - User specified key
         * @param integer $window
         * @param boolean $useTimeStamp
         * @return boolean
         **/
        public static function verify_key($b32seed, $key, $window =
4, $useTimeStamp = true) {

                    $timeStamp = self::get_timestamp();

                    if ($useTimeStamp !== true) $timeStamp = (int)
```

```php
$useTimeStamp;

            $binarySeed = self::base32_decode($b32seed);

            for ($ts = $timeStamp - $window; $ts <= $timeStamp
+ $window; $ts++)
                    if (self::oath_hotp($binarySeed, $ts) ==
$key)
                        return true;

            return false;

        }

    /**
     * Extracts the OTP from the SHA1 hash.
     * @param binary $hash
     * @return integer
     */
    public static function oath_truncate($hash) {
        $offset = ord($hash[19]) & 0xf;

        return (
            ((ord($hash[$offset+0]) & 0x7f) << 24 ) |
            ((ord($hash[$offset+1]) & 0xff) << 16 ) |
            ((ord($hash[$offset+2]) & 0xff) << 8 ) |
            (ord($hash[$offset+3]) & 0xff)
        ) % pow(10, self::otpLength);
        }

    }

// this is an MFA implementation in PHP
// call it from the command line with:
// php <mfakey>
// it will return an mfa code

// get the MFA key from command line
$InitalizationKey = $argv[1];

$TimeStamp      = Google2FA::get_timestamp();
$secretkey      = Google2FA::base32_decode($InitalizationKey);
// Decode it into binary
$otp            = Google2FA::oath_hotp($secretkey, $TimeStamp);
// Get current token

echo $otp;

// Use this to verify a key as it allows for some time drift
//$result = Google2FA::verify_key($InitalizationKey, "123456");
// result is true if MFA succeeded

// you could easily use the class above to implement MFA in you
PHP apps
```

You can call it with:

```
php mfa.php PEHMPSDNLXIOG65U
```

Change the MFA Key to your Key. The output is a 6 digit number.

To integrate into a bash script you could use:

```
mfakey=PEHMPSDNLXIOG65U
mfacode=$(php mfa.php $mfakey)
echo mfacode=$mfacode
```

Just be careful...

And a big thanks to Phil @ idontplaydarts!

Appendix E - UnBrick a Brick

'Bricking' is the term used to describe what happens when you screw up a configuration file which then stops you being able to get back into your instance via ssh. Basically, you turned your box into a 'brick'...

In the course of this book, I must have bricked a thousand boxes. Luckily, they were all disposable boxes, so I just terminate and retry. But every now and then something happens and there's data you need on a brick. There is a way to rescue your bricked data, or even fix the affected volume. It basically involves shifting the kaput root volume to a new instance (as a non-root volume), mounting it and fixing it or downloading your data. If you want, you can then reattach to the original instance (as a root volume) and you should be able to get back in.

If you look on the Internet, you'll find various articles, like "How to Recover an Unreachable Linux Instance" in the AWS Articles & Tutorials at **http://aws.amazon.com/articles/5213606968661598**. (Watch out, the instructions don't work... the command 'sudo mount /dev/xvdf /bad' should read 'sudo mount /dev/xvdf1 /bad').

But we all hate silly long lists of instructions, don't we? Yep, which is why I scripted it out. Here the first script which builds a server tagged 'brick' and bricks it.

[appendixe/make.sh]

```
#!/bin/bash

# this script makes a simple instance
# then ssh in and breaks ssh
# it bricks the instance

# include globals
. ./../globals.sh

# base name for this instance
ibn=brick

# show variables
echo AMI: $baseami
echo instance base name: $ibn
echo VPC name: $vpcname
```

```
# get our ip from amazon
myip=$(curl http://checkip.amazonaws.com/)
echo myip=$myip

# make a new keypair
echo "making keypair"
rm "$ibn".pem
aws ec2 delete-key-pair --key-name "$ibn"
aws ec2 create-key-pair --key-name "$ibn" --query 'KeyMaterial'
--output text > "$ibn".pem
chmod 600 "$ibn".pem
echo "$ibn" keypair made

# get the vpc id
vpc_id=$(aws ec2 describe-vpcs --filters Name=tag-
key,Values=vpcname Name=tag-value,Values=$vpcname --output text
--query 'Vpcs[*].VpcId')
echo vpc_id $vpc_id

# make a security group
sgid=$(aws ec2 create-security-group --group-name "$ibn"sg
--description "$ibn security group" --vpc-id $vpc_id --output text
--query 'GroupId')
# tag it
aws ec2 create-tags --resources $sgid --tags
Key=sgname,Value="$ibn"sg
# now get the security group id again by using the tag
sgid=$(aws ec2 describe-security-groups --filters Name=tag-
key,Values=sgname Name=tag-value,Values="$ibn"sg --output text
--query 'SecurityGroups[*].GroupId')
echo sgid=$sgid

# allow ssh in on port 22 from our ip only
aws ec2 authorize-security-group-ingress --group-id $sgid
--protocol tcp --port 22 --cidr $myip/32

# get a vpc subnet
subnet_id=$(aws ec2 describe-subnets --filters Name=vpc-
id,Values=$vpc_id Name=tag-key,Values=subnet Name=tag-
value,Values=1 --output text --query 'Subnets[*].SubnetId')
echo subnet_id=$subnet_id

# make the instance
instance_id=$(aws ec2 run-instances --image $baseami --key "$ibn"
--security-group-ids $sgid --instance-type t2.micro --subnet-id
$subnet_id --associate-public-ip-address --output text --query
'Instances[*].InstanceId')
echo instance_id=$instance_id

# tag the instance (so we can get it later)
aws ec2 create-tags --resources $instance_id --tags
Key=instancename,Value="$ibn"

# wait for it
echo -n "waiting for instance"
while state=$(aws ec2 describe-instances --instance-ids
$instance_id --output text --query
'Reservations[*].Instances[*].State.Name'); test "$state" =
"pending"; do
   echo -n . ; sleep 3;
done; echo " $state"

# get the new instance's public ip address
ip_address=$(aws ec2 describe-instances --instance-ids
$instance_id --output text --query
'Reservations[*].Instances[*].PublicIpAddress')
echo ip_address=$ip_address
```

AWS Scripted 2   224

```
# wait for ssh to work
echo -n "waiting for ssh"
while ! ssh -i "$ibn".pem -o ConnectTimeout=5 -o BatchMode=yes -o
StrictHostKeyChecking=no ec2-user@$ip_address > /dev/null 2>&1
true; do
  echo -n . ; sleep 5;
done; echo " ssh ok"

# ssh to the box and screw up the sshd config file
echo ssh in and screw up sshd_config
# make and run expect script
echo "#!/usr/bin/expect -f" > expect.sh
echo "set timeout -1" >> expect.sh
echo "spawn ssh -i "$ibn".pem ec2-user@$ip_address" >> expect.sh
echo "expect \"]\"" >> expect.sh
echo "send \"sudo su\n\"" >> expect.sh
echo "expect \"]\"" >> expect.sh
echo "send \"sed -e 's/#Port 22/Port X/g' /etc/ssh/sshd_config
> /etc/ssh/sshd_config2\n\"" >> expect.sh
echo "expect \"]\"" >> expect.sh
echo "send \"mv -f /etc/ssh/sshd_config2
/etc/ssh/sshd_config\n\"" >> expect.sh
echo "expect \"]\"" >> expect.sh
echo "send \"chown root:root /etc/ssh/sshd_config\n\"" >>
expect.sh
echo "expect \"]\"" >> expect.sh
echo "send \"chmod 600 /etc/ssh/sshd_config\n\"" >> expect.sh
echo "expect \"]\"" >> expect.sh
echo "send \"/etc/init.d/sshd restart\n\"" >> expect.sh
echo "expect \"]\"" >> expect.sh
echo "send \"sleep 5\n\"" >> expect.sh
echo "expect \"]\"" >> expect.sh
echo "send \"exit\n\"" >> expect.sh
echo "expect \"]\"" >> expect.sh
echo "send \"exit\n\"" >> expect.sh
echo "interact" >> expect.sh
cat expect.sh
chmod +x expect.sh
./expect.sh
rm expect.sh

# test ssh (won't work)
ssh -i "$ibn".pem ec2-user@$ip_address

echo now use unbrick.sh to fix it...
```

Here's a script which makes an 'unbricker' box, handles all the drive shuffling and fixes the drive. Even if you don't use it, it showcases some useful code for starting and stopping instances, as well as attaching and detaching EBS volumes.

[appendixe/unbrick.sh]

```
#!/bin/bash

# use this script to get access to a bricked server volume
# so you can fix whatever is wrong

# the tag of the server which is broken
# if you used appendixe/make.sh, this is 'brick'
brickibn=brick
```

```
echo brickibn=$brickibn

# get the instance id
brickid=$(aws ec2 describe-instances --filters Name=tag-
key,Values=instancename Name=tag-value,Values=$brickibn
Name=instance-state-name,Values=running --output text --query
'Reservations[*].Instances[*].InstanceId')
echo brickid=$brickid

# get the volume id
volid=$(aws ec2 describe-instances --filters Name=tag-
key,Values=instancename Name=tag-value,Values=$brickibn --output
text --query
'Reservations[*].Instances[*].BlockDeviceMappings[*].Ebs.VolumeId')
echo volid=$volid

# stop the bricked instance
aws ec2 stop-instances --instance-ids $brickid

# wait for it to stop
echo -n "waiting for instance stop"
while state=$(aws ec2 describe-instances --instance-ids $brickid
--output text --query 'Reservations[*].Instances[*].State.Name');
test "$state" != "stopped"; do
  echo -n . ; sleep 3;
done; echo " $state"

# detach ebs volume from bricked instance
aws ec2 detach-volume --volume-id $volid --instance-id $brickid

# wait for detachment
echo -n "waiting for volume detach"
while state=$(aws ec2 describe-volumes --volume-ids $volid
--output text --query 'Volumes[*].State'); test "$state" !=
"available"; do
  echo -n . ; sleep 3;
done; echo " detached"

# now make a 'debug' instance

# include globals
. ./../globals.sh

# tag for unbricker instance   .
ibn=unbricker

# show variables
echo AMI: $baseami
echo instance base name: $ibn
echo VPC name: $vpcname

# get our ip from amazon
myip=$(curl http://checkip.amazonaws.com/)
echo myip=$myip

# make a new keypair
echo "making keypair"
rm "$ibn".pem
aws ec2 delete-key-pair --key-name "$ibn"
aws ec2 create-key-pair --key-name "$ibn" --query 'KeyMaterial'
--output text > "$ibn".pem
chmod 600 "$ibn".pem
echo "$ibn" keypair made

# get the vpc id
vpc_id=$(aws ec2 describe-vpcs --filters Name=tag-
key,Values=vpcname Name=tag-value,Values=$vpcname --output text
--query 'Vpcs[*].VpcId')
```

AWS Scripted 2

```
echo vpc_id=$vpc_id

# make a security group
  sgid=$(aws ec2 create-security-group --group-name "$ibn"sg
--description "$ibn security group" --vpc-id $vpc_id --output text
--query 'GroupId')
  # tag it
  aws ec2 create-tags --resources $sgid --tags
Key=sgname,Value="$ibn"sg
  # now get the security group id again by using the tag
  sgid=$(aws ec2 describe-security-groups --filters Name=tag-
key,Values=sgname Name=tag-value,Values="$ibn"sg --output text
--query 'SecurityGroups[*].GroupId')
  echo sgid=$sgid

# allow ssh in on port 22 from our ip only
  aws ec2 authorize-security-group-ingress --group-id $sgid
--protocol tcp --port 22 --cidr $myip/32

# get a vpc subnet
  subnet_id=$(aws ec2 describe-subnets --filters Name=vpc-
id,Values=$vpc_id Name=tag-key,Values=subnet Name=tag-
value,Values=1 --output text --query 'Subnets[*].SubnetId')
  echo subnet_id=$subnet_id

# make the unbricker instance
  unbrickid=$(aws ec2 run-instances --image $baseami --key "$ibn"
--security-group-ids $sgid --instance-type t2.micro --subnet-id
$subnet_id --associate-public-ip-address --output text --query
'Instances[*].InstanceId')
  echo unbrickid=$unbrickid

# tag the instance (so we can get it later)
  aws ec2 create-tags --resources $unbrickid --tags
Key=instancename,Value="$ibn"

# wait for it
  echo -n "waiting for instance"
  while state=$(aws ec2 describe-instances --instance-ids
$unbrickid --output text --query
'Reservations[*].Instances[*].State.Name'); test "$state" =
"pending"; do
    echo -n . ; sleep 3;
  done; echo " $state"

# get the new instance's public ip address
  ip_address=$(aws ec2 describe-instances --instance-ids $unbrickid
--output text --query
'Reservations[*].Instances[*].PublicIpAddress')
  echo ip_address=$ip_address

# wait for ssh to work
  echo -n "waiting for ssh"
  while ! ssh -i "$ibn".pem -o ConnectTimeout=5 -o BatchMode=yes -o
StrictHostKeyChecking=no ec2-user@$ip_address > /dev/null 2>&1
true; do
    echo -n . ; sleep 5;
  done; echo " ssh ok"

# attach the volume to the unbricker
  aws ec2 attach-volume --volume-id $volid --instance-id $unbrickid
--device /dev/xvdf

# wait for attachment
  echo -n "waiting for volume attach"
  while state=$(aws ec2 describe-volumes --volume-ids $volid
--output text --query 'Volumes[*].Attachments[*].State'); test
"$state" != "attached"; do
```

```
    echo -n . ; sleep 3;
  done; echo " $state"

  # ssh to the unbricker box and fix the sshd_config file
  echo ssh in and fix sshd_config
  # make and run expect script
  echo "#!/usr/bin/expect -f" > expect.sh
  echo "set timeout -1" >> expect.sh
  echo "spawn ssh -i "$ibn".pem ec2-user@$ip_address" >> expect.sh
  echo "expect \"]\"" >> expect.sh
  echo "send \"sudo su\n\"" >> expect.sh
  echo "expect \"]\"" >> expect.sh
  echo "send \"lsblk\n\"" >> expect.sh
  echo "expect \"]\"" >> expect.sh
  echo "send \"mkdir /brick\n\"" >> expect.sh
  echo "expect \"]\"" >> expect.sh
  echo "send \"mount /dev/xvdf1 /brick\n\"" >> expect.sh
  echo "expect \"]\"" >> expect.sh
  echo "send \"sed -e 's/Port X/Port 22/g'
/brick/etc/ssh/sshd_config > /brick/etc/ssh/sshd_config2\n\"" >>
expect.sh
  echo "expect \"]\"" >> expect.sh
  echo "send \"mv -f /brick/etc/ssh/sshd_config2
/brick/etc/ssh/sshd_config\n\"" >> expect.sh
  echo "expect \"]\"" >> expect.sh
  echo "send \"chown root:root /brick/etc/ssh/sshd_config\n\"" >>
expect.sh
  echo "expect \"]\"" >> expect.sh
  echo "send \"chmod 600 /brick/etc/ssh/sshd_config\n\"" >>
expect.sh
  echo "expect \"]\"" >> expect.sh
  echo "send \"exit\n\"" >> expect.sh
  echo "expect \"]\"" >> expect.sh
  echo "send \"exit\n\"" >> expect.sh
  echo "interact" >> expect.sh
  cat expect.sh
  chmod +x expect.sh
  ./expect.sh
  rm expect.sh

  # stop the unbricker
  aws ec2 stop-instances --instance-ids $unbrickid

  # wait for it to stop
  echo -n "waiting for instance stop"
  while state=$(aws ec2 describe-instances --instance-ids
$unbrickid --output text --query
'Reservations[*].Instances[*].State.Name'); test "$state" !=
"stopped"; do
    echo -n . ; sleep 3;
  done; echo " $state"

  # detach ebs volume from unbricker
  aws ec2 detach-volume --volume-id $volid --instance-id $unbrickid

  # wait for detachment
  echo -n "waiting for volume detach"
  while state=$(aws ec2 describe-volumes --volume-ids $volid
--output text --query 'Volumes[*].State'); test "$state" !=
"available"; do
    echo -n . ; sleep 3;
  done; echo " detached"

  # attach volume to brick
  aws ec2 attach-volume --volume-id $volid --instance-id $brickid
--device /dev/xvda

  # wait for attachment
```

```
echo -n "waiting for volume attach"
while state=$(aws ec2 describe-volumes --volume-ids $volid
--output text --query 'Volumes[*].Attachments[*].State'); test
"$state" != "attached"; do
  echo -n . ; sleep 3;
done; echo " $state"

# start the bricked instance
aws ec2 start-instances --instance-ids $brickid

# wait for it to start
echo -n "waiting for instance start"
while state=$(aws ec2 describe-instances --instance-ids $brickid
--output text --query 'Reservations[*].Instances[*].State.Name');
test "$state" != "running"; do
  echo -n . ; sleep 3;
done; echo " $state"

# terminate unbricker
aws ec2 terminate-instances --instance-ids $unbrickid

# wait for termination
echo -n "waiting for instance termination"
while state=$(aws ec2 describe-instances --instance-ids
$unbrickid --output text --query
'Reservations[*].Instances[*].State.Name'); test "$state" !=
"terminated"; do
  echo -n . ; sleep 3;
done; echo " $state"

# delete unbricker key
rm "$ibn".pem
aws ec2 delete-key-pair --key-name "$ibn"

# delete unbricker security group
aws ec2 delete-security-group --group-id $sgid

echo brick fixed and unbricker terminated

# ssh to the fixed box
# get the new instance's public ip address
brickip=$(aws ec2 describe-instances --instance-ids $brickid
--output text --query
'Reservations[*].Instances[*].PublicIpAddress')
  echo brickip=$brickip

# wait for ssh to work
echo -n "waiting for ssh"
while ! ssh -i "$brickip".pem -o ConnectTimeout=5 -o
BatchMode=yes -o StrictHostKeyChecking=no ec2-user@$brickip >
/dev/null 2>&1 true; do
  echo -n . ; sleep 5;
done; echo " ssh ok"

ssh -i "$brickibn".pem ec2-user@$brickip
```

Hopefully, you'll never need to use them.

Appendix F - Bash Script Essentials

Bash is a tricky language, mainly because there seem to be a whole host of ways to do any one thing. Below are some of the essential methods you will need for automating AWS.

Getting Values from Commands

One of the most common things you need to do on the command line is get some output from a command and save it to a bash variable. Here's an example that gets your IP from Amazon and puts into the myip bash variable:

```
myip=$(curl http://checkip.amazonaws.com/)
echo myip=$myip
```

Use the $(...) notation to execute a command and put the output into a variable.

Waiting for Something to Complete

Many AWS commands do not complete immediately. Examples are creating new instances and RDS databases. In addition, even if an instance has been created, it may take a few seconds for something like SSH to come online (the box needs to boot after all).

Therefore, you will need to be able to run a wait loop as follows:

[appendixf/waitforinstance.sh]

```
  # wait for instance
  echo -n "waiting for instance"
  while state=$(aws ec2 describe-instances --instance-ids
$instance_id --output text --query
'Reservations[*].Instances[*].State.Name'); test "$state" =
"pending"; do
    echo -n . ; sleep 3;
  done; echo " $state"
```

What this does is execute the command "aws ec2 describe-instances --instance-ids $instance_id --output text --query 'Reservations[*].Instances[*].State.Name'" repeatedly until the output changes from 'pending'. I print a '.' (to know something is happening) and wait 3 seconds in between calls. This is an effective way to pause the script until any resources are ready to be used.

SSH is another important wait situation:

[appendixf/waitforssh.sh]

```
# wait for ssh
echo -n "waiting for ssh"
while ! ssh -i credentials/admin.pem -p 38142 -o ConnectTimeout=5
-o BatchMode=yes -o StrictHostKeyChecking=no ec2-user@$ip_address >
/dev/null 2>&1 true; do
   echo -n . ; sleep 5;
done; echo " ssh ok"
```

Here I am trying to connect to a server (the Admin Server) but SSH takes a few seconds to be ready. I am executing "ssh -i credentials/admin.pem -p 38142 -o ConnectTimeout=5 -o BatchMode=yes -o StrictHostKeyChecking=no ec2-user@$ip_address > /dev/null 2>&1" repeatedly. The " > /dev/null 2>&1" portion simply redirects stdout and stderr to /dev/null so you don't see any output. However, if the command succeeds, boolean true will be returned, and false if it fails. Hence "while ! XXX true" repeats if the XXX is unsuccessful.

Automating Search and Replace

The bash command for replacing text in a file is 'sed'. I use this extensively to build files on the fly in scripts. Here is an example:

```
sed -e "s/SEDdbhostSED/$dbendpoint/g" -e "s/SEDdbnameSED/
$dbname/g" -e "s/SEDdbpass_adminrwSED/$password4/g"
ami/admin/httpd_template.conf > ami/admin/httpd.conf
```

This excerpt takes the template file httpd_template.conf and runs it through 'sed' and pipes the output to httpd.conf (you don't want to overwrite or change the template files). The three '-e' options specify 3 search and replaces: SEDdbhostSED with $dbendpoint;

SEDdbnameSED with $dbname; and SEDdbpass_adminrwSED with $password4. The variables $dbendpoint, $dbname and $password4 are all defined earlier in the script. I use the SEDxxxSED notation (in the file being searched and replaced) because this string won't occur in the template script for any other reasons.

One new thing I started using for this book is a command to *escape* the search and replace strings. Things like IAM User or Role ARNs contain the '/' character which breaks 'sed'. So if you execute the following, it won't work, because the '/' before dummy needs to be escaped to '\/':

```
sed -e "s/SEDuserarnSED/arn:aws:iam::000000000000:user/dummy/g"
script_template.sh  > script.sh
```

The three characters that need to be escaped are: / \ and &. To do it, use the following 'sed':

```
strsafe=$(echo $str | sed -e 's/\/\\/g' -e 's/\//\\//g' -e
's/&/\\&/g')
```

which converts the bash variable 'str' to its safe counterpart 'strsafe'. Now you can use $strsafe in 'sed' search and replace specifiers.

Splitting Strings

You will sometimes receive data back from the aws command which is a space separated string. Chopping this string up can be achieved with this:

[appendixf/splitstring.sh]

```
# split a space delimited string
teststring="apple banana orange"
testarray=$(echo $teststring | tr " " "\n")
for i in $testarray
do
 echo found $i
done
```

If the delimiter is not a space, but something else, change the third line to reflect this, for instance for comma separated:

```
testarray=$(echo $teststring | tr "," "\n")
```

Running a Script on a Remote Server

A variant of the ssh command involves setting the BatchMode=yes option and appending the command to be executed:

```
ssh -i credentials/admin.pem -p 38142 -t -o ConnectTimeout=60 -o
BatchMode=yes -o StrictHostKeyChecking=no ec2-user@$ip_address sudo
./install_admin.sh
```

In this case, you would connect to the server and run "sudo ./install_admin.sh". Note that if you have disabled password-less sudo su, you will need to use the more complex procedure involving expect.

Copying Files to and from a Remote Server

Once instances have launched and SSH is available, you invariably need to send some files. Here's how with the scp command running on the box you are transferring from:

```
scp -i credentials/admin.pem -P 38142 ami/admin/httpd.conf ec2-
user@$ip_address:
```

This would copy the local file ami/admin/httpd.conf to the remote server into the /home/ec2-user directory. Note the trailing ':' and how the port is specified with a capital P (ssh uses a lowercase p).

Getting files back from the server is as follows:

```
scp -i credentials/admin.pem -P 38142 ec2-
user@$ip_address:httpd.conf .
```

This would copy the file /home/ec2-user/httpd.conf from the remote server to the current directory, specified by the '.' character. Obviously, port 38142 needs to be open in the AWS Security Group involved.

Including a Script in a Script

I make extensive use of the bash 'source' command, which can be abbreviated to the '.' character. Without modification, the bash shell won't let you execute a script just by typing its name - you need to issue commands like this:

```
./test.sh
```

A slight variant is:

```
. ./test.sh
```

and again:

```
source ./test.sh
```

last:

```
source test.sh
```

There is much confusion on the Internet concerning this topic. There are 4 examples above and different people have different opinions about what they mean. So let me explain: the 'source' command includes and runs a script *inline* in the current shell or script. That means all variables currently defined are available to the called script and if the script sets any variables, these persist in the calling environment. It's as though you copied and pasted the commands in. The '.' notation is a shorthand for 'source' and behaves in exactly the same way. so 'source test.sh' and '. test.sh' are exactly the same. The first example above is NOT a 'source' command - the dot represents the '.' meaning 'this directory'. And calling a script like that starts a new process so variables are separate. The last three examples above are synonymous. Have a look at this script which runs some tests:

```
[appendixf/sourcetests.sh]
```

```
#!/bin/bash

# write a test script
echo '#!/bin/bash' > test.sh
echo 'echo input=$input' >> test.sh
```

```
echo 'output=output' >> test.sh
chmod +x test.sh

# set a variable in the top context
input=input
echo input=$input

# show that output is empty
echo output=$output

# run just the filename (we get an error)
echo running: test.sh
test.sh

# run ./ version
echo running: ./test.sh
./test.sh
echo output=$output
# reset output
unset output

# run . ./ version
echo running: . ./test.sh
. ./test.sh
echo output=$output
# reset output
unset output

# run source ./ version
echo running: source ./test.sh
source ./test.sh
echo output=$output
# reset output
unset output

# run source version
echo running: source test.sh
source test.sh
echo output=$output
# reset output
unset output
```

which when run produces:

[appendixf/sourcetestsresult.txt]

```
input=input
output=
running: test.sh
./snippet_sourcetests.sh: line 18: test.sh: command not found
running: ./test.sh
input=
output=
running: . ./test.sh
input=input
output=output
running: source ./test.sh
input=input
output=output
running: source test.sh
input=input
output=output
```

As you can see, the first call ('./test.sh') has input and output blank
- so $input is not available to test.sh and test.sh does not set
$output in the parent script. But the last three ways of calling the
script ('. ./test.sh', 'source ./test.sh' and 'source test.sh') all print
input and output correctly - so $input is available to test.sh and
test.sh sets $output in the calling script.

AWS CLI Query Methods

Almost all AWS CLI commands return some form of data. The
standard return format is JSON. To demonstrate this, let's create a
dummy IAM User:

```
aws iam create-user --user-name dummy
```

This returns:

```
[appendixf/createuseroutput.txt]
```

```
    "User": {
        "UserName": dummy",
        "Path": "/",
        "CreateDate": "2019-10-19T03:37:48.351Z",
        "UserId": "somestring",
        "Arn": "arn:aws:iam::000000000000:user/dummy"
    }
}
```

Delete the user and redo the creation with output set to text:

```
aws iam delete-user --user-name dummy
aws iam create-user --user-name dummy --output text
```

The output is now not in JSON:

```
 USER  arn:aws:iam::000000000000:user/dummy     2019-10-
19T06:49:44.225Z          somestring         dummy
```

Let's say you wanted to retrieve a single variable form the output,
you can do this with the --query option:

```
aws iam delete-user --user-name dummy
aws iam create-user --user-name dummy --query 'User.UserName'
```

This returns a JSON string:

```
"dummy"
```

Normally, you don't want JSON data back because it is more difficult to parse. So you can execute the same commands with the text output option to get a cleaner return:

```
aws iam delete-user --user-name dummy
aws iam create-user --user-name dummy --output text  --query
'User.UserName'
```

And this returns clean data:

```
dummy
```

which you can put in a bash variable with the $(...) construct.

Setting the query string can be a bit confusing. Run the command without query or output options and you'll get a lump of JSON. Then you need to specify what you want by drilling down into the returned JSON. In the example above I jumped into the 'User' aggregation and then extracted the value for 'UserName'. It's always case sensitive.

Also, if the returned JSON has arrays, you need to specify the array position or * for all items, for example, if you have no instances:

```
aws ec2 describe-instances
```

returns:

```
[appendixf/describeinstancesoutput.txt]
```

```
{
    "Reservations": []
}
```

The square brackets are a giveaway that the Reservations aggregation is an array, so any query string would start with 'Reservations[*].' (for all Reservations) or 'Reservations[0].' for the first Reservation only. However, you need to test, because the aws command doesn't like some combinations.

So the command:

```
aws ec2 describe-instances --output text --query
'Reservations[*].Instances[*].State.Name'
```

would return a space separated list of the State.Name property for each instance in all Reservations. However, I recommend using options in the command to return only one piece of data and avoid space separated lists if at all possible.

Note that if you want to use a variable in a query string, you need to close and open the single quotes (because bash treats text inside single quotes as real text and does not evaluate it). An example can be seen when you check if an SES email address has been verified:

```
aws ses get-identity-verification-attributes --identities
"$emailsendfrom" --region $deployregion --output text --query
'VerificationAttributes."'$emailsendfrom'".VerificationStatus'
```

Very rarely, you execute an AWS command which returns more than one piece of data that you need and which can only be run once. An example is the SES User Key generation. In this case you need to use a more cumbersome but equally effective JSON bash parser function:

[appendixf/jsonval.sh]

```
# extract from aws/ami/email/make.sh
# this function allows us to extract data from a json string
function jsonval {
        temp=`echo $json | sed 's/\\\\\//\//g' | sed 's/[{}]//g' |
awk -v k="text" '{n=split($0,a,","); for (i=1; i<=n; i++) print
a[i]}' | sed 's/\"\:\"/\|/g' | sed 's/[\,]/ /g' | sed 's/\"//g' |
grep -w $prop | cut -d":" -f2| sed -e 's/^ *//g' -e 's/ *$//g'`
        echo ${temp##*|}}
        }

# make ses user
aws iam create-user --user-name sesuser

# we need to get 2 values from this returned data but can only
call the function once
# hence the laborious jsonval method
json=$(aws iam create-access-key --user-name sesuser)

# get key id
prop='AccessKeyId'
AccessKeyId=`jsonval`
```

```
# get secret key
prop='SecretAccessKey'
SecretAccessKey=`jsonval`
```

I have found that this 'jsonval' method fails in some circumstances.
Another way to do it is to get output as text, chop it up and select
the right 'bits', for example:

```
# make an access key for the user
# you need to get 2 values from this returned data but can only
call the function once
# so you cant use --query
cred=$(aws iam create-access-key --user-name $username --output
text)
bits=($cred)
AccessKeyId=${bits[1]}
SecretAccessKey=${bits[3]}
```

Fun with Quotes

It took me a long time to realise there was a difference in bash
between the quote types " and '... Most of the time they work
interchangeably. But they are subtly different. " evaluates it's
contents (so things like variables are replaced) but ' treats it's
contents as a literal string. Hence:

```
str=someval
echo "str=$str"
```

prints

```
str=someval
```

but

```
str=someval
echo 'str=$str'
```

prints

```
str=$str
```

And when I realised that's what explains similar PHP behaviour it
hit me like a rock and I shall now be on the lookout for other
bashisms in my PHP. You sort of always knew PHP was built on
top of bash, or something bash-like, but this really exemplifies it.

AWS Scripted 2

One thing to be really careful about is those annoying curly quotes word processors love to convert your nice straight quotes to. They don't work on the command line and you get all sorts of weird errors. So just be careful copying and pasting from any editor or file which is not pure ASCII text.

About the Author

You already know my mantra: "Divide! Automate! Conquer!"

So I won't go on about it...

Keep in touch at **http://www.quickstepapps.com**!

Copyright Notice

Please help others to find this book by leaving a review. Your feedback is always appreciated.

Download

All code in this book can be downloaded at **http://www.quickstepapps.com** free of charge. You will also find related Articles and an interactive Support Forum. All code examples are tested on OSX and Amazon Linux platforms and in working order as of publishing.

Contact

Should you have questions, suggestions, difficulties or corrections, please contact the author at:

http://www.quickstepapps.com

Made in the USA
San Bernardino, CA
03 July 2017